STUDIES IN EARLY HEBREW METER

Harvard Semitic Museum
Harvard Semitic Monograph Series

edited by

Frank Moore Cross, Jr.

Number 13

STUDIES IN EARLY HEBREW METER

by

Douglas K. Stuart

SCHOLARS PRESS
Missoula, Montana

STUDIES IN EARLY HEBREW METER

by

Douglas K. Stuart

Published by

SCHOLARS PRESS

for

Harvard Semitic Museum

Distributed by

SCHOLARS PRESS
University of Montana
Missoula, Montana 59801

STUDIES IN EARLY HEBREW METER

by

Douglas K. Stuart

Library of Congress Cataloging in Publication Data

Stuart, Douglas K
Studies in early Hebrew meter.

(Harvard Semitic monographs ; 13)
Bibliography: p.
1. Hebrew poetry, Biblical — History and criticism. 2. Hebrew language — Metrics and rhythmics. I. Title. II. Series.
BS1405.2.S8 892.4'1'1 76-6134
ISBN 0-89130-100-3

PRINTED IN THE UNITED STATES OF AMERICA

Edwards Brothers, Inc.
Ann Arbor, Michigan 48104

ABBREVIATIONS

AJSL	*American Journal of Semitic Languages and Literatures*
ArOr	*Archiv Orientální*
b	*colum breve*
BANE	Wright, G. E., (ed.). *The Bible and the Ancient Near East: Essays in Honor of William Foxwell Albright.* Garden City: Doubleday, 1961.
BASOR	*Bulletin of the American Schools of Oriental Research*
CBQ	*Catholic Biblical Quarterly*
EHO	Cross, F. M. and Freedman, D. N. *Early Hebrew Orthography*. New Haven: American Oriental Society, 1952.
HSCP	*Harvard Studies in Comparative Philology*
HTR	*Harvard Theological Review*
HUCA	*Hebrew Union College Annual*
ICC	*International Critical Commentary*
IDB	*Interpreter's Dictionary of the Bible*
IEJ	*Israel Exploration Journal*
JAOS	*Journal of the American Oriental Society*
JBL	*Journal of Biblical Literature*
JCS	*Journal of Cuneiform Studies*
JJS	*Journal of Jewish Studies*
JNES	*Journal of Near Eastern Studies*
JPOS	*Journal of the Palestine Oriental Society*
JQR	*Jewish Quarterly Review*
JSS	*Journal of Semitic Studies*
JTS	*Journal of Theological Studies*
l	*colum longum*
LXX	Septuagint
MT	Masoretic Text

SAYP Cross, F. M. and Freedman, D. N. *Studies in Ancient Yahwistic Poetry*. Missoula, Montana: Scholars Press, 1975.

SOTP Rowley, H. H., (ed.). *Studies in Old Testament Prophecy: Presented to Theodore H. Robinson*. Edinburgh: T and T Clark, 1957.

ZAW *Zeitschrift für die Alttestamentliche Wissenschaft*

ZDMG *Zeitschrift der Deutschen Morgenländischen Gesellschaft*

In the transliteration of Hebrew, Ugaritic, and Akkadian, x signifies a vowel of unknown quantity. Since the final forms of *kaph*, *mem*, *nun*, *peh*, and *ṣadeh* were late developments, they are not used in the Hebrew transcriptions.

The spirantization of the letters *b*, *g*, *d*, *k*, *p*, *t*, probably a late development under Aramaic influence, is not indicated in the transliteration.

⌜⌝ indicates an omission from the received text.
<> indicates an addition to the received text.

TABLE OF CONTENTS

CHAPTER I

PREVIOUS RESEARCH INTO HEBREW METRICS

In the last century Julius Ley,[1] followed by Karl Budde[2] and later, with considerable refinement by Edward Sievers,[3] developed a basic approach to Hebrew metrics which continues to enjoy very wide acceptance. This approach, which is sometimes called the Ley-Sievers-Budde method,[4] combined the traditional Masoretic accentual and vocalic system with critical insights into the parallelistic nature of Old Testament poetry and arrived at a workable description for the various types and lengths of meter in Hebrew. It is so well known and so widely employed that we shall discuss only those features of the method that are appropriate to our discourse at various points. The method itself has worked sufficiently well to have become predominant among all theories. We shall thus label its circle of advocacy the "traditional" school.

The originators of this method had a limited number of inscriptions and original texts available to them as they approached the study of Hebrew metrics.[5] Little investigation had been attempted into historical Hebrew phonetics, and the disciplines of orthographic analysis and paleography were barely emergent. As a result Ley, Sievers, and Budde, like their predecessors and nearly all students of Hebrew metrics, were very much dependent upon the text and vocalizations of the Masoretes. It was normal that their school would also depend significantly upon the musical word accents developed for chanting in medieval Judaism, preserved by the Masoretes in their texts.[6]

Following this line of development the traditional school described poetry by units of stress. These may be called feet, each of which is a discernable morphosyntactic mass of between one and six syllables. As it is often practiced today (although somewhat errantly, since each of the writers of this school presents a highly nuanced theory) this system involves little more than counting the Masoretic accents in one line of a couplet or triplet and comparing the result with that of the other line(s). Careful attention to the parallelism determines the limits of each line or colon.[7] Thus are produced the familiar 3+3, 4+3, 3+2, 2+2, etc. which constitute "traditional" Hebrew scansion. This method has gained wide acceptance. It is by no means, however, the only theory of Hebrew metrics to have been promulgated.

Other schools have developed, some with many proponents. We must discuss these schools according to their general characteristics in spite of the individualities of their representative members. It should be noted that two of the schools are outgrowths of approaches to meter borrowed (riskily as Jakobson observes[8]) from students of classical Greek prosody.

At least three main schools, and numerous offshoots, may be discerned. We shall treat each of these briefly. The most prominent of them, the "traditional" school, began with Bellermann and culminates in the work of Sievers. The "semantic parallelism" school began with Lowth's definitive study of *parallelismus membrorum* and is represented today by T. H. Robinson. Another major school we may designate the "alternating meter" school (as it is in fact described by some of its proponents). Here we include scholars who find Hebrew meter to be based exclusively or nearly so[9] on a two-syllable foot (i.e. either iambic or trochaic accentually) such as Hölscher, Mowinckel,[10] Horst, and Segert. We shall deal individually with theorists whose work is of special interest.

Early in the nineteenth century Bellermann[11] published what is commonly regarded as the first modern theory of Hebrew meter. Heavily influenced by classical metrics (as have been most studies of Hebrew meter), his system measured syllable lengths by the classical units of time, *morae*. Syllables with greater numbers of *morae* were considered tonic and were accentuated. Syllables with few *morae* were either unaccented or ignored. Vocal *shewa* was often completely disregarded in this system, so that phrases such as בְּסוֹד and לְכוֹל were treated as monosyllables. In spite of these and other peculiarities Bellermann's work produced results still considered valuable in many circles. He posited strophes of from three to eight verses in length; he anticipated Budde's recognition of 3+2 Qinah meter; he did not shy away from emendation when necessary. His decisions as to placement of stress were as inconsistent as those of any scholar who followed him, yet he opened up Hebrew prosody to scientific examination.

Saalschütz[12] refined and popularized Bellermann's views, differing with him largely on the matter of *morae*, a concept he rejected. While Bellermann had often judged Hebrew poems to be at least roughly hexameter (in 3/8 time) Saalschütz now found Hebrew poetry to be exclusively hexameter. Whereas Bellermann had, with the Masoretes, tended to place the stress on the ultima of most Hebrew words, Saalschütz placed it wherever possible on the penult. In the first quarter of the nineteenth century the metrical questions had already become complicated, even within a single tradition of scansion.

Ten years after Saalschütz, Heinrich Ewald published an independent approach to Hebrew meter in his *Dichter des Alten Bundes*.[13] Ignoring Bellermann and Saalschütz he carefully examined a number of possible approaches to Hebrew meter based on classical notions, and rejected them all. Instead he devised a meter which emphasized the *approximate* length of cola (e.g. seven or eight syllables), but affirmed that Hebrew was not inclined to any syllabic rhythm in verse. He stressed rather thought units and their parallelism.[14] Ewald made little distinction between what the traditional school would designate as 2+2, 3+3, 4+4, etc. He was rather concerned with the general length of lines and, like Mowinckel, with natural units of meaning within lines. While this is different from the "word meter" of the semantic parallelism school, it contains similarities to that school's approach. Further, Ewald's concern for overall length of cola has some affinity to the stance of the present study. Ewald's notable weakness was his imprecision; his genius is seen in his anticipation of so many modern positions.

In the middle of the last century Ernst Meier[15] developed an elaborate system of rising and falling tones to describe Hebrew meter. He judged all Hebrew poetry to be essentially 2/4 time and thus prefigured the alternating meter school. His notion of tonality follows the Alexandrian classicists' designation of rising (*arsis*) and falling (*thesis*) tones rather than accentuation. Most modern proponents of a two-syllable foot ignore tonal modality and concentrate on accentuation.[16]

In the last third of the century Julius Ley produced three studies[17] which continue to hold great influence. His theories, as expanded by Budde, have been only partially superceded. Even Sievers' contention that Hebrew poetry was primarily anapestic has not altered, but merely expanded the basic theory. Ley's approach has been described briefly above. Its most significant feature is its disregard for unaccented[18] syllables. One counts accents wherever they may occur, whether they form anapestic patterns, as Sievers believes, or not. Neither Ley nor Budde claimed to find the accentuation within "feet" to comprise any exclusive pattern. Even Sievers' anapest is such a variable foot with potential for compression or expansion that his metrical counts almost always duplicated those of Ley and Budde. Thus we are justified in treating these three scholars as a group notwithstanding their individually nuanced positions.

A still popular school of metrics may be traced from Lowth[19] through Buchanan Gray to T. H. Robinson. Their approach to meter we call the semantic parallelism school.[20]

Buchanan Gray[21] returned almost two centuries in time to revive Lowth's emphasis on parallelism and make it the basis for meter as well as meaning in poetry. He subordinated most considerations of stress or tone and spoke instead of *units* of indivisible words and word elements. These are comprised of verbs, nouns, prepositions, suffixes, and constructs as they are normally grouped in Hebrew composition. One group receives one count. Intrinsic word accentuation is of diminished importance; Gray did not believe it was a determining factor in the original composition of the poems. He also expanded upon Lowth's three well-known types of parallelism so as to describe a more detailed range of poetic types. In his terminology, for example, Qinah meter is "incomplete parallelism without compensation."

Few scholars would disagree with Gray's sense of semantic parallelism. Most would, like Mowinckel, agree that it is not really an element of meter but of style. Interestingly the patterns produced by counting *units* are often exactly those produced by counting *accents* by the traditional school.

T. H. Robinson[22] has built directly upon the foundation laid by Gray with comparatively little change. His contributions to the system include a willingness to recognize mixed meter, tonal and vocalizational factors, and a plastic sense of strophic length. To ameliorate the problem of unusual counts sometimes produced by the semantic parallelism method Robinson has borrowed and refurbished the classical device of *anacrusis*.[23]

Two doctrines thus distinguish the Lowth-Gray-Robinson school: the belief that semantic parallelism is the main determinant of Hebrew meter and the belief that phonetic considerations are of secondary importance.

A third school may be seen represented in the recent works of Horst, Mowinckel, and Segert. They are not in total agreement with one another on many details. Their metrical counts for Hebrew poetry tend often to be almost identical, however. We call this school the alternating meter school in keeping with its designation by Segert and Horst. As mentioned, both Ewald and Ernst Meier anticipated some features of this school's approach. But so did Gustav Bickell,[24] a maverick in his day, whose views we may summarize immediately.

Bickell believed that all Hebrew poetry was either iambic or trochaic. He counted the syllables of a colon and assigned to them a regular interchange of toned and untoned so that a colon with an even number of syllables was always iambic. An uneven number of syllables meant that a line was trochaic. Bickell's sense of vocalization was remarkably sophisticated; he undid Masoretic contractions and syncopes fearlessly (e.g. *bă'elōhīm*). He also counted syllables, but not for the same purposes espoused later in this study. His weaknesses were an unreasonably heavy reliance on Syriac prosodic principles and too free a willingness to emend the text *metri causa*. In his writings there appear thousands of suggested alterations of the received text of the Psalter alone.

Among other members of this school there is very little difference between the positions of Hölscher and Mowinckel or between Horst and Segert. We may thus review the positions of the latter man in each pair.

Mowinckel[25] has revived Hölscher's[26] stress upon the iamb as the basic Hebrew foot. The iamb's three-syllable counterpart, the anapest, is occasionally to be found, but not so often as to affect significantly the predominance of the two-syllable foot. Mowinckel's metrical counts are usually about one stress greater than those of either the traditional school or the semantic parallelism school. Qinah is 4+3; fully parallel standard meter is 4+4, etc. The extra stress comes usually from units contextually endowed with meaning but not weighted as independent by the semantic parallelism school. Examples of these are object suffixes, pronouns, and sometimes even prepositions. Secondary accents not unlike those first posited by Ley and commonly used by metrists (e.g. *yᵉrùšaláyim*) are also sources of a higher count. Mowinckel describes the traditional school as both subjective and inconsistent. His own choice of which morphemes in a given colon are sufficiently meaningful to receive a stress may also be characterized as subjective and inconsistent, although the iambic framework adds a degree of precision. Mowinckel is fully aware that his unwavering reliance upon Masoretic vocalization and consonantal tradition is methodologically risky. But he, like Segert and David Noel Freedman, prefers this risk to that of the arduous and uncertain reconstruction of a theoretically original poetic form, as attempted in the present study.

Segert's approach to meter[27] is relatively similar to that of Mowinckel and Hölscher. It involves placing the stress upon primary and secondary natural tones and alternating on-off stresses. The result is normally iambic and occasionally trochaic. That it is never anapestic is the only significant difference between Horst-Segert and Hölscher-Mowinckel. Segert's work recalls Bickell's most strongly, although it does not relate stress to an even or uneven number of syllables. Every syllable is part of the scansion regardless of its import to the meaning of the colon. This approach is characteristic of theories of alternating meter, and is precisely contrary to the traditional school's view that only naturally stressed syllables are determinative for a metrical count.

Each work on Hebrew metrics in the last two centuries has offered at least something different from what had been published before. Nevertheless one may clearly discern broad outlines of schools, and may summarize the schools discussed above as follows.

The traditional school: Bellermann, Saalschütz, Ley, Budde, Sievers.

The semantic parallelism school: Lowth, Gray, Robinson.

The alternating meter school: Ewald, Meier, Bickel, Hölscher, Horst, Mowinckel, Segert.

Obviously many scholars who wrote on Hebrew meter do not appear in these groups. Each of the schools which in fact are still viable do receive notice. There remain to be discussed the works of two scholars whose labors in Hebrew metrics have laid the groundwork for the newest school of all, that represented in this study. These men are Paul Haupt and W. F. Albright.

Both Haupt and his student Albright trace their lineage to the traditional school. Neither departed radically from it. Their refinements are nevertheless important.

Haupt[28] carefully catalogued words and phrases according to their prosodic characteristics: words with two stresses, words with recessive accents, enclitics, proclitics, etc. He rarely found any mixed meter in Hebrew poetry. Most of his poems scanned either 3+3 or 3+2 with occasional 2+2, all in the manner of the traditional school. He isolated triplets where many had failed to see them and he rigorously used meter as a means of excising non-genuine material from poetic texts.

Albright's approach to Hebrew meter[29] stemmed directly from that of Haupt. He was also aware of the symmetry produced by counting syllables, but never departed from Haupt's counts in the manner of the traditional school. Further, neither Albright nor Haupt depended rigidly upon Masoretic accentuation and vocalization. Both scholars, Albright in particular, possessed the requisite linguistic tools to reconstruct Hebrew poems according to supposed original pronunciations and both used their skill in textual criticism to great advantage. This willingness and ability to improve upon the received text separated them from their predecessors.

Albright's studies of Old Testament and Ugaritic poetry published during the last fifty years have finally provided new bases for the study of metrics. While Albright had continued to employ the traditional scansion in print, his highly informed use of textual criticism, paleography, orthographic analysis, and other tools enabled him to produce convincing approximations of the original forms of many poems. We are deeply indebted to scholars such as Speiser, Harris, and others[30] who studied vocalization indicators from cuneiform transcriptions, Qumran, the Hexapla, and many new or newly understood Northwest Semitic inscriptions.[31] These all support efforts to understand the pronunciation, structure, and vocabulary of Old Testament poetry as it would have appeared at various periods in the history of Israel. From this we may move toward the precision appropriate to a scansion based upon syllable count.

The recent development of this newer scansion is primarily the work of Frank Moore Cross and David Noel Freedman. Their approach to syllabic scansion was developed during joint studies of numerous Old Testament poems[32] and has recently been employed in critical studies of Hebrew and Ugaritic texts.[33]

There exist some differences between the approaches of Cross and Freedman. Freedman's recent work[34] has used the MT without emendation as the basis for a controlled experiment. Although highly skilled in the techniques necessary to reconstruct original vocalizations and forms, he has purposely limited himself to the received text. In this way scholars hostile to or unacquainted with reconstructive techniques are able and willing to follow his arguments for the newer syllabic scansion. While Freedman knows that using the MT uncritically involves a certain degree of error, he is also aware that a margin of error accompanies reconstructions of supposed original texts as well.

In contrast to this, Cross has stressed the importance of the various versions as controls upon the text (no single tradition of which is free from error), of the need to emend the text whenever necessary, and of the desirability of attempting to reconstruct poetry according to an approximated original form and vocalization. Cross believes that in this manner at least the precise number of *syllables* will more likely be discovered in a careful reconstruction than in the unedited MT. Uncertainties as to vowel quality or length do not in fact alter the discernment of syllables in words, and it is the quantity of syllables that the newer scansion is dependent upon.

Recently A. J. Ehlen[35] has completed a study of metrical patterns employing the newer scansion, in a psalm found at Qumran. These patterns are quite different from those of the league and monarchy and show syllabic balance metrically in few cases. This is due in part to the fact that late poetry became more a literary than a musical enterprise.

Most past attempts at Hebrew metrics have suffered from the limitations of the MT. Freedman has shown that one *can* use the MT while demonstrating the superiority of syllabic meter over stress meter.[36] It is nevertheless advantageous to go beyond the MT. This requires much careful work involving textual revision, revocalization, orthographic, paleographic, and other linguistic controls, and the systematic deletion of whatever prosaic matter may have been interpolated within the original wording of poems.

Understandably these procedures and the assumptions behind them have not been universally accepted. D. W. Watson[37] has thus sought to refute some of them, especially as they are practiced by Albright and his students. In this he has been less than entirely successful, especially in light of discoveries from early inscriptions now recognized as poetic,[38] the particulars of which tend to vindicate the assumptions of this school.

The present study builds upon and expands recent research into syllabic meter. It is a survey of Ugaritic and early Hebrew poetry designed to demonstrate that the newer system of scansion is even more precise than those which have preceded it.

It should be noted that a system of meter based on the quantity of syllables per colon does not ignore the possibility of internal feet of various types. It merely gives primary consideration to the variable most neglected in past approaches to Hebrew meter: overall colon length in number of syllables and the patterns discerned therefrom.

Problems of Establishing Meter

A number of theoretical problems present themselves at the outset of our stated task. Most of them are the same problems that would occur in the course of inducing the metrical structure of poetry in any language. Some are peculiar to the incomplete graphic notation and oral-aural transmission of Hebrew and Ugaritic poetry.

It is likely that both Ugaritic and early Hebrew poetry were composed formulaically. That is, the poets in question recited and re-recited their songs according to rhythmic patterns making use of a repertoire of phrases and clauses to express many given essential ideas. This method of composition was clearly more extensively used by the Ugaritic poets than by the Hebrew poets, although it appears in both literatures. According to the lengthy studies of Lord and Parry[39] it is common to find evidences of oral metrical composition in the epic and narrative literature of both ancient and modern peoples. Enough is known of both Ugaritic and early Hebrew poems to determine that they were composed orally rather than in written form. This is evidenced by the presence in these works of the three earmarks of oral musical composition: formulae, thematic structure, and lack of enjambment.[40] Since such poetry was composed to be performed rather than read we may be sure that it was put into writing only for purposes of preservation.

Ugaritic provides the first transcription of dictated oral poetry in West Semitic literature. Errors are found in the written texts, but they are few compared to those in early Hebrew poems, and are of a given type. Nearly all arise from improperly dictated formulae, or formulae that are reversed or misplaced.[41] Frequent repetition of lengthy sections of narrative enables us to isolate many of the errors and to judge how and why they were made.

In the case of Hebrew poetry the isolation of dictation errors is complicated and conjectural. In some cases dual texts such as II Samuel 22=Psalm 18 serve the purpose of the repetitions in Ugaritic. Otherwise the critic is unsure whether a garbled text is miscopied or misdictated or both.

These considerations affect an inductive study of meter. Formulaic composition depends upon a precise meter. When formulae are present in abundance in poetry one may expect to find consistency in metrical patterns as well. Meter may be mixed, but given formulae will occur in like metrical contexts. Where formulae appear to be repeated in Hebrew poems one expects and finds repeated metrical patterns, as with Ugaritic poetry. The number of repetitions which in fact occur in a Hebrew poem are usually relatively few, however. Formulaic analysis proves therefore to be of only occasional use with Hebrew poetry, and then only in conjunction with other critical techniques.

The question of internal feet within individual cola continues to be unresolved.[42] It is in fact unresolved even in the traditional school. This is because the traditional school's definition of an internal foot is so variable as to be nearly uninformative. Advocates of this method have found cola to have two, three, or four feet; a foot may contain one, two, or even three words (free forms);[43] it could have from one to six syllables. Here is a system so variable and inexact that anything poetic (and often prosaic) in either Hebrew or Ugaritic could be made to fit it. It is, however, a method suited to the analysis of Hebrew poetry in the Masoretic tradition, assuming that the poetry was chanted rather than sung to a precise metrical melody.

The meter of the alternating school often resolves the question of internal feet in an almost mechanical way: normal feet usually have two syllables in either iambic or trochaic fashion, although many feet are still monosyllabic. The arbitrary nature of this approach adds to its doubtfulness. It is, moreover, still a somewhat inexact system.

By contrast the method based on syllable count is exacting. Although internal stresses and feet are not subjects of our investigation we nevertheless follow a method which describes meter according to the relatively precise standard notation of European hymnic meter.[44] The newer method produces a firm and less ambiguous count of the meter without ignoring or abandoning the possibility of internal feet. It describes to the syllable the meter of any given tune or poem. All other methods tell only whether a given line is short ("2"), medium ("3"), or long ("4" or "5"). The newer method now reveals the exact length of a line from four to thirteen or more syllables.

Within couplets and triplets, it appears that Ugaritic and Hebrew poets used lines or cola which were purposely either relatively short or relatively long. The exact length in numbers of syllables was not as important as the *relative* length. For example, if a poet composed in Qinah meter, he tended to alternate *relatively* long lines with *relatively* short ones. His meter, described in terms of syllables, might be something like: 9:7::7:9, or 8:6::8:6, or 9:7::9:7, etc. In such cases it would appear that the poet is consciously alternating relatively long lines with relatively short ones.

Borrowing Latin terminology, Cross has suggested the designation *colum longum* for the relatively long lines, and *colum breve* for those which are relatively shorter. We usually abbreviate these designations to "l" and "b." To be called "l" a colon or line should be discernably rather long relative to other lines; to be called "b" it should be rather short.

In practice, lines which contain from eight to thirteen syllables prove to be "l" lines. Lines with from three to five syllables are always "b" lines. Six or seven syllables may prove to constitute either an "l" or a "b" line. The precise identification must be determined by careful examination of the context. A line with six syllables, for example, would certainly be considered "l" if it occurred within a pattern such as 8:8, 9:9, 6:6, 8:8, etc. (all "l" meter) and showed no qualitative difference from the type of meter manifest in the immediate context. In a pattern such as 5:5::5:5, 4:4::4:4, 6:6::6:6, however, we would count the six-syllable lines as "b" meter, if it is qualitatively similar to the other lines of the immediate context. Similar principles apply to Ugaritic poetry, except that Ugaritic cola have, on the average, a syllable or two more than Hebrew cola. Double lines, in which a cesura is either not present or difficult to place, may be designated by the appropriate capital letter: "L" or "B."

It may be helpful to the reader to note that couplets described by the three major schools as "2+2" will usually turn out to be b:b short couplets (technically half-couplets and only one part of a full b:b::b:b couplet) in the newer notation. Couplets scanned by the other schools as "3+3" or "4+4" normally appear as 1:1 here, since they rarely exhibit anything other than normal overall parallelism. Furthermore traditional Qinah meter, which is characteristically an unbalanced meter, appears to show a hitherto unrecognized variety of possible combinations. These are 1:b::1:b, 1:b::b:1, b:1::b:1, and b:1::1:b. Qinah is apparently unbalanced stylistically as well as metrically. In this the semantic parallelism school, although it confuses style with meter, is right.[45]

How prevalent is mixed meter? Haupt and Albright (in his early studies only) found almost none.[46] Their counts showed long rows of a single pattern, often extending through several strophes. Haupt regularly exicsed couplets that contradicted the prevailing meter of a poem as textual interpolations. Most members of the three major schools admit some mixed meter, but seem to indicate in their publications that repeating meter (i.e. a given count such as 3+3 recurring repeatedly) is the norm. In the case of Qinah meter there is virtual consensus among the schools that it is unmixed. The traditional and semantic parallelism schools scan 3+2, and the alternating meter school scans 4+3.

The syllable counting method obviates such rigid positions. Meter of various types appears to be mixed in most poems of any length. b:b::b:b couplets vary freely with 1:1 couplets. b:b:b and 1:1:1 triplets appear frequently in no set patterns. Strophes, if they exist, are of varying lengths.[47] Clearly, "regularity" (repetition of a given colon length) is manifest primarily *within* a couplet or triplet rather than among groups of couplets or triplets.

Fairly long sections of couplets or triplets of one count do occur, for example, in II Isaiah and Ugaritic. They are in the minority even in those contexts, however.

Poetry is an art, and an artistic feel for the material under analysis is essential to its study. Nevertheless the actual formal description of the meter of poetry can only be technical. The original poets probably composed naturally and freely without consciously laboring to fit their material into any elaborate scansion. This by no means implies a lack of meter (or even very complicated meter) but merely a lack of *conscious* formal metrical composition. Lord and Parry have shown that orally composed poetry, especially when formulae are present, can achieve a high level of symmetry. This symmetry is an aid to memorization and recitation, as well as hearing and understanding.

The speed of composition is an important factor. The oral poet who is reciting a lengthy narrative is essentially recomposing the piece each time he recites it. He thus recites under pressure of time; formulae and repetition give him time both to recall and to plan ahead. Ugaritic and Hebrew poets, once they had recited the first line (or two) of a couplet or triplet, could begin to plan the particulars of following couplets or triplets while still singing the final line according to a tune and meter that had already been fixed by its use in the prior line(s).

Most popular songs can be learned and repeated easily, even by children, if they are heard many times. Certain sections of Ugaritic and Hebrew songs must have enjoyed general popularity in this manner. The full content of lengthy epics is another matter. This is the specialty of the professional singer, who is probably the source of nearly all of our Ugaritic and early Hebrew poetry.[48]

The ancient professional singer might well have been surprised to have his syllables counted and his sentences grouped into cola, couplets, triplets, and strophes. Most modern folk composers would as well. Yet the analyst must indicate with objective precision how these poets' minds were in fact working. He must show what visible forms their art took so as to be regular, memorizable, and repeatable. Our goal is thus to describe meter as rigorously as possible without imputing to it symmetries which it does not have. We do this regardless of how the poetry was understood technically by its composers.

Irregular meter, though sometimes confusing to the student, is not an insurmountable problem. It is not to be confused with either mixed meter or unbalanced meter. *Mixed* meter is the juxtaposition of couplets and triplets of varying lengths, such as 7:7, 8:8, 6:6:6, 9:9, etc. *Irregular* meter is unexpected and unrepeated unevenness in the lengths of cola within couplets or triplets, such as 7:6, 9:7, 7:8:8, 10:7, etc.[49] *Unbalanced* meter occurs when the lines of a couplet are of different counts, yet the couplets (or triplets) themselves form a consistent pattern, such as 7:5::5:7, 7:5::5:7, etc. (which is one type of Qinah).

Irregularity of meter need not imply complexity or obscurity in a poem. Many English hymns of irregular meter[50] are among the most popular and easily learned songs in our culture, in spite of the fact that the vast majority of English hymns are regular[51] in meter (couplets have even cola, or unbalanced cola are repeated in a regular pattern). Irregular songs need not be hard to learn or difficult to reproduce.

The few cases[52] of truly irregular meter which do occur in this study are likewise neither a threat to the overall theory of syllabic meter nor complex in themselves. They are, however, not to be lightly dismissed. In some cases, they are irregular only according to the rubrics induced for syllabic meter and for the traditional approach they are no problem.

Textual integrity is usually correlated with metrical integrity. In a well-preserved text such as Exodus 15 there are very few metrical anomalies or problems. In Judges 5 the poor state of the text before emendation produces many unusual and broken patterns. Likewise, Ugaritic symmetry within couplets or triplets is easily demonstrable in well-preserved contexts.

The melodies to which Hebrew and Ugaritic poems were composed are irrecoverable. Since in the poetry of both languages the basic units are the couplet and triplet, we may assume that the basic tune lines to which the poems were set were primarily of couplet and triplet length. With variations and combinations, verses and refrains are built, much in the manner of music around the world. As some relatively long psalms in the Old Testament with tune titles[53] suggest, complete songs were indeed built up from the various primary units.

The incomplete graphic notation of Hebrew and Ugaritic writing adds an element of uncertainty to the process of reconstructing pronunciation and therefore meter. This does not mean that a reasonably accurate reconstruction cannot be made;

only that it must be substantiated and must depend upon a careful induction of linguistic information by empirical means.[54]

A further although minor complication is the occasional practice of *inconsistent* orthography in the Canaanite tradition. The effect of this phenomenon is to produce a healthy skepticism about the condition of the text in question. It need not always disturb reconstruction or vocalization.[55]

It does not yet appear that the intrinsic word accents in Hebrew and Ugaritic prose give any clue as to poetic meter. In the case of Hebrew the Masoretic accent marks, highly unreliable at any rate,[56] do not seem to occur in poetry in any regular sequence.[57] Two major accentual shifts in the history of Hebrew complicate the picture. One probably occurred circa 1200 B.C. when case endings were dropped. This would have effectively moved many verbal stresses, for example, from penult to ultima.[58] Between the time of the Qumran writings and the vocalization of the MT there is evidence of another shift in the verbal accent. This was toward the ultima of many forms.[59] The shifts may have confused the Masoretes' ability to scan early Hebrew poetry.

Moreover, intrinsic prose accents, difficult as they are to recover, may be of no help in discerning meter, if not in fact misleading.[60] Reliance on the MT as a basis for any stress meter is highly unsatisfactory.

Syllabic meter is likely to remain useful always. Its worth would not be diminished should a convincing system of internal feet be discovered. Its symmetry does not depend upon any theory of internal stress. The quantity of syllables per colon will continue to be a precise measure of couplet and triplet length regardless of other advances. A couplet whose cola are each eight syllables in length (8:8), for example, will remain 8:8 whether found to be iambic, trochaic, anapestic, dactylic, or any combination of rhythms.

An ever-present indeterminate factor in prosodic analysis is the possibility of poetic license. Under any system of scansion an unusually short or long line normally calls for emendation or special treatment of some sort. So does a strange metrical pattern surrounded by regular patterns.

Nevertheless there always exists the possibility that a poet has exercised his right to irregularity, whether by one syllable or many.

It is not possible for us to be sure that poetic license is present in a piece unless we thoroughly understand the ground rules to which a given poet is bound. If we find him obviously breaking a rule we may call it poetic license. It is an easier task to isolate instances of poetic license in classical poetry, for example, where metrical rules are so well understood.[61] But in Hebrew, if we find a couplet that appears to scan 10:7, we may call it "unbalanced" or the like yet we have no justification in labelling it "improper." Besides this, we are already acquainted with the fact that some of our early poetry is of irregular meter, which breaks rules only if the rules have been set too rigidly by the modern analyst. In short, we as yet have no control over poetic license in Hebrew and Ugaritic poetry. We assume that it must have existed, but we may not attribute any anomaly to it with certainty.

One may rarely emend a passage *metri causa*. On occasion, when well-known formulae are obviously confused or reversed one may set them right by an appeal to meter.[62] Likewise in Hebrew poetry, unusual meter *may* serve as an indication of incompleteness or expansiveness in the text, but only if logic, parallelism, grammar, or some other feature suggests a faulty text. Therefore one must refrain from emendation of any line, no matter what its meter, unless emendation is also indicated by phenomena other than syllable count.

An occasional couplet may be metrically strange yet otherwise acceptable. The critic is in no position to intervene in such a case. The composition of poetry is not so rigid a process that all its component parts are totally predictable. This is to the delight of the hearer and should be to the caution of the critic.

As Jakobson[63] has shown, poetry is primarily distinguished by factors relating to repetition. Repetition occurs in both prose and doggerel, however, so that one is ultimately dependent upon his esthetic judgment in identifying poetry. This judgment obviously differs from person to person, as an examination of those passages treated as poetry throughout Kittel's

Biblia Hebraica proves. If syllabic meter proves to be an accurate description of Hebrew prosody it will provide a further objective basis, at least in many cases, for the isolation of poetry from prose.

General Factors in Prosodic Analysis

Ugaritic poetry and early Hebrew hymnic poetry appear to have been composed orally rather than in writing. Yet all which has been preserved comes to us in written form. During and after their composition, and until the time of their fixing in writing,[64] certain influences typical of oral poetry presumably affected these materials. The student of this poetry must therefore be alert for indications of transmission or dictation errors, textual variances due to confusion of poetic cliches, reversals of epithets within couplets and triplets, and the like. All of them may influence or obscure scansion. The work of Lord and Parry[65] is of immense value in this area. Its application to the poetry of Ugarit and ancient Israel has proved to be highly fruitful.[66]

Throughout this study there appear discussions of phenomena first explained by them in their pioneering works on folk literature, even though they derived their principles of analysis from literature other than that treated here.

Musical factors were influential upon our material. There are ample indications that most of the early poetry of any people is composed to music.[67] Ugaritic and Hebrew show no variance from this tendency. Many of the early Hebrew poems are in fact specifically called "songs" in the text.[68] More elusive is the ability to identify what sort of songs they were. The metrical approach of most members of the traditional school, following for the most part indices from the Masoretes, lends itself to the theory that the songs were chanted. Chanting of these songs continues to be the uniform practice in Judaism. Chanting allows for the pairing of almost any number of syllables and words to a given melody note and thus conveniently handles any poetry or prose regardless of formal meter.[69] Thus, in a typical Jewish synagogue worship service both congregation and cantor sing sections of Hebrew and Aramaic prose and poetry without differentiation. It is our centention, however, that the poems with which we deal in this study were originally composed and sung to melodies with discernable and distinct metrical patterns. Both melody and meter were more precise than those of a chant.

In a few specific instances it may be possible to demonstrate that whole sections of poems had the same meter and thus perhaps even the same melody as other poems or sections of poems. In most cases it is probable that the smaller units of poetry--the couplets and triplets--were composed to given tunes and are interchangeable with other couplets of similar meter. Because of the possibility of internal stress (feet) it is not safe to assume that *all* couplets of 8:8 meter, for example, are metrically identical with all other couplets of 8:8 meter. But as is the case with European hymnic prosody, a song of given meter may normally be sung to another melody of like meter without great distortion. This is, after all, the reason for the metrical indexes which commonly appear in hymnals. Ample notation of these phenomena appears in conjunction with the texts studied in the following chapters.

As poetry is an art rather than a science the practice of its analysis, scientific in its formal aspects, must involve the sorts of subjective judgments that were also the original author's own prerogative. Thus determinations such as placement of strophic boundaries, combination of couplets into a quatrain, identification of "short" vs. "long" meter, etc. are decided by esthetic judgment rather than firm means of quantification.

Rhyme appears at a number of points in Ugaritic and early Hebrew poetry.[70] Rhyme does not usually seem to be the product of a conscious effort or intent. This would be too easy in a language with case endings such as Ugaritic, or a language with as many repetitions of common final sounds as has Hebrew. Rhyme in these languages is rather a specialized type of *assonance*. Assonance is thus the actual operative factor in the composition of poetry which happens to rhyme, and rhyme is merely a sub-category of assonance. This is suggested by the observation that the vast majority of Hebrew and Ugaritic poems exhibit no rhyme patterns whatever, although assonance of various types is widespread. It is further confirmed by the fact that nearly all occurrences of rhyme in Hebrew and Ugaritic are manifested in parts rather than the whole of the poems in question. The student must deal therefore with the full range of assonance: vocalic or consonantal repetitions, paranomasia, *figura etymologica*, alliteration, rhyme, etc., all of which occur to a remarkable degree. Any key to how the poetry itself was originally composed may give the analyst more information upon which to base his decisions as to form, stichometry, and meter.

A chronological typology for much of the early Israelite poetry has now been offered in expanded form by Albright.[71] It is based primarily upon styles of repetitive parallelism, but also on other formal criteria such as the occurrence of paranomasia, *figura etymologica*, etc.

Few metrical patterns may now be given chronological boundaries. Most are found in such a variety of contexts that their use in a poem is of no help in fixing its date.[72]

Each of the preceding considerations, from factors of oral transmission through the dating of metrical patterns, is part of the necessary groundwork which must be performed in the course of poetic analysis. Failure to do this groundwork has resulted in the failure of many attempts at metrics in the last two centuries.

While none of these factors in itself may be crucial to a poem, all provide the fabric from which the poet weaves his product, and all must be evaluated when a study of prosody is undertaken.

Textual Criticism

The study of poetry in the Old Testament necessarily involves the student in text-critical activity. This is true to a lesser extent in the case of Ugaritic because of the more permanent nature of the writing medium. Every proper analysis of the meter of a poem eventually requires a reconstruction of the poem into a form as hypothetically close to the original as possible.

While there are many difficulties connected with such a process, both theoretical and practical, it is a necessary undertaking. Many factors influenced the accurate transmission of any piece of ancient literature as it was recited and re-recited, copied and recopied. They were sufficiently strong so as to be able to corrupt the text of even the most popular of compositions.[73]

Serious difficulties such as might have arisen from incorrect copying, dictation, or interpretation of archaic documents written in the orthography and calligraphy of a previous age, may often be resolved by recasting the piece in question into its assumed original orthography and stichometry.[74] It is best to reconstruct a text to its original and (in the case of the Semitic alphabetic languages) more ambiguous form both morphologically and semantically as one goes back in time. This provides a minimally interpreted base from which to proceed without influence from later and sometimes provincial traditions of interpretation, including that of the Masoretes.

Textual emendation may be required, sometimes on a major scale. Moreover, in the process of analyzing a poem one should turn not only to the information supplied him by the practice of text-critical methods. He may find it necessary to improve upon the received text, with or without compelling evidence from the versions.

Emendation has been studiously avoided in most studies of Old Testament prosody, frequently on dogmatic grounds. One loses the confidence of many of his readers if he dares to tamper with the MT. The failure to emend a senseless text is, however, a greater insult to the inspired writer than the attempt to translate and annotate nonsense.[75]

The dogmatic avoidance of textual criticism has been carefully refuted by Housman.[76] Further, Orlinsky[77] and Albright[78] have argued specifically in the area of the Hebrew Bible that obeisance to a solitary text is unacceptable. As classicists have long known, emendation is always desirable if in fact it produces out of chaos a reading which is appropriate to the parallelism, imagery, style, vocabulary, and overall sense of the piece in question.

Emendation is never to be attempted, however, merely to make readable or to fill out a corrupt or nonsensical text. It must result in an elimination of incoherence or inappropriateness rather than in simple ease of comprehension or scansion. That many texts will continue to remain obscure in parts is certain. When no convincing emendation is at hand, none should be offered. A blank line is preferable to pure conjecture.

Nor can an inconsistent text-critical methodology be tolerated. Critics for centuries have turned to the versions *only* when the MT was obviously faulty. This would imply that copy errors at various stages were always preserved by the scribes and never altered or misread into different forms or words. We know this to be false from the changes visible in the Qumran texts alone. Copyists often changed at least a letter or two of a word that they could not recognize or make sense of in a given context. Many textual problems are hidden beneath passages in the MT which appear to read smoothly because of haplography or expansion or scribal correction. They can come to light only when one consistently refers to the versions and parallels at every verse without exception.

Textual study and emendation when necessary have felicitous results. As an example, the poetry of the Song of Deborah is often garbled or disturbed. Yet, as we shall see, this poem unlocks itself to a remarkable degree when subject to the critical processes discussed above. In turn, the metric analysis proceeds in a superior manner, having a more accurate base upon which to rest its quantification.

The production of good poetry by these means is always the highest consideration. One is not justified in making a translation of a text that is simply not poetry, and pretending that it is. But any emendation involves more than mere mechanical operations. A thorough familiarity with and feel for the material is requisite. Lower criticism therefore eventually requires the intervention of higher criticism. It is a combination of science and art.

Emendation may rarely be attempted *metri causa* alone. One must satisfy the demands of coherence and appropriateness before changing what has been received. This is true both for

Hebrew and for Ugaritic in spite of the differences between the two stemming from their different writing media.

The received Hebrew text did not enjoy any unique protection or preservation from the sorts of influences which can corrupt a text. We must look to other families and versions with as much interest and care as we accord to the MT. For example, the Septuagint, when retroversion is clear, may be given equal status as an authoritative witness to the supposed original, along with the MT. The Vulgate and Targum are of much less interest and use owing to the fact that they are translated from the Masoretic tradition (the received consonantal text). The Samaritan Pentateuch originally derives from a Palestinian text which has often been corrected toward the MT. The Peshitta is in some ways more valid than all other versions with the exception of the LXX and Samaritan Pentateuch because its origin was a comparatively early Palestinian targum. It has been secondarily revised, however, sometimes toward the LXX and sometimes toward either the Hexapla or MT.

Importantly, any of the versions may hold the key to the convincing reconstruction of an original text.

The Qumran texts, although they do not cover the poems studied here except in fragments, would command equal attention to the MT or LXX or any other version. In no case can an approach to the MT so conservative as to permit the translation of illegible texts be accepted. Emendation is superior to bad poetry or prose instead of poetry; nothing at all is superior to something invented to fill space.

Since the present study is not primarily a text-critical work most of the textual comparisons receive little mention. Whenever the MT is to be rejected for a superior reading, however, notation is ample. Specific matters are treated in the notes to the various poems. On occasion, when a decision between two variant reads is not possible, both readings are presented.[79] In other cases no solution to a corrupted text is forthcoming, and a space is left blank.[80]

Of the many examples offered in this study in support of the quantitative theory of meter, only a small percentage involve serious textual problems. The purpose of our activity in textual analysis is to provide an optimal base for poetic analysis; the main thesis of the study does not depend upon *any* text-critical method.[81]

Vocalization

Essential to metrical analysis in both Hebrew and Ugaritic is some knowledge of the pronunciation of the language at the time of the composition of a given poem. Since neither Hebrew nor Ugaritic orthography fully indicated vowels it is obvious that a certain degree of subjectivity will be present in reconstructing these spoken languages. It is nevertheless mandatory that such an attempt be made as a prelude to metrical analysis, in spite of the pitfalls involved. To do otherwise would be to ignore the manifestly oral-aural nature of the poetry. Phonetic features (*contra* the semantic parallelism school) are inherently determinative in the composition, memorization, and vocal reproduction of our poems.

Every past theory of metrics has relied heavily upon Masoretic vocalizations. As a result, every system has had at least some trouble with the treatment of vocal *shewas*, furtive *pataḥs*, anaptyctic vowels, etc. As is well known, the Masoretes represented only one tradition of spoken Hebrew in matters such as these. To expect their pronunciation(s) of Hebrew from ca. 600 to 900 A.D., both provincialized and influenced by other Semitic tongues,[82] to reflect accurately the language of our poems from a period as much as two millennia earlier, is most unreasonable.[83]

We are, however, indebted to them for their precision and candor in attempting to describe Hebrew as it was read in their time, even with its inconsistencies and uncertainties. Their indications of the fluidity of the language, revealed in such devices as the pausal form and composite pointing, have furnished us with much data useful for our reconstruction of the spoken text.

Ugaritic presents problems of vocalization often more troublesome even than those of Hebrew. The theoretical principles upon which this study's vocalization proceeds are those worked out by Albright and Cross and, in some cases, certain of

Cross's students.[84] Clearly, Ugaritic shows evidences of fluidity and inconsistency[85] of pronunciation no less than Hebrew.

A complication affecting Ugaritic but not Hebrew is the fact that case endings, while very much alive in the language, were probably also the least semantically informative of its morphemes. Thus in many cases represented in the following chapters it becomes clear that case endings may have been omitted at the whim of the composer in the context of construct chains and proper nouns. On occasion it seems that even the construct of a word may vary its exact form depending on certain contextual factors.[86]

For our purposes (primarily the determination of overall syllable quantity) there is a saving grace which serves to ameliorate the problems associated with such a subjective enterprise. We need only *approximate* the shadings of vowels or diphthongs, weakness or strength of consonants, spirantizations, doublings, etc. as long as we can be fairly sure of the actual number of syllables in a given word, and thus in the successively larger units of poetry.

Even the position of accents in individual words is of only secondary concern to our study, since syllabic meter leaves open the question of internal stress.

The importance of careful orthographic analysis cannot be overemphasized as a precurser of any attempt at vocalization. Every text treated in this study has been reconstructed in the orthography of the period of its presumed composition. Ample groundwork for such a practice has been laid by Albright,[87] Cross,[88] and Freedman.[88] Their work, combined with the extensive studies of original Hebrew pronunciation by Harris,[89] Speiser,[90] Sperber,[91] and others[92] provides some basis for vocalizing ancient Hebrew materials. Further information on Hebrew vocalization, extrapolated from such sources as Latin and Hexaplaric transliterations, Qumran, Akkadian, Punic, etc. has only served to strengthen our knowledge.

We have, however, *no* contemporary vocalized texts. Nothing of early Hebrew vocalization is certain. We deal in probabilities and extrapolations rather than firm data. But we judge the scholar dependent only upon the MT to be on even less solid ground. We are likely to be closer than he is to the phonetic realities.

While most discussions of Hebrew vocalization procedures are to be found in the notes to the various poems in following chapters, it is appropriate here to list some of the major features assumed to be operative. Based on those notes and the published studies cited above, the following observations should be made:

1. Case endings were almost never preserved in Hebrew.

2. Diphthongs were preserved in the southern dialect at least until the time of the Exile. They were normally contracted in the north, except in some final positions (e.g. *šadday*).

3. The feminine singular noun had two potential endings, from *-*tu* and *-*atu* of the old Canaanite, pronounced -*t* and -*ā* in Hebrew.

4. The segholate plural of the masculine was uniformly of the pattern *qəṭalīm*.

5. The dual is formed upon the singular stem.

6. MT *mayim*, *samayim*, etc. were originally segholates rather than plurals (*maym*, *šamaym* in the south; *mēm*, *šamēm* in the north).

7. Several "Canaanite" particles (*lu*, *la*, *limma*, -*mi*,[93] etc.) are proper to early Hebrew poetry.

8. Although the shading of vowels varied greatly with geography and period, the root Semitic vowels (a, i, u) were presumably more original in many positions than their derivatives (o, e). The latter were used from the earliest periods in the north, and probably to a lesser extent in the south.[94] Sperber[95] has argued convincingly that only three vowels were consistently distinguished as phonemic even by the Masoretes themselves: a, i, and o/u. In biblical Hebrew the distribution of Masoretic pointings makes clear that the various vowel shadings (*seghol* as opposed to *ṣere*, for example) are allophonic rather than phonemic. Vocalizational systems other than the Tiberian serve to support this contention.

All pre-monarchical Hebrew poems preserved were probably of northern provenance since the north was the site of the central sanctuary, and therefore league traditions, until David's time. We therefore reconstruct all pre-monarchical poetry in northern orthography and dialect.

The following decisions as to vocalization are also made:

1. Vowels whose length is uncertain are usually left short. The date of most tone-lengthening, for example, is unknown.

2. Long *a* in some pointings of the MT was probably not original; e.g. in the cohortative, where it may have been either short or *anceps*; and the locative, where the original ending was probably *-*ha* or the like rather than MT -*āh*.

3. The shift from **ā* to *ō* (e.g. in the participle *kōtēb*, or in the f. pl. -*ōt*) is assumed to have taken place as in the MT. Amarna evidence, though scanty, supports this.

4. The *i* to *ē* shift under stress in some positions is assumed, although it is of unknown date, to preserve consistency with the MT.

5. Short *i* in closed positions, not fully shifted to *e* (seghol) in the MT (e.g. *bin*, Joshua 1:1; *'ōyibka*, Exodus 23:4) is retained generally. This shift is likewise merely allophonic.

6. Segholation did not occur until after the composition of Old Testament texts. It is still in process at the time of Origen's work.[96]

7. Short *o* in some positions (from **u*) is assumed as in MT.

8. The construct plural is arbitrarily vocalized as -*ē* in both north and south. Its origin was perhaps the old oblique plural **-ī*. Masoretic traditions suggesting an origin in **-ay* may be wrong, although firm proof is not forthcoming. **-ay* to -*ē* in the dual is secondary. Cross and Freedman discuss the entire question in *Studies in Ancient Yahwistic Poetry*, 141f.

9. Long vowels are indicated by macron regardless of origin.

10. Alternate forms of constructs, suffixes, prepositions, etc. were varied in poems *metri causa*: e.g. *bām/bahem*,

ᶜal/ᶜalē, -ka/-ak, ēka/ēk, ka/kamō, quṭul/quṭl-, ṣədaqōt/ ṣidqōt, -in/-inna (or *an/anna*).

11. Such personal suffixes as *ka* and **ki* were apparently not appended directly to forms ending in consonants. A vowel usually represented in Masoretic pointing by *seghol* or *shewa* was interjected (e.g. *suseka*; *yadəka*, etc.). Thus "your hand" (*ydk*) may be given three syllables in the scansion.

12. Other vocalization problems are dealt with *ad loc.*

Past studies of Hebrew meter have relied almost exclusively on the Tiberian Masoretic dialect's pronunciations. Even the recent studies by Mowinckel, Segert, and Freedman, which acknowledge MT vocalization to be doubtful or erroneous in many parts, remain with the received pointings. Segert, moreover, commits a common but inexcusable error by abandoning MT vocalization, except in the case of segholate nouns, *only* when Qumran evidence demands another vocalization. This is methodological chaos of the sort well refuted by Housman and others.[97]

Examples of the Newer Metrical Analysis

It is our general theory that the poetry of the early Israelites was in the Canaanite tradition. This is not to say that the Hebrew is directly descended from the Ugaritic. Rather, they *both* partook of Northwest Semitic musical and poetic traditions. Like Ugarit, Israel had a musical poetry, oral in composition. It was sung to musical lines the exact length of which in syllables (and probably in some sort of musical measures) was an important determinant.

The loss of case endings from the time of Ugaritic to the time of classical Hebrew made for different lengths of cola. Hebrew tended to be a syllable or two shorter per colon in its various patterns than did Ugaritic. This would also have necessitated development of different (shorter) melodic lines in most cases, although one may speculate that both traditions may have shared not a few tunes.

At all events the exact number of syllables per colon was important to the prosody of both poetries. In the following pages we shall demonstrate how the newer method of syllable counting describes the meter of Hebrew poetry more precisely than the scansions of other schools. We select examples from a variety of Hebrew poems and compare the results of the four methods. Obviously individual scholars within a given school would sometimes differ with one another as to a count. Also, some couplets which follow present analytical problems for any school but the newest. Possible alternate counts are therefore given. Since the representatives of these schools follow the MT we must give their counts according to the Masoretic vocalization rather than force them to accept our reconstructed vocalization.

The following examples are taken from the full treatments of various poems in the succeeding chapters.[98] While these examples are in no way exhaustive, they serve initially to demonstrate the advantages of syllable counting compared to the other approaches.

Example No. 1: Genesis 4:23-24

Here the stichometry is a problem. In *BH* Kittel assumed that עדה וצלה was not part of the poem, creating unnecessary problems in scansion. Below is a better stichometric arrangement with each ictus placed as *most* members of the traditional school would do. (The ictus is indicated here by the letter *x*.)

x x x x
ʿādāh w^{e}ṣillāh *š^{e}maʿan qôlî̂*

x x x
n^{e}šê lemek *ha'zēnnāh 'imrātî*

x x x x (x) x
kî 'îš hāragtî l^{e}piṣʿî *w^{e}yeled l^{e}ḥabburātî*

x (x) x x x x
kî šibʿātayim yuqqam qāyin *w^{e}lemek šibʿîm w^{e}šibʿāh*

The unusual results (a scansion of 4+3, 3+3/2, 3/2+3) may have been the reason for Kittel's adoption of an alternate stichometry which is less satisfactory in its parallelism but easier to scan according to his understanding of the traditional method:

š^{e}ma^{c}an qôlî n^{e}šê lemek   *ha'zēnnāh 'imrātî*

kî 'îš hāragtî l^{e}piṣ^{c}î   *w^{e}yeled l^{e}ḥabburātî*

kî šib^{c}ātayim yuqqam qāyin   *w^{e}lemek šib^{c}îm w^{e}šib^{c}āh*

This yielded 3+2, 3+2/3, 2/3+3 (if no secondary accents are assumed it is 3+2, 3+2, 2+3) which would perhaps have satisfied most members of the school. Sievers and Ley might have placed a secondary accent (x) within *l^{e}ḥabburātî*; someone might have been tempted to accent *kî* in the third couplet and shift the accent to the first syllable of *yuqqam*, etc. But basically the advocates of the traditional scansion would have scanned these lines as shown above, either with Kittel's or the revised stichometry.

The semantic parallelism school would read 4+3, 3+2, 3+3/2 for the revised stichometry and 3+2, 3+2, 3+3/2 for the Kittel arrangement. Sometimes Robinson or Gray will accent a *kî*, especially if it means "if" as in the third couplet of this song. But here it is not likely that they would do so, to avoid too high a count. As expected, the count of the semantic parallelism school is very close to that of the traditional school.

Most members of the alternating meter school would scan the revised arrangement as follows:

^{c}ādāh w^{e}ṣillāh š^{e}ma^{c}an qôlî   *n^{e}šê lemek ha'zēnnāh 'imrātî*

kî 'îš hāragtî l^{e}piṣ^{c}î   *w^{e}yeled laḥabburātî*

kî šib^{c}ātayim yuqqam qāyin   *w^{e}lemek šib^{c}îm w^{e}šib^{c}āh*

Some representatives of this school would be dissatisfied with the results from the first two lines. They might, by various means, reduce the count, probably to 4+4 in the first line and 4+3 in the second. This would be done either by syncope of the vocalic *shewas*, by dismissal of some secondary accent (all of which do not have to be stressed),[99] by finding anapests, by employing anacrusis, by redividing the line (the first line above could be made into a 3+2, 3+2), etc. Bickell, among others, would retain the higher count.

The alternating meter school would scan the Kittel arrangement as follows:

x x x x x x x

šᵉmaᶜan qôlî nᵉšê lemek   ha'zēnnāh 'imrātî   etc.

The resultant 4+3 is typically the count for the alternating school's view of Qinah, although the Song of Lamech is hardly representative of normal Qinah.

None of the major schools would feel entirely comfortable with the Song of Lamech. Ley, for example, treated the poem in two different ways in his *Grundzüge* and *Leitfaden*. Even with the adoption of the questionable stichometry offered by Kittel these approaches are not wholly satisfying.

Syllabic scansion offers an entirely different view of this poem:

ᶜadā waṣillā šamaᶜn qōlī   9

našē lamk ha'zēnna 'imratī   9

ᵓīš haragtī lapiṣᶜī   7

wayald laḥabburatī   7

kī šibᶜatēm yuqqam qēn   7

walamk šibᶜīm wašibᶜā   7

The syllable count shows that in fact the couplets are each precisely balanced, and that the meter of the final two couplets is the same rather than different as the other systems might have suggested.

The nature of the parallelism is simply 1:1, 1:1, 1:1.[100] The deletion of *kī* at the outset of the second couplet is not *metri causa*. Particles such as *kī*, *'et*, *'ašer*, and others are patently prosaic and usually suspicious in a poetic context. Where *kī* means "if," however, as in the third couplet of this song, it must be retained.

Example No. 2: Genesis 49:10

Here the traditional school would read 3+3, 3+3/2, as reference to Kittel's arrangement in BH would show. The grouping of the various small words in the first line of the second couplet is obviously a problem.

The semantic parallelism school would scan the two couplets as 3+3, 3/4+3. The alternating meter school would probably read 4+3, 3+3. We suggest the adoption of minor emendations which do not affect the meter of any school but make sense out of an otherwise corrupt passage: for שׁבט read שׁפט; revocalize MT *yābō'* to *yūbā'*; change שׁילה to שׁי לה. We assume these changes in our conjectures as to the meter obtained above by the various schools.

In the scansions of the three major schools these two couplets are of either identical or nearly identical meter (the alternating meter shows the differences in length between the two most clearly). Syllabic scansion shows how different the two couplets really are:

lō' yasūr šōpēṭ miyyahudā	9
wamuḥōqēq mibbēn dagalēw	9
ᶜad kī yūbā' šay lō	6
walō yiqhat ᶜammīm	6

There is no lack of balance within each couplet, yet their metrical lengths are very different. Both of these features are shown most clearly by the newer method. The metrical length may be described schematically as 1:1, 1:1. Although the second couplet is relatively short, it does not exhibit internal parallelism and is not therefore part of a b:b::b:b full couplet, so we choose to label it 1:1. That it contains many words and much information in contrast to the usual b:b couplet is added proof that it should be considered a "long" couplet.

Example No. 3: Exodus 15:14

Quell arranged this verse in *BH* to scan 3+3/4. The semantic parallelism school would read 3+3. Alternating meter yields 4+4. While these methods tend to demonstrate the balance of the couplet's lines, they do not distinguish it from couplets of very different length. For example, the 3+3 of the traditional and semantic parallelism schools is the same count these schools might give to the short couplet above from Genesis 49:10. The 4+4 of the alternating school shows no differentiation from their count for the longer couplet of that same section.

Syllabic meter exhibits a greater precision. It proves the Exodus 15:14 couplet to be longer than the second (6:6) couplet of Genesis 49:10, yet shorter than the first couplet of that verse (9:9). It is:

šamaᶜū ᶜammīm yirgazūn	8
ḥīl 'aḥaz yōšibē pališt	8

Example No. 4: Numbers 21:29

Our treatment of this verse in a following chapter includes the insertion of מלכ between לכ and מאב of the MT.[101] Otherwise the text is satisfactory. We will assume that the various schools are also reading this change into the MT.

Each of the schools allows for the possibility of a somewhat "unbalanced" scansion. The traditional meter might be 3+2/3, 3+2/3+3. The semantic parallelism method gives 3+2/3, 3+2+3. Alternating meter could be 3/4+3/4, 4/3+3/4+4/3. The apparent possibility of irregular meter is removed with syllabic scansion:

'ōy laka malk mō'āb	6
'abadta ᶜam kamōš	6
natan banēw palēṭīm	7
wabanōtēw bašabīt	7
lamalk 'amōrī sīḥōn	7

While the meter is mixed, it is neither unusual nor unbalanced, nor even *possibly* unbalanced. The general length may be labelled 1:1, 1:1:1.

Example No. 5: Numbers 23:24

The arrangement of this verse by Rudolph in BH was according to the traditional scansion. It read 3+3, 3+3, normal for nearly all Hebrew meter. The semantic parallelism method gives something on the order of 3/4+2, 3/4+3/2. Alternating meter is approximately 3/4+3/4, 4+3/4. Except in the case of the highly malleable traditional meter, the schools suggest at least possibility of imbalance within these couplets. Syllabic met meter, however, reflects a balanced *and* precise picture of the metrical realities:

hēn ᶜam kalabi' yaqūm	7
waka'arī yitnaśśā'	7
lō' yiškab ᶜad yō'kal ṭarp	7
wadam ḥalalīm yištē	7

In terms of syllabic length these couplets are not unbalanced in any way. While one might argue in the manner of the semantic parallelism school that there is some sort of incomplete parallelism here, he would not be justified in finding incomplete metrical parallelism. The couplets are normal 1:1, 1:1 rather than the 1:b::1:b or the like that might reflect true imbalance (as in Qinah).

Example No. 6: Deuteronomy 33:26-27

Hempel was aware of the minor textual difficulties of these verses, but was able to arrange them in BH in a generally acceptable manner. Our suggested textual emendations would not threaten the scansion of either the traditional school or the semantic parallelism school. They alter the count of the alternating meter school slightly; this is considered in that school's presumed count of 3+3/4+3, 4+4/3. Traditional meter theoretically yields 3+3+2/3, 3+3. Semantic parallelism meter scans 3+3+2, 3+3. The syllable count is:

'ēn ka'ēl yašurūn	6
rōkēb šamēm ba^{c}az	6
⌐bagē'ūt šaḥaqīm	6
ma^{c}ōnō 'elōhē qadm	7
⌐mittaḥt zarō^{c}ōt ^{c}ōlam	7

None of the popular methods depicts the meter of these verses so precisely as the method of syllabic scansion. V. 26 may be described as either b:b:b or l:l:l. The context would suggest l:l:l. V. 27 is l:l.

Example No. 7: II Samuel 1:21b-22

Members of the various schools would find these verses to be short metrically. The traditional school would read mostly 2+2: 2+2, 2+2/3, 2+2, 2/3+2, 2+2. The results of semantic parallelism meter are similar: 2/3+2, 2+2/3, 2+2, 2+2, 2+2. Alternating meter is probably 2+3/2 throughout. It is at least somewhat awkward, however, to fit these couplets into any of the above meters.

Syllabic meter gives a precise and detailed picture of the metrical realities:

kī šam nig^{c}al	4
magēn gibbōrīm	5
magēn ša'ūl	4
bal mašūḥ bašamn	5
middam ḥalalīm	5
miḥḥilb gibbōrīm	5
qašt yōnatan	4
lō' naśag 'aḥōr	5
waḥarb ša'ūl	4
lō' tašūb rēqam	5

Schematically this is b:b::b:b, b:b::b:b::b:b, a couplet and triplet each with internal parallelism. The parallelism in this case (except for the 5:5 short couplet) is reflected in the staccato nature of the composition. There is no rigid internal parallelism here, but it is obvious that the poet composed his short couplets in four and five syllable cola. The 5:5 couplet is special in this context: it alone is fully parallel internally. As one traces the logical progression of these verses he notes that without this 5:5 couplet the following two short couplets are not completed in thought. This is perhaps the reason why it is specially composed and differs slightly in count from its neighbors.

The popular methods of scansion could not be expected to call attention to such phenomena.

Example No. 8: II Samuel 1:25

The stichometry of v. 25 is not obvious. In BH Kittel was able to construe it as a tricolon and scan 3+2+3 by making a cesura after *milḥamāh*. The verse reads awkwardly when divided in such a manner, however, and he noted the possibility of textual corruption. Here is an example of how commitment to an imprecise metrical theory may lead one to impute imprecision to a sound text.

We suggest an alternate stichometry, with the cesura after *yōnatan* (the tenth-century form of the name) as follows:

'ēka napalū gibbōrīm	8
batawk milḥamā yōnatan	8
ᶜalay bamōtēka ḥalal	8

Arranged in this way, the simple balanced triplet might have appeared unbalanced in the traditional scansion, 3+3+2. To the semantic parallelism school it would have been 3+3+2 (3+2+3 for the Kittel arrangement). Alternating meter might give a count of 4+4+4 (4+3+5 for the Kittel stichometry).

We may describe such a triplet simply as 1:1:1.

Example No. 9: II Samuel 22 (=Psalm 18): 35-36

These two verses contain a couplet and triplet which could scan 3+4/3, 3/4+3/2+3/2 in the traditional manner. The scansion of the semantic parallelism school would be 3+4, 3/4+2+2. Alternating meter might be 4/4+5, 4+4+4. Each of these methods either allows for or clearly describes some sort of imbalance. This is not the case if syllabic meter is employed and our assumption about its accuracy is correct. The newer scansion yields a completely balanced couplet and triplet, which may be represented as 1:1, 1:1:1. A minor emendation, which does not affect meter, is made in the final colon on the basis of the Qumran text:

mulammēd yaday lamilḥamā	9
⌜⌝*niḥḥēt qašt naḥušt zarō*^{c}*ōtay*	9
⌜⌝*tittēn lī magēn yiš*^{c}*eka*	8
⌜⌝*yamīneka tis*^{c}*adēnī*	8
wa^c*i‹z›rateka tarbēnī*	8

Example No. 10: Amos 5:12

Here we would assume a slight emendation to be in order, omitting the word *kī* at the outset of the verse as a typical prosaic interpolation. Otherwise there are no differences in text between our reconstruction and that of Procksch in BH. No school's meter would be affected in this case by the omission of *kī*. Traditional meter is 3+3, 4+3 (or 2+2+3). Semantic parallelism meter is approximately 3+2, 4+3 (or 2+2+3). Alternating meter is 4/5+4, 4/5+4/5. None of these depicts the meter so exactly as the syllabic count:

yada^c*tī rabbīm piša*^{c}*ēkim*	9
wa^c*aṣūmīm ḥaṭṭōtēkim*	8
ṣōrirē ṣaddīq lōqiḥē kopr	9
wa'ibyōnīm baša^c*r hiṭṭū*	8

Schematically this is l:l, l:l, unusual neither in logic nor meter. While there is a one-syllable imbalance between individual cola within the couplets, the couplets themselves are metrically equivalent. Such meter is best described as *regular* and *unbalanced*. Since the patterns of couplets in proximity to these two couplets in Amos 5 are not 9:8, we may also note that these couplets are part of a *mixed* metrical context.

It is interesting to note that Lord and Parry's recordings of Serbo-Croation folk-poets' songs reveal that the number of distinct notes in each melody is usually greater than the number of syllables in the words sung. This means, of course, that some syllables are held while the voice intones a multiplicity of sounds, as in music of all ages. Therefore, any attempt at a stress meter which insists upon a rigid equation of syllables with musical beats might well be self-defeating. Examination of the types of cantillation applied to various passages of scripture in the Yemenite, Sephardic, and Ashkenazic traditions shows that great diversity exists as to both the melodies and timing of the music to which these passages are set.[102]

The foregoing examples are intended to demonstrate that the newer scansion based on syllable count is both more precise and more adaptable than the scansions offered by the three prevailing schools of metrics. With careful syllable counts and the use of a simple length notation (l and b) one may now differentiate regular and irregular meter, balanced and unbalanced couplets, mixed and unmixed metrical contexts, and exact colon length in a manner unmatched by other methods of scansion.

It is especially noteworthy that other methods of scansion often suggest balances or imbalances in metrical parallelism that may in fact be quite spurious. These are often obviated only by syllabic scansion.

We continue to be indebted to the fine scholars who represent the major schools. They have nothing less than the highest appreciation of Hebrew poetry. Working with limited approaches to prosody they have produced frequently brilliant studies of Old Testament poetry from which all students of the texts benefit. Their excellence in using a limited system of analysis demonstrates, when problems arise, that a newer method with greater precision would be welcome.

In the following chapters several hundred lines of Ugaritic and early Hebrew poetry are analyzed prosodically. The Ugaritic poetry is taken from three long sections of the Baal and Keret myths. The Hebrew poetry studied includes most of the early poems from the Pentateuch and Former Prophets. Selections from the book of Amos are also included in an effort to apply the principles of the newer scansion to the earliest of the classical prophets. The results show that even though Amos' prophecies were different from the earlier material in length and subject matter (and frequently vocabulary) many of them display metrical patterns common to the earlier period.

Our purpose in producing the whole of lengthy poems, both Hebrew and Ugaritic, is to demonstrate the reliability of syllabic scansion under all metrical conditions. In each case the poems are arranged in a form as close as possible to what we believe to have been original; otherwise they are unchanged.

NOTES

CHAPTER I

[1]J. Ley, *Grundzüge des Rhythmus, des Vers- und Strophenbaues in der hebräischen Poesie*, Halle, 1875; *Die metrischen Formen der hebräischen Poesie*, Leipzig, 1886; *Leitfaden der Metrik der hebräischen Poesie*, Halle, 1887.

[2]K. Budde, "Das hebräische Klagelied," *ZAW* 2 (1882), 1-52; *Der Segen Mose's*, Tübingen, 1922.

[3]E. Sievers, *Metrische Studien. I: Studien zur hebräischen Metrik*, Leipzig, 1901; *II: Die hebräischen Genesis*, Leipzig, 1904.

[4]We, however, refer to it as the "traditional" method, both to indicate its widespread acceptance, and not to exclude its other advocates.

[5]These included a relatively small number of coins and seals, as well as inscriptions from Moab, Jerusalem (Siloam), coastal Phoenicia, Zinjirli, and Teima.

[6]This traditional dependency upon the Masoretes continues: "Meter may be reduced to nothing more than a tallying of accents provided by the Masoretes." (Gottwald, "Hebrew Poetry," *IDB*, Abingdon, 1962, Vol. III, p. 835). By contrast, Alexander Sperber in his brilliant *Historical Grammar of Biblical Hebrew* (Leiden, 1966) demonstrates both the inconsistency of Hebrew accentuation and the lack of relationship of accent marks to intrinsic word stress (pp. 457-476).

[7]The following terms are hereafter interchangeable: colon = line; bicolon = couplet; tricolon = triplet; accent = stress. The Masoretic signs supposedly indicating accentuation are called here "accent marks."

[8]R. Jakobson, "On Ancient Greek Prosody," *Selected Writings I*, The Hague, Mouton, 1962, 262-271.

[9]"Based exclusively" means that other types of feet are occasional and incidental to the primary meter. Nearly all critics are forced to posit an occasional syncope or anacrusis to explain an unusual prosodic pattern.

[10]Mowinckel might particularly object to being grouped with this school, since his arrival at iambic meter is dependent upon a programmatic interpretation of accentuation. For him, accents are partly phonetic, partly semantic. Nevertheless his metrical counts place him ultimately in the alternating meter school.

[11]J. Bellermann, *Versuch über die Metrik der Hebräer*, Berlin, 1813.

[12]J. Saalschütz, *Von der Form der hebräischen Poesie*, Königsberg, 1825.

[13]Göttingen, 1835.

[14]This is much in the manner of Mowinckel, certain of whose arguments Ewald anticipated.

[15]E. Meier, *Die Form der hebräischen Poesie*, Tübingen, 1853; *Das Hohelied*, Tübingen, 1854; *Die poetischen Bücher*, Tübingen, 1854.

[16]Cf. Jakobson, *op. cit.* and "Über die Beschaffenheit der prosodischen Gegensätze," *Selected Writings I*, The Hague, Mouton, 1962, 254-261

[17]See note 1.

[18]"Unaccented" is used here in the sense of "unstressed" or "non-tonic."

[19]R. Lowth, *The Sacred Poetry of the Hebrews* (trans. and new ed.), New York, 1829.

[20]All scholars recognize that parallelism is characteristic of Hebrew poetry. Most recognize the importance of various categories of parallelism including grammatical parallelism, phonetic parallelism, metrical parallelism, and semantic parallelism. The semantic parallelism school is unique in subordinating all types of parallelism except the latter, and further in quantifying it as "meter."

[21]G. B. Gray, *The Book of Numbers*, *ICC* Vol. IV, 1903; *The Forms of Hebrew Poetry*, Cambridge, 1915; (also in reprint with new prolegomenon by D. N. Freedman, New York, KTAV, 1973).

[22]T. H. Robinson, *The Poetry of the Old Testament*, Cambridge, 1947; "Basic Principles of Hebrew Poetic Form," *Festschrift Alfred Bertholet*, Tübingen, 1950, 438-450; "Hebrew Poetic Form," *Supp. to Vetus Testamentum* I (1953), 128-149.

[23]As used by classicists and occasionally by Semitic scholars, anacrusis refers to a syllable remaining at the end of a foot or colon which is not included in the basic pattern or its count. As Robinson uses the term it becomes a means for explaining the presence of a word or even short phrase at the end of a colon which does not otherwise fit into the predominating meter of a section of poetry.

[24]G. Bickell, *Metrices Biblicae regulae exemplis illustrae*, Innsbruck, 1879; "Die hebräischen Metrik," *ZDMG* (1880), 557ff.

[25]S. Mowinckel, "Zum Problem der hebräischen Metrik," *Festschrift Alfred Bertholet*, Tübingen, 1950, 379-94; "Zur hebräischen Metrik II," *Studia Theologica* VII (1953), 54-85.

[26] G. Hölscher, *Hesekiel*, Giessen, 1924; *Das Buch Hiob*, Tübingen, 1937.

[27] S. Segert, "Vorarbeiten zur hebräischen Metrik," *ArOr* 21 (1953), 481-510; "Zur Habakkuk Rolle aus dem Funde Beim Toten Meer, IV (F., Metrisches)," *ArOr* 23 (1955), 178-83; "Problems of Hebrew Prosody," *Supp. to Vetus Testamentum* VII (1960), 283-291.

[28] P. Haupt, "The Poetic Form of the First Psalm," *AJSL* 19 (1903), 129-42; "Moses' Song of Triumph," *AJSL* 20 (1904), 149-72; *Biblische Liebeslieder*, Baltimore, Johns Hopkins Press, 1907; "Critical Notes on Micah," *AJSL* 26 (1910), 201-252.

[29] Albright's poetical studies range from "The Earliest Forms of Hebrew Verse," *JPOS* 2 (1922), 69-86, to *Yahweh and the Gods of Canaan*, New York, 1968. See the bibliography here and in Wright (ed.), *The Bible and the Ancient Near East*, Garden City, 1961.

[30] See notes 89-92.

[31] Particularly the inscriptions from Gezer, Jerusalem, and Arslan Tash, all of which may be poetic. The Arslan Tash inscription is certainly poetry, and many of its features confirm poetic theories advanced by the newer school (e.g. that the article does not normally belong to poetry, that mixed, syllabic meter prevails in the Syro-Phoenician area as well as in Israel, etc.). Cf. Cross and Saley, "Phoenician Incantations on a Plaque of the Seventh Century B.C. from Arslan Tash in Upper Syria," *BASOR* 197 (1970), 42-49.

[32] Cross, F. M., and Freedman, D. N., *Studies in Ancient Yahwistic Poetry*. Dissertation Series #21. Missoula, Montana: Scholars Press, 1975.

[33] E.g. Cross, "The Song of the Sea and Canaanite Myth," *Journal for Theology and the Church* 5 (1968), 1-25.

[34] See especially, "Archaic Forms in Early Hebrew Poetry" (1960), "The Structure of Psalm 137" (1971), "Acrostics and Metrics" (1972), "Strophe and Meter in The Song of the Sea" (1974), and "Psalm 29: A Structural Analysis" (with C. F. Hyland, 1973).

[35] A. Ehlen, *The Poetic Structure of a Hodayah from Qumran*, Th.D. Thesis, Harvard University, 1970.

[36] See note 34.

[37] D. W. Watson, *Text-Restoration Methods in Contemporary U. S. A. Biblical Scholarship*, Naples, 1969.

[38] See note 31.

[39]A. Lord, *The Singer of Tales*, New York, Atheneum, 1968; M. Parry, L'Epithète Traditionelle dans Homère, Paris, 1928; "Studies in the Epic Technique of Oral Verse-Making," I (*HSCP* 41: 73-147, 1930); II *HSCP* 42: 1-50, 1932); Parry and Lord, Serbocroation Heroic Songs, Cambridge, Mass., Harvard University Press, 1954.

[40]See Lord, *The Singer of Tales*.

[41]Parry's original definition of a formula: "...a group of words which is regularly employed under the same metrical conditions to express a given essential idea." Cf. Lord, *The Singer of Tales*.

[42]The possibilities of internal feet are also discussed by S. A. Geller in a Harvard Ph.D. thesis to be completed in 1976.

[43]We assume the components of some construct chains to be technically free forms. The definition of "word" in any language may be a problem, although "minimal free form" is commonly used. The reader may wish to differ with our analysis and speak of "bound syntactic units" or the like as constituting "feet."

[44]The modern system, centered upon the number of syllables per colon, has never needed replacement, even though it does not pretend to provide an exhaustive description of metrical characteristics.

[45]The entire question of Qinah needs reexamination in light of syllabic meter. It is possible that the number of words or bound forms in Qinah cola may be completely irrelevant to the imbalance characteristics of the meter. Or, semantic factors may indeed play a role in addition to phonetic considerations, as part of the overall grammatical parallelism.

[46]Albright was characteristically willing to change a position quickly when new evidence warranted it. By the 1940's he had apparently reversed his earlier position against mixed meter.

[47]The classical concept of the strophe may, in fact, be entirely irrelevant to Ugaritic and early Hebrew poetry.

[48]See Lord, *The Singer of Tales*, pp. 13ff. for a description of the making of an oral poet and the special expertise required for his craft.

[49]Cf. the various discussions, *ad loc.* in Chapter III, where uneven couplets (e.g. 6:7) or triplets (e.g. 7:8:8) occur. Truly irregular meter involves imbalance of *two* or more syllables (except in the case of Qinah) or erratic patterns of one-syllable imbalance. A one-syllable difference between cola in b:b (::b:b) meter is not a problem and is not necessarily irregular.

[50]E.g. "God Rest Ye Merry, Gentlemen," "The First Noel," "O Come All Ye Faithful," "The Ninety and Nine," "Blessed Assurance," "Great Is Thy Faithfulness," etc., all of which have simple, popular tunes.

[51]"Regular" in the sense of English meter is of course slightly different from "regular" in Hebrew-Canaanite.

[52]Deut. 32, however, seems to have much irregular meter.

[53]E.g. Psalms 6, 8, 9, 22, 45, 46, 56, etc.

[54]The groundwork for this has been laid by Cross and Freedman, *Early Hebrew Orthography* and many others. Cf. notes 87-92.

[55]The writer has studied scribal inconsistencies in various ancient Near Eastern texts in an unpublished Yale University paper, 1966. Inconsistencies are normally survivals of historical spellings placed side by side, and often purposely varied one after another sequentially, on the part of a scribe. The Moabite Stone appears to exhibit a tendency to use historical spellings except where place names required the use of a more explicit orthography. A more recent example comes from the plaque at the Johnston Gate to Harvard Yard, quoting from an original founding document of the college: "...shal*bee* called Harvard College at Newtowne, to henceforward *be* called Cambridge."

[56]See Sperber, *Historical Grammar of Biblical Hebrew*, Leiden, 1966, pp. 457-476.

[57]They do not, as well, in Greek. Cf. Goodwin and Gulick, *Greek Grammar*, Boston, Ginn and Co., 1958, 343-362, and the following:

> Greek verse, being developed in intimate connection with music, is regulated by the quantity of syllables, not the accent of words....Sometimes the word-accent seems to correspond with meter...but in general we may disregard the accent.... (*ibid.*, 343)

While there are obviously many differences between Greek and Hebrew poetry, it is interesting to note that Greek meter *originally* disregarded completely any intrinsic accentuation (or tonal quality as the accents may have indicated) even when internal feet were basic to the meter. Goodwin and Gulick (*ibid.*, 344) have also shown that modern Greek poetry has shifted away from the original principles to depend upon accentuation rather than syllabic quality. Could a parallel situation have occurred within Hebrew so as to distance the Masoretes from the original principles of composition of Old Testament poetry?

[58]E.g. the 3.m.s. form **yiqṭólu* > *yiqṭṓl*.

[59]E.g. the 3.m.pl. form *yiqṭốlû* > *yiqṭ*^{e}*lû́*.

[60] If Sievers were right that classical Hebrew verse was composed in combinations of anapests, proto-Hebrew verse would have been composed in combinations of trochees and pyrrhics. Later (post-Qumran) feet would often have been amphibrachs or the like.

[61] But cf. Jakobson, "On Ancient Greek Prosody," which warns against an exclusive reliance on Alexandrian grammarians, and their doctrines of the three-syllable rule, the three-mora rule, etc.

[62] Cf. the Ugaritic evidence in Chapter II, Text 5 II 3.

[63] R. Jakobson, "Grammatical Parallelism and its Russian Facet," *Language* 42 (1966), 399-429.

[64] Considering the delicate materials upon which most Hebrew was written and the complex nature of the transmission of written texts, we mean by "fixed" the earliest point at which all textual evidence agrees or changes no further.

[65] See note 39.

[66] Cf. Cross, "The Song of the Sea and Canaanite Myth," p. 1, note 3, and R. Whitaker, "A Formulaic Analysis of Ugaritic Poetry," Ph.D. dissertation, Harvard University, 1970.

[67] Cf. Lord, *The Singer of Tales*, 1-29 *et passim*.

[68] E.g. Exodus 15:1; Numbers 21:17,27; Deuteronomy 31:30; Judges 5:1, etc.

[69] See the brief but excellent discussion by Eric Werner, "Masoretic Accents," in the *IDB*, Vol. III, pp. 295-299, and the bibliography given there.

[70] See 2 IV 10 and Genesis 4:23-4, 49:3; Numbers 21:27f.; Judges 14:18b, 16:24; Amos 5:11.

[71] W. F. Albright, *Yahweh and the Gods of Canaan*, New York, 1968, 1-52. See also Robertson, David A., *Linguistic Evidence in Dating Early Hebrew Poetry*. Dissertation Series #3. Missoula, Montana: Scholars Press, 1972.

[72] Some patterns may, in a general sense, be datable. For example, the Qinah pattern does appear to have a *terminus a quo* (Amos) although not a clear *terminus ad quem*. Short meter (6:6::6:6, etc.) occurs almost exclusively in early contexts. The very long (1:1::1:1) pattern occurs in Ugaritic poetry but only once perhaps (Numbers 24:6) in early Hebrew poetry.

[73] In fact the more popular compositions may have suffered textual corruption first and most if their popularity led them to be more widely and frequently copied.

[74] The effectiveness of this approach may be seen in Albright, "The Psalm of Habakkuk," *SOTP*, 1-18; and in Cross and Freedman, *SAYP*.

[75]An alternate opinion is evident in Dahood's *Psalms I-III* (*Anchor Bible*, 1966, 68, 70). Dahood never emends the consonantal MT no matter how strange a translation it may result in.

[76]A. E. Housman, *Selected Prose*, Cambridge, 1962. See especially Chapter IV, "The Application of Thought to Textual Criticism," 131-150, and Chapter VII, "The Name and Nature of Poetry," 168-95. See also, J. Strugnell, "Notes on the Text and Transmission of the Apocryphal Psalms 151, 154, 155," *HTR* 59 (1966), 257-81; "Notes on I Q S 1, 17-18; 8, 3-4 and I Q M 17, 8-9," *CBQ* 29 (1967), 580-82; Review of Goshen-Gottstein, *M. H. Text and Language*, *JBL* 80 (1961), 199-200; Review of Di Lella, *The Hebrew Text of Sirach*, *CBQ* 30 (1968), 88-91.

[77]H. Orlinsky, "The Textual Criticism of the Old Testament," *BANE*, 113-132.

[78]Albright, "The Oracles of Balaam," *JBL* 63 (1944), 207-33; "The Psalm of Habakkuk," *SOTP*, 1-18; *Yahweh and the Gods of Canaan*, 34ff.

[79]Cf. the treatment of Genesis 49:20, 24, 26; I Samuel 2:8; etc. in Chapter III.

[80]E.g. Numbers 21:30; Judges 5:19, etc.

[81]As witnessed in the recent works of Freedman and Dahood who accept syllabic meter but do not depart from the consonantal MT.

[82]Presumably most by Aramaic. See Cross and Freedman, *EHO*, 68f. and Albright, "The Gezer Calendar," *BASOR* 92 (1943), p. 22.

[83]For a convincing critique of the Masoretic vocalizations, see Sperber, *Historical Grammar of Biblical Hebrew*.

[84]See Cross, "The Song of the Sea and Canaanite Myth"; *Canaanite Myth and Hebrew Epic*; "Prose and Poetry in the Mythic Texts of Ugarit"; and R. Clifford, *The Cosmic Mountain in Canaan and the Old Testament*, Cambridge, Harvard University Press, 1972.

[85]A typical example: *rištkm* (2 I 24) vs. *raštkm* (2 I 27) in close proximity. Cf. note 52, and *passim* in the notes to Chapter II.

[86]See the introduction to the treatment of 2 I 7-41 and Keret A 7-43, 55-123.

[87]See especially "The Psalm of Habakkuk," *SOTP*, 1-18.

[88]Cross and Freedman, *Early Hebrew Orthography* and *Studies in Ancient Yahwistic Poetry*.

[89]Z. Harris, *A Grammar of the Phoenician Language*, New Haven, 1936; *The Development of the Canaanite Dialects*, New Haven, 1939.

[90]E. A. Speiser, "The Pronunciation of Hebrew According to the Transliterations in the Hexapla, Chapters I-II," *JQR* 16 (1925-6), 343-382; "The Pronunciation of Hebrew Based Chiefly on the Transliterations in the Hexapla (Chapter II cont.)," *JQR* 23 (1932-3), 233-265; "(Chapter III)," *JQR* 24 (1933-34), 9-46.

[91]A. Sperber, "Hebrew Based upon Greek and Latin Transliterations," *HUCA* 12-13 (1937-8), 103-274; "Hebrew Based upon Biblical Passages in Parallel Transmission," *HUCA* 14 (1939), 153-249; *Historical Grammar of Biblical Hebrew*, Leiden, 1966.

[92]E.g. E. Brønno, *Studien über hebräische Morphologie und Vokalismus*, Leipzig, 1943; W. Chomsky, "The History of Our Vowel System in Hebrew," *JQR* N.S. 32 (1941-2), 27-49. These studies by Brønno and Chomsky are of limited value. See also the bibliographies here and in Cross and Freedman, *EHO* and *SAYP*.

[93]The Amarna texts show a vocalization of *mi*; Mari evidence favors *ma*. The vocalization may have varied, or else was medial (œ or the like). Cf. Moran, "The Hebrew Language in its Northwest Semitic Background," *BANE*, p. 60.

[94]Moran, *ibid.*, 59f. Albright assumed $\bar{a} > \bar{o}$ and $\bar{i} > \bar{e}$ in Ugaritic pronunciation, although there is no clear evidence for or against these shifts. They are, at any rate, merely allophonic variations.

[95]*Historical Grammar of Biblical Hebrew, passim.*

[96]Cf. Sperber, *Historical Grammar of Biblical Hebrew.*

[97]Housman, *Selected Prose.*

[98]In each case the reader is urged to consult the fully annotated treatments in the following chapters. Vocalization and, especially, textual problems are examined there.

[99]Mowinckel's justification would be somewhat more elaborate, involving the programmatic combination of semantic and phonetic features in determining placement of ictus.

[100]The following observations as to "l" and "b" cola may be made: l cola have six or more syllables, apparently never less. b cola have 4 to 7 syllables, never more. Thus 6 or 7 are syllable counts that may vary between l and b and must be decided upon in each case by careful examination of the text. When 6 and 7 equal b, they are so designated because there is internal parallelism within cola or because one is certain that the poet is purposely composing in short units in a context of other b:b (::b:b) meter. When 6 and 7 equal l, this indicates no internal parallelism within cola and intentionally long units of composition. Thus a 6:6 couplet in the context of 8:8 and 9:9 couplets would best be judged l:l if it showed no internal parallelism and did not seem to depart radically from

the general characteristics of the 1:1 cola in the immediate vicinity. l and b are thus convenient indicators of the critic's judgment, but not rigid, precise indicators. "b" poetry appears to the critic to have been consciously composed in short units; "l" poetry is longer, with apparently indivisible cola.

[101]Cf. P. Hanson, "The Song of Heshbon and David's *Nîr*," *HTR* 61 (1968), 297-320.

[102]See A. Idelsohn, *Jewish Music in its Historical Development*, New York, Holt, Rinehart and Winston, 1929.

CHAPTER II

UGARITIC POETRY

Keret A: 7-43, 55-123

The lengthy section of the Keret epic which follows provides examples of a variety of Ugaritic metrical types. Especially beneficial is the opportunity to follow metrical patterns through dozens of uninterrupted lines, with textual problems at a minimum.

The existence of extensive parallels between lines 62-123 and lines 156-227 of the epic aids in fixing a superior text and provides helpful material by way of metrical comparison. The exact vocalization of many words continues to be uncertain, but we may be sure of the number of syllables in all but a few problematical cases. In these particular lines, there remains the difficulty of deciding whether some of the verbs in lines 92-108 are to be understood as imperatives or perfects. At one or two points we will see that the choice affects the meter.

It would be cumbersome to duplicate the consonantal text found in the now standard Herdner corpus, and unnecessary as well. Any reading adopted in our text which is not either accepted by Herdner or discussed by her is noted.

The most significant problem in vocalization is perhaps that presented by the case ending in a construct chain. When composed poetically the language must have allowed for variability. The case ending, containing a minimum amount of semantic information precisely when part of a construct chain, would have been liable to omission *metri causa*.[1] In any language whose prosody involves the counting of syllables means will be employed to lengthen and shorten certain words.

In other cases the case ending must have been preserved in construct.[2] The resultant inconsistency should not be surprising to the student of poetry. It does, however, require an appreciation for the ancient poet's willingness to elide or pronounce a given "expendable" syllable according to the demands of the metrical parallelism. In unvocalized poetry, this is an uncertainty with which the analyst must live.

The problem is eased by the fact that any given phrase, clause, or epithet of formulaic nature apparently tends to be "frozen" and exhibit the same number of syllables, and the same retention or deletion of case endings wherever it occurs. These formulaic elements are the basic building blocks of the oral poet and are changed or substituted for only in standard, predictable ways.

Very little short (b:b::b:b, etc.) meter is evidenced in Ugaritic poetry. There is none in Keret A. As in early Hebrew poems, couplets and triplets vary freely and unpredictably. Meter is fully mixed; while couplets and triplets are almost precisely balanced, they may differ greatly in syllabic length from one another. Sequences of couplets of the same syllabic length are clearly as rare as they are in early Hebrew poetry. It would be very unusual, for example, to find several 8:8 couplets in succession.

The average couplet or triplet is roughly 9:9 (9:9:9). Approximately the same number of 8:8 (8:8:8), 9:9 (9:9:9) and 10:10 (10:10:10) couplets and triplets occur. Cola of less than eight or more than ten syllables are relatively infrequent. Yet it is impossible to speak of a "standard" of "ideal" length for Ugaritic couplets. Much of the beauty of Ugaritic meter lies in its free variation between couplets and triplets of differing lengths. It is even possible that a poet who produced long sequences of a metrical pattern in singing his poetry would have been considered by his audience an inferior craftsman.

We avoid dividing Ugaritic poetry into strophes (as usually in Hebrew poetry) because no evidence of purposeful strophic composition may be discerned in the text:

The meter of Keret A: 7-43, 55-123 may be diagrammed as follows:

(approximately six lines missing)

triplet	1:1:1	7f.
couplet	1:1	10f.
couplet	1:1	12f.
couplet	1:1	14f.
quintuplet[3]	1:1:1:1:1	16f.

triplet	1:1:1	21f.
couplet	1:1	24f.
couplet	1:1	26f.
triplet	1:1:1	28f.
couplet	1:1	31f.
couplet	1:1	33f.
triplet	1:1:1	35f.
couplet	1:1	38f.
couplet	1:1	41f.

(approximately ten lines missing)

couplet	1:1	55f.
couplet	1:1	57f.
triplet	1:1:1	59f.
triplet	1:1:1	62f.
couplet	1:1	65f.
couplet	1:1	67f.
couplet	1:1	69f.
couplet	1:1	71f.
triplet	1:1:1	73f.
triplet	1:1:1	76f.
triplet	1:1:1	79f.
couplet	1:1	83f.
couplet	1:1	85f.
triplet	1:1:1	87f.
couplet	1:1	90f.
couplet	1:1	92f.
couplet	1:1	94f.
couplet	1:1	96f.
triplet	1:1	98f.
couplet	1:1	101f.
couplet	1:1	103f.
couplet	1:1	106f.
couplet	1:1	107f.
couplet	1:1	108f.
couplet	1:1	110f.
couplet	1:1	111f.
couplet	1:1	113f.
triplet	1:1:1	114f.

couplet	1:1	116f.
couplet	1:1	118f.
couplet	1:1	120f.
couplet	1:1	122f.

etc.[4]

Vocalized Text: Keret A. 7-43, 55-123

(approximately six lines missing)

7.	*bētu malki 'itabida*[6]	8	The royal house is destroyed,
	dū šab^{c}u 'aḫūma lahu	8	Which had seven sons,
	ṯamānatu banī 'ummi	8	Eight mother's sons.
10.	*kirta ḥatikuna rašu*	8	Kirta is poor of fatherhood,
	kirta gardiš mankānati	8	Kirta is bereft of establishment.
12.	*'aṯṯata ṣidqihu la yapaqa*	10	His lawful wife he obtained,
	maturraḫta yušrihu[7]	7	His rightful wife.
14.	*'aṯṯata taraḫa wataba^{c}at*	10	He married the wife and she departed.
	ṯa'ru 'ummuti takīnu lahu	10	Flesh of kinship he built for himself.
16.	[8]*muṯallaṯāta kāṯirūma tamūtū*	12	By threes the choice young men died,
	murabba^{c}āta zubulānūma	10	By fours, the young princes,
	muḫammašāta yi'tasip rašpu	10	By fives Rašpu gathered them,
	muṯaddaṯāta ġalama yammu	10	By sixes Yam covered them,
	mušabba^{c}āta bašilḥi tattapilū	12	By sevens they fall by the sword.
21.	*ya^{c}īnu ḥatikahu kirta*	9	Kirta sees his offspring,
	ya^{c}īnu ḥatikahu rašu	9	He sees his offspring ruined,
	ma'idā[10] *gardišu ṯibtuhu*	9	Wholly undermined his seat.
24.	⌜[11]*bātammi hin šipḥu yi'tabidu*	10	In its entirety, behold a posterity perishes,
	wabapuḫayyirihu yariṯu	10	And in its totality, an inheritance.

26.	*ya^{c}rubu baḥadrihu yabkiyu*	10	He enters his chamber, he weeps,
	baṯani rigamīma[12] *wayidma^{c}*	10	In the . . . . . . and sheds tears.
28.	*tinnatikna 'udma^{c}ātuhu*	9	His tears pour out
	kamā ṯiqalīma 'arṣaha	9	Like shekels to the ground,
	kamaḫmašāti miṭṭatahu	9	Like pieces of five on his bed.
31.	*bamā bakyihu wayīšanu*	9	In his weeping, he falls asleep,
	badam^{c}ihu nahamimatu	9	In his tears, slumber.
33.	*šinatu tal'u'annu*[13] *wayiškab*	10	Sleep overtakes him when he lies down,
	banahamimati[14] *wayaqmuṣu*	10	Slumber when he curls up.
35.	*wabaḥulmihu 'ilu yaridu*	10	And in his dream El descends,
	baḏahratihu 'abū 'adami	10	In his vision, the father of man,
	wayiqrab baša'āli kirta[15]	10	And he approaches, asking Kirta,
38.	[16] *minnu kirta kiyabkiyu*	8	"What ails Kirta that he weeps,
	yidma^{c}u nu^{c}mān ġulm 'ili	8	Weeps the beloved lad of El?
41.	*mulka ṯōri 'abīhu ya'arrišu*	11	Is it the kingship of Bull, his father, he desires,
	himma darkata ka'abī 'adami	11	Or dominion like the father of man?"
55.	*ṯalāṯa suswī-mi markabti*	9	Three chariot steeds,
	batarbaṣi banī 'ammati	9	In the dwarfs' stable.[17]
57.	*tina banīma 'aqniya*	8	Grant that I may beget children,
	tina ṯa'ra-mi 'am'ida	8	Grant that I may multiply flesh.
59.	*waya^{c}ni ṯōr 'abūhu 'il*	8	And Bull, El, his father replied,
	dayyuka babakī kirta	8	Enough for you of weeping, Kirta,
	badam^{c}i nu^{c}mān ġulm 'ili	8	Of shedding tears, beloved lad of El.

62.	*tirtaḥiṣa wata'addima*	9	Wash yourself and rouge yourself,
	raḥaṣ yadēka 'ammat‹ā›ha[18]	9	Wash your hands to the elbow,
	'uṣbaᶜātika ᶜadē ṯakmi	9	Your fingers to the shoulder.
65.	*ᶜuruba baẓilli ḫēmati*	9	Enter the shade of the tent,
	qaḥa 'immira bayadēka	9	Take a lamb in your hand,
67.	[][19]*dabḥa bamā yamīni*	7	A sacrifice in your right hand,
	lal'a kil'atanēmi	7	A kid in both your hands.
69.	*kxlxtx*[20] *laḥmxka dī nazli*	9	Take all (?) your most tempting food,
	qaḥa mxsrxra[21] *ᶜiṣṣur dabḥi*	9	Take the . . . of a bird of sacrifice.
71.	*ṣaqa bagulli ḥattuṯi yēna*	10	Pour wine in a silver bowl,
	bagulli ḫarusi nubta[22]	8	In a golden bowl, mead.
73.	*ᶜalī laẓāri migdāli*	8	Go to the top of the tower,
	[][23]*rakab ṯikmēmi ḥāmiti*	8	Ascend to the upper parts of the wall,
	ša'a yadēka šamīma	8	Lift your hands to heaven.
76.	*dabaḥ laṯōr 'abīka 'ili*	9	Sacrifice to Bull, your father, El,
	šarida baᶜla badibḥika	9	Do homage to Baal with your sacrifice,
	bin dagani bamaṣidika	9	The son of Dagan with your food offering.
79.	*wayarid kirta lagaggati*	9	Then let Kirta descend from the roof,
	ᶜadaba 'akla laqiryati	9	Prepare corn for the city,
	ḥiṭṭata labēti ḫuburi	9	Grain for Bet-Hubur.
83.	*yi'api laḥmu dū ḫamiši*	9	Let bread be baked for five,
	mxgxda ṯidṯi yaraḫīma	9	Bread for six months.
85.	*ᶜadana nagba wayaṣi'*	8	Muster the nobility and let them come forth,
	ṣaba'ū ṣaba'ī nagbi	8	All the hosts of the nobility.

87. *wayaṣi' ᶜadanu maᶜi*	8	And let the multitude come forth indeed,
ṣaba'uka 'ūli ma'idi[24]	9	Your host, an exceedingly great force,
ṯalāṯu mi'atu rabbāti	9	Three hundred myriads.
90. *ḫupṯu dū balī supuri*	8	Soldiery without number,
ṯannānī dū balī hagī	8	Spear-carriers without count.
92. *halaka la'alapīma ḫaḏiḏu*	11	The common folk march by the thousands,
walarabbāti kumayyiru[25]	9	And by the tens of thousands massed.
94. *'aṯaru ṯinē ṯinē halakū*	10	They marched two by two, they walked,
'aṯaru ṯalāṯa kulluhumu	10	They marched by threes, all of them.
96. *yaḥīdu bētahu sagara*	9	The bachelor's family is cut off,
'almanatu šakkār taššakir	9	The widow hires herself out.
98. *zibbilu ᶜarša-mi yiššaʾu*	9	The sick man carries his own bed,
ᶜiwwiru mazzāl yamazzilu	9	The blind man[26] divines by the stars,
wayaṣi' tariḫu ḥadaṯu	9	And the newly-wed goes forth.
101. *yibᶜaru laṯinē 'aṯatahu*	10	He brings to another his wife,
lamā nikari mōdadatahu	10	To a stranger, his beloved.
103. *‹kamā›*[27] *'irbayī taškunū šadi*	10	Like locusts that dwell on the steppe,
ka[28]*ḥasinī pi'ati madbari*	10	Like grasshoppers at the edge of the desert,
106. *‹h›alakū*[29] *yāma waṯanī*	8	They march a day and a second,
ṯalīṯa rabīᶜa yāma	8	A third, a fourth day,
107. *ḫamīša ṯadīṯa yāma*	8	A fifth, a sixth day,
muk šapšumma bašabīᶜi	8	Lo, at sunrise on the seventh,
108. *watamġiyū la'udum rabbati*	10	They arrive at Udum the great,
wala'udum ṯurrarati	8	And at Udum the grand.

110.	*wagarrīnan*[31] *ʿira-mi*	7	And attack the city,
	šuranna padara-mi	7	Harass the town.
111.	*saʿat bašadīma ḥaṭibīha*	10	Sweep from the fields her hewers of wood
	bagurānāti ḥāpišāta[32]	8	From the threshing-floors the straw-pickers.
113.	*saʿat banipki*[33] *šāʾibāta*	9	Drive from the well the drawers of water,
	bamaquri[34] *mumalliʾāta*	9	From the spring those that fill.
114.	*duma yāma waṯanī*[35]	7	Stay a day and a second,
	ṯalīṯa rabīʿa yāma	8	A third, a fourth day,
	ḫamīša ṯadīṯa yāma	8	A fifth, a sixth day.
116.	*ḥiẓẓīka ʾal tišʿala qirtaha*	10	Surely you shall shoot your arrows at the city,
	ʾabnī yadēka mušaddipāti	10	Your handstones flung headlong.
118.	*wahin šapšumma bašabīʿi*	9	And behold, at sunrise on the seventh,
	wala yīšanu pabil malku	9	And king Pabil will be sleeping,
120.	*laqāri ṯiʾgati ʾibbīrīhu*	10	Until the noise of his stallions' neighing,
	laqāli nahaqti ḥimārīhu	10	Until the sound of his he-asses' braying,
122.	*lagaʾati ʾalpī ḥariṯi*	9	Until the lowing of the plow-oxen,
	lazaǵatti kalbi ṣāpiri	9	Until the bark of the watch-dog.

NOTES

Keret A: 7-43, 55-123

[1]E.g. lines 39-40, 59, 61, 70, 78, etc.

[2]E.g. lines 7, 15, 73, 82, 120-1, etc.

[3]These lines may also be divided into a triplet and a couplet. See also note 8.

[4]We end reconstruction of the text here since it is the point at which the parallel in 156-227 ends, and textual uncertainty is thus increased.

[5]Ugaritic vocalization is both theoretical and possibly variable. The incomplete graphic notation contributes to the uncertainty. For example, *yqṭl* may have been either *yaqṭul*, *yaqṭulu*, or *yaqṭula*. An imperative such as *qḥ* may be either *qaḥ* or *qaḥa*. Proper names may be given the case ending or not (*mōt/mōtū*). The same situation pertains to the case ending in a construct chain (*puḫru/puḫr*). One can only assume that a given form was chosen by the poet *metri causa*, and reconstruct accordingly. We assume, moreover, that Ugaritic vocalization maintained the primitive Semitic three-vowel system except in the case of contracted diphthongs.

[6]Or *'ītabida*, from **'i'tabida*.

[7]An unbalanced couplet such as this calls for comment. The semantic parallelism school would call such a couplet the product of "incomplete parallelism without compensation," their term for Qinah. The second line of such a couplet is called by some an "echo variant." Because normal, although incomplete parallelism is present, we may designate the couplet as 1:1. There is no parallelism within cola. Lines of this type often occur when a poet is moving his audience into a new scene or context, but that is not the case here.

When one examines unbalanced lines of this sort, he finds that they are commonly unbalanced by precisely the number of syllables of the verbal form in the first colon, which is missing in the second colon. Thus here, if *yapaqa* were supplied in the second colon, the couplet would be completely balanced. This is the case with the unbalanced couplet in line 71f. (where two syllables' imbalance would be resolved by supplying the verb in the first colon again in the second), and in line 111f. (which is again unbalanced by two syllables, the number if the first line's verb). Whether we are to assume the verb to repeat from the first line to the second of such couplets, or whether this is some sort of stylistic (and therefore purposeful) imbalance is not clear. True scene-changing or "rubric" couplets (e.g. line 108f.) are a separate matter.

[8]A quintuplet is highly unusual in either Ugaritic or Hebrew poetry. Nevertheless these five cola may be divided (into a couplet and triplet?) only with difficulty. It is further unusual that the long cola should be found at both the beginning and the end of such a configuration. On the analogy of the triplets, one might expect a longer line at either the beginning or the end, but not both.

[9]Correcting the text from *mšb^{c}thn* according to the parallelism.

[10]The exact vocalization of this form is unsure. Note that line 88 has *m'ad*. It is probably not merely a reflex of Hebrew *m^e'ōd* (< **ma'du*). *ma'id-* is therefore adopted here, being a stative pattern.

[11]It is most unusual (but not impossible in some cases, e.g. line 35) to find the first line of a couplet beginning with the conjunctive *w*. We therefore delete *w* here, with further notation that the tablet is difficult to read at this point.

[12]The meaning and vocalization of *bṯn rgmm* are difficult. We assume two nouns in a construct combination, and vocalize accordingly.

[13]*tl'u'an* is an unusual form because of the two vocalized *alephs* together. It is from **tal'iwanhu*, the *iw* having shifted to *u* (*'u*), etc.

[14]This now widely accepted emendation originated with Engnell. It involves the recognition of simple haplography of the *b*.

[15]This line might also be understood as an extra-metrical or "rubric" line.

[16]Even if the tablet has *m'at*, *mn* or the like must have been the intention. Cf. Herdner, 62, note 10.

[17]Cf. Albright, "Dwarf Craftsmen in the Keret Epic and Elsewhere in Northwest Semitic Mythology," *IEJ* 4 (1954), 1-4.

[18]Read the locative with the parallel in line 157.

[19]Omit *'mr* as conflate. Cf. the parallel in line 160, but note that both contexts are slightly corrupt, perhaps due to confusion of the formulae.

[20]The etymology and meaning of *klt* is unclear. It could relate to *kly*, "container," to *kwl*, "to weigh out," or to *klh/kly*, "to consume." A verbal form is likely since *qḥ* in the following line can hardly be expected to serve as the only verb for the couplet.

[21]The meaning and vocalization of *msrr* are unclear.

[22]See note 7.

[23]Omit all but the last word of line 74 as obvious dittography.

[24]The text has *m'ad*. See note 10. *r'iš* varies with *r'aš* in this same way.

[25]An imbalance by one syllable is not severe. If there were no *w* at the outset of the second colon we might assume that *hlk* were to be understood, or was lost by haplography, as discussed in note 7.

[26]Or, with Albright, the "half-blind man."

[27]Reading with the parallel in line 192. A confusion about the placement of such particles is often found in dictated oral poetry because the slow speed of the dictation disturbs the poet's sense of rhythm. See Lord, *The Singer of Tales*, Chapter 6.

[28]Reading with the parallel in line 193. See note 27.

[29]Reading with the parallel in line 94.

[30]Arrival at Udum is regularly described by means of an unbalanced couplet. It is a scene-changing device, and the imbalance may well be purposeful.

[31]Reading the short form of the energic ending. The longer form simply would add -*na*. Read imperatives in 110-16.

[32]See note 7. But note also that a 9:9 couplet follows and is very similar. Perhaps the poet made his cesura in such a way as to divide the line in two before the final syllable in the first colon, thus producing 9:9.

[33]This emendation is commonly proposed. Cf. Herdner, 64, note 1.

[34]Reading with the parallel in line 217.

[35]The imbalance of one syllable in this triplet is not severe, and not a textual problem. In a sequence of numerical adjectives such as this, a poet's choice of formulae is greatly restricted, and some imbalance is hard to avoid. *ṯani*, "second," has only two syllables and the *y* would have been indicated if *ṯaniya* or the like had been an acceptable form.

[36]*nahaqqati* is also a possible vocalization. Herdner has, incorrectly, *nqht*.

[37]Assuming the root to be *zġd*. If it is *zġġ*, read *lazaġġati*, metrically equivalent. Restore the preposition with the parallel.

Herdner 2, Col. 1, lines 7-41

With the exception of three short broken or illegible parts of the tablet (lines 9f., 12f., 31) this section of the Baal cycle is well preserved and thus lends itself to poetic analysis. Triplets constitute slightly more than one-third of the total text, and freely interchange with couplets. Various types of metrical patterns occur including, possibly, the b:b short couplet twice (lines 11f., 20f.). In both of these cases the b:b couplet occurs in balance with l cola of 10 syllables. This makes suspect the identification as a b:b couplet, since its count is 5:5 (=10). It appears to be composed in purposely short units of five syllables each, however, and is not to be summarily dismissed as "l."

A number of purposely unbalanced triplets occur, all involving a special type of ellipsis. This imbalance is discussed in the notes to the several triplets in question.

One must assume the potential variability of the two forms of the 2.m.pl. possessive/objective suffix, *-*kum* and *-*kumu*, and their third person counterparts, *-*hum* and *-*humu*. Although the shorter form is generally presumed in our readings, the two-syllable fuller form seems to be required in at least one case (line 33f.). The fragmentary nature of the text before line 7 and after line 41 sets the boundaries for this section.

The metrical structure may be outlined as follows:

triplet	l:l:l	6f.
couplet (?)	(obscured)	9f.
couplet	l:l	11f.
triplet (?)	(obscured)	12f.
couplet	l:l	13f.
couplet	b:b[1]	14
couplet	l:l	14f.
couplet	l:l	15f.
triplet	l:l:l	16f.
couplet	l:l	18
couplet	l:l	18f.
couplet	l:l	19f.
couplet	b:b[2]	20

triplet	1:1:1	20f.
triplet	1:1:1	21f.
triplet	1:1:1	23f.
couplet	1:1	24f.
couplet	1:1	25
triplet	1:1:1	25f.
triplet	1:1:1	27f.
couplet	1:1	28f.
triplet	1:1:1	29f.
couplet	1:1	30
couplet	1:1	30f.
couplet	1:1	31f.
couplet	1:1	32f.
triplet	1:1:1	33f.
couplet	1:1	34f.
couplet	1:1	35f.
couplet	1:1	36
couplet	1:1	36f.
triplet	1:1:1	37f.
triplet	1:1:1	38f.
couplet	1:1	40
couplet	1:1	40f.

Vocalized Text: Herdner 2, Col. 1, lines 7-41

7.	*yaṯabbira ‹ḥōrānu ya-yammu›*[3]	10	May Horon break, O Yamm,
	yaṯabbira hōrānu ri'šaka	10	May Horon break your head,
	ʿaṯtartu šim baʿli qudqudaka	10	Astart, name of Baal, your pate.
9.	. . . .		- - - - - - - - - - - - - - - -
	. . . .[4]		- - - - - - - - - - - - - - - -
11.	*mal'akīma yil'aku yammu*	9	Yamm send messengers,
	taʿudatē ṯipṭu naharu	9	The deputies of Judge River.
12.	. . . .		- - - - - - - - - - - - - - - -
	. . . .		- - - - - - - - - - - - - - - -
	. . . .[5]		- - - - - - - - - - - - - - - -

13.	*tabaᶜā ġalmami 'al taṯibā*	10	Depart, lads, do not tarry.
	'idaka panīma 'al tattinā	10	Then they set their faces
14.	*ᶜim puḫr*[6] *mōᶜidi*	5	To the assembled body,
	tōka ġur 'ili[7]	5	To the mount of El.
14.	*lapaᶜnē 'ili 'al tappulā*	9	At the feet of El fall,
	'al tištaḥwiyā puḫr mōᶜidi	9	Do obeisance to the assembled body.
15.	*qumā-mi* [8]*˹waṯaniyā daᶜtikum*	10	Stand and repeat what you know,
	rugumā laṯōr 'abīya 'ili	10	Speak to Bull, my father, El.
16.	*ṯaniyā lapuḫri*[9] *mōᶜidi*	9	Repeat to the assembly,
	tuḥuma yammi baᶜlikum	9	Message of Yamm, your master,
	'adānikum ṯipṭi nahari	9	Of your lord, Judge River.
18.	*tinū*[10] *'ila-mi dī taqūhu*	9	Hand over the god whom you serve,
	dī taqiyūna hamūlātu	9	Whom the multitudes worship.
18.	*tinū baᶜla waᶜananīhu*	9	Hand over Baal and his Clouds,
	bin dagan 'ariṯa-m[11] *paḏahu*	9	The son of Dagan that I might spoil his wealth.[12]
19.	*tabaᶜā ġalmami lā yaṯibā*	10	The two messengers depart, they do not tarry,
	'idaka panīma la yattinā	10	Then they set face
20.	*tōka ġur 'ili*	5	To the mount of El,
	ᶜim puḫr mōᶜidi[13]	5	To the assembled body.
20.	*'appa 'ilūma lalaḥmi*[14] *yaṯibū*	11	Now the gods are sitting to eat,
	banū qudši laṯurumi	8	The holy ones to dine,
	baᶜlu qamu ᶜalē 'ili[15]	8	Baal waits upon El.

21.	*halum*[16] *'ilūma tipāhūhum*	9	As soon as the gods see them,
	tipāhūna mal'akē yammi	9	See the messengers of Yamm,
	ta^{c}udatē ṯipṭi nahari	9	The deputies of Judge River,
23.	*taġliyū 'ilūma ri'ašātihum*	11	The gods bow their heads,
	laẓāri birakātihum	8	Upon their knees,
	walakaḥṯi zubulihum[17]	8	And upon their lordly thrones.
24.	*bahumu yaga^{cc}iru ba^{c}lu lama*[18]	11	Them Baal rebukes (saying), Why
	ġalitum 'ilūma ri'ašātikum	11	O gods, have you drooped your heads
25.	*laẓāri birakātikum*	8	Upon your knees,
	⸢[19]*la-ni-kaḥṯi zubulikum*[20]	8	And upon your lordly thrones?
25.	*'aḥdi 'ilīma tu^{c}niyū*	8	I see that the gods are cowed
	laḥatti mal'akē yammi	8	From terror of the messengers of Yamm,
	ta^{c}udatē ṯipṭi nahar	8	Of the deputies of Judge River.
27.	*ša'ū 'ilūma ri'ašātikum*	10	Lift up, O gods, your heads,
	laẓāri birakātikum	8	From your knees,
	la-ni kaḥṯi zubulikum[21]	8	From your lordly thrones.
28.	*wa'anāku ^{c}anāyu*[22] *mal'akē yammi.*[23]	12	I will answer the messengers of Yamm,
	ta^{c}udatē ṯipṭi nahari.[24]	9	The deputies of Judge River,
29.	*tišša'ū 'ilūma ri'ašātihum*	11	The gods lift up their heads
	laẓāri birakātihum	8	From their knees,
	la-ni kaḥṯi zubulihum[25]	8	From their lordly thrones.
30.	*'aḫra*[26] *timġayāni mal'akē yammi*	11	Then come the messengers of Yamm,
	ta^{c}udatē ṯipṭi nahari	9	The deputies of Judge River.
30.	*lapa^{c}nē 'ili la tappulā*	9	At the feet of El they fall,
	la tištaḥwiyā puḫr mō^{c}idi	9	They do obeisance to the assembly.

31.	*qamāmi . . . . . .*[27]	(9?)	Standing - - - - - - -
	'amarā ṯaniya da^ctihum	9	They say their memorized speech.
32.	*'ištu 'ištāmi yi'tamirā*	9	One fire, two fires speak(?),
	ḥarbu laṭuštu ‹lašānuhum›[28]	9	A whetted sword is their tongue.
33.	*rigmu laṯōr 'abīhu 'ili*	9	Report to Bull, his father, El,
	tuḥumu yammi ba^clikumu	9	Message of Yamm your master,
	'adānikum ṯipṭi nahari	9	Of your lord, Judge River:
34.	*tinū 'ila-mi ḏī taqūhu*	9	Give over the god whom you serve,
	ḏī taqiyūna hamūlātu	9	Whom the multitudes serve.
35.	*tinū ba^cla wa^cananīhu*	9	Give over Baal and his Clouds,
	bin dagan 'ariṯa-m[29] *paḏahu*	9	The son of Dagan that I may spoil his wealth.
36.	*waya^cni ṯōr 'abūhu 'ilu*	9	And Bull, his father, El, answered,
	^cabduka ba^clu ya-yammu-mi	9	Baal is your servant, O Yamm,
36.	*^cabduka ba^clu la^cālami*	9	Baal is your servant forever,
	bin dagani 'asīruka-mi	9	The son of Dagan is your captive.
37.	*huwa yabilu 'argamānaka*	10	He will bring your tribute,
	kī 'ilu-mi ‹ṯa^cayaka›[30] *yabilu*	10	For a god brings your tribute,
	wabanū qudši manuḥayēka	10	And the holy ones your gifts.
38.	*'ap 'anaša zubulu ba^clu*	10	Then Prince Baal sickened,
	yu'ḫadu bama[‹›-31] *yadi masḫaṭa*	10	He seized a cudgel in his hand,
	• *bêyamīni*[32] *maḥaṣa ġalmēmi*	10	With his right hand he struck the lads.
40.	*yamīnahu ^canatu tu'ḫadu*	10	Anat seizes his right hand,
	šim'ālahu tu'ḫadu ^caṯtartu	10	Astart seizes his left hand.

40. *'īk maḫaṣta mal'akē yammi* 9 How can you strike the messengers of Yamm,

ta^{c}udatē ṯipṭi nahari 9 The deputies of Judge River?

NOTES

Herdner 2, Col. 1, lines 7-41

[1]See note 7.

[2]See note 13.

[3]On the restoration, see Herdner, p. 7, note 2.

[4]The broken area is about the length of a couplet, although too fragmentary to read.

[5]The broken area is about the length of a triplet, and also too fragmentary to read.

[6]The vocalization of the two initial words in this line is uncertain. Also possible are *ᶜimma puḫri*, *ᶜim puḫr*, and *ᶜim puḫri*. Note the vocalization *puḫr mōᶜidi* of the following couplet (14f.) as compared with *puḫri mōᶜidi* of the triplet in 16f. Both are tentative vocalizations.

[7]Note that this b:b couplet balances precisely the preceding l lines. It could well be considered as combining with them to complete a triplet. The decision to take the line as b:b rather than l is a subjective one. The halves of the couplet are at least somewhat independent, however, since they are reversed in line 20f. There is, moreover, obvious internal parallelism within these ten syllables.

[8]Read *w* rather than the meaningless *r*, following Gordon. Cf. Herdner, p. 7, note 6.

[9]Here we assume one of three possible vocalizations for *pḫr*. Also possible would be *puḫr* and *puḫur*.

[10]Or read possibly *tina* if El is being addressed.

[11]We assume here the unvocalized form of the enclitic *m*, as often in Hebrew. If the vocalized form *-mi* is to be read, adjust the line to ten syllables.

[12]Or the like meaning for *pdh*. *'rṯ* may be read "possess."

[13]Note that the order of the short cola is reversed here from that of the otherwise identical couplet in line 14. This is a common phenomenon in dictated oral poetry. The fact that the two cola were interchangeable with respect to the musical line suggests their metrical equivalence.

[14]The restoration is based on Herdner 18, IV, 18f. and 29f.

[15]The first line of this triplet is overly long by precisely the number of syllables contained in the verb in the first line, omitted in the following lines. This sort of

triplet occurs commonly in the remainder of the section. It is probably a stylistic device, and it is surely purposeful. The poet may have sung the verb as a cadenza and then proceeded with his triplet, or he may even have supplied the verb in each line, our text being elliptical. See the discussion at note 7 to Keret A.

[16]The *-um* is adverbial, as in *šapšum(ma)*. Also possible is *halumma*.

[17]On the imbalance of the triplet see note 15.

[18]Or read *limma* or the like from **lū + himma*, "indeed."

[19]Omit the *w* as conflate since only two formulae, either *wala* or *la-ni* are found before *kḥṯ* in all other contexts.

[20]Note that the poet has added to the 11:8:8 triplet an initial line (line 24), and divided its cola in such a way as to produce two couplets (or a quatrain). He could as easily add an eight-syllable colon at the end of the pattern. Formulaic composition allows him to make additions or subtractions to set patterns as the subject matter requires. The set pattern, which he uses frequently, is easy to sing and affords him time to prepare ahead.

[21]On the imbalance, see note 15. Note that the imbalance in this case is by two syllables, precisely the number of syllables of the verb in the first colon of the triplet.

[22]On the imbalance see note 15. Although *w'ank ᶜny* is perhaps more prosaic than *waᶜaniti* or the like would be, we may judge the imbalance to be purposeful, again by precisely the number of syllables in the first line's verb. Here, as in line 30, it is a couplet rather than a triplet in which the imbalance is found.

[23]Note the slightly different length of the corresponding line (line 30), where the extra element is of one less syllable (*'aḫra*). The formulaic substitution is quite precise.

[24]On the imbalance see notes 22, 23, and 15.

[25]On the imbalance see note 15.

[26]*'ḫr* appears to correspond to the element which lengthens these first lines of couplets and triplets, even though that element is normally a verb and *'ḫr* is adverbial. Like *š'* of line 27f., it unbalances the couplet by precisely two syllables.

[27]The text is illegible at this point.

[28]This convincing restoration is suggested by Professor Cross.

[29]See note 11.

[30]The restoration is suggested by Professor Cross on the basis of Genesis 49:10. Cf. W. L. Moran, "Genesis 49:10 and its Uses in Ezekiel 21:32," *Biblica* 39 (1958), 405-25.

[31]The fuller form of the preposition belongs with the shorter word *yd* rather than with *ymn*, and thus is supplied here. This parallels the situation in Keret A, 103f., where a similar transposition of *-m* has occurred, as is proved by the parallel in Keret A lines 192-193.

[32]See note 31.

Herdner 5, Col. I, lines 1-16; Col. II, lines 2-23

This section of the Baal cycle contains a number of interesting metrical patterns, including an extra-metrical one-word command (Col. II, line 8) and the interchange of two formulaic elements in the process of oral dictation (Col. II, line 3f.). At a few points the tablet is somewhat marred, and there is an occasional uncertainty as to the meaning and vocalization of a line (e.g. Col I, line 5f.). Nevertheless the overall result serves to confirm the trends visible in other Ugaritic poetry. These include oral composition and dictation, as evidenced by the presence of formulae, lack of enjambment, and thematic structure; unpredictable variation between couplets and triplets; precise balance between the cola of couplets and triplets; no indication of strophe; etc.

In the two sections presented here there is only one case of possible imbalance within a couplet (Col. I, line 4f.). The couplet presents textual problems, however, and the imbalance may well be only apparent. A rare short triplet (b:b:b) is found in Col. II, line 5f. The remainder of the meter is long.

The metrical scheme may be outlined as follows:

Col. I	triplet	1:1:1	1f.
	couplet	1:1	4f.
	(couplet)	(1:1)	5f.
	couplet	1:1	6f.
	triplet	1:1:1	9f.
	triplet	1:1:1	11f.
	couplet	1:1	14f.
Col. II	couplet	1:1	2f.
	couplet	1:1	3f.
	short triplet	b:b:b	5f.
	couplet	1:1	6f.
	(extra-metrical command)		8
	couplet	1:1	8f.
	couplet	1:1	10f.
	couplet	1:1	11f.
	couplet	1:1	13f.
	couplet	1:1	14f.
	couplet	1:1	15f.

triplet	1:1:1	16f.
couplet	1:1	19f.
couplet	1:1	20f.
couplet	1:1	21f.

Vocalized Text: Herdner 5, Col. I, lines 1-16

1.	*kī timḫaṣ lōtana baṯna barīḥa*	11	When you smote Lotan, the ancient dragon,
	takalliya baṯna ᶜaqallatāna	11	Destroyed the crooked serpent,
	šilyaṭa dī šabᶜati ri'ašīma	11	Shilyat with the seven heads;
4.	*tiṯkaḥū titrapū šamūma*	9	The heavens withered, they drooped,
	karukusī[1] 'ipādīka	8	Like the folds of your garments.
5.	*'anāku 'isp'i 'uṭm*	?	- - - - - - - - - - - - - - -
	ḏrqm 'mtm[2]	?	- - - - - - - - - - - - - - -
6.	*lu yaratta banapši bin 'ili-mi mōt*	12	You shall indeed go down to the throat of the son of El, Mot,
	bamahamārati yadīd 'ili ġazri	12	Into the watery pit of the beloved of El, the hero.
9.	*tibaᶜā[3] lā yaṯibā 'ilāmi*	10	The gods depart, they do not stay,
	'idaka la yattinā panīma	10	Then they set face
	ᶜimma baᶜli mxryxmx[4] ṣapāni	10	Toward Baal at the heights (?) of Sapon.
11.	*wayaᶜnā gapnu wa'ugaru*	9	And Vine and Field said,
	tuḥumu bin 'ili-mi mōti	9	Message of El's son, Mot,
	hawatu yadīd[5] 'ili ġazri	9	Word of the beloved of El, the hero.
14.	*panapšu napši[6] labi'i-mi tahwī*	11	And it is (His) will that creates the lust of the lioness,
	himmu bxrxlxtu[7] 'anḫari bayammi	11	As well as the appetite of the dolphin in the sea.[8]

2.	*šaptu la'arṣi šaptu lašamīma*	11	A lip to earth and a lip to heaven,
	‹ya'riku›[9] *lašāna lakabkabīma*	11	He stretches his tongue to the stars.
3.	*ya*^{c}*rubu ba*^{c}*lu ba‹pīhu›*[10]	8	Baal enters into his mouth,
	ba‹kabidihu›[11] *yaridu*	8	Into his innards he descends.
5.	*kī ḥarira zēta*	6	Indeed he was parched like an olive,
	yabilu‹bul›[12] *'arṣi*	6	He who brings in the produce of the field,
	wapirī ^{c}*iṣṣīma*[13]	6	And the fruit of the trees.
6.	*yīra'unnu 'al'iyānu ba*^{c}*lu*	10	Afraid of him is valiant Baal,
	ṯata^{c}*unnu rākib* ^{c}*arapāti*	10	In dread of him is the cloud rider.
8.	*taba*^{c}*ā*[14]	(extra-metrical)	Be gone!
8.	*rugumā labin 'ili-mi mōti*	10	Say to the son of El, Mot,
	ṯaniyā layadīd 'ili ġazri	10	Repeat to the beloved of El, the hero:
10.	*tuḥumu 'al'iyāni ba*^{c}*li*	9	Message of valiant Baal,
	hawatu 'al'iy qarradīma[15]	9	Word of the conqueror of the heroes:
11.	*bahaṯā labinu 'ili-mi mōtu*	11	Hail, O son of El, Mot,
	^{c}*abduka 'anā wadū* ^{c}*ālamika*	11	Your slave am I, and yours eternally.
13.	*taba*^{c}*a ⸢lā*[16] *yaṯibā 'ilāmi*	10	The gods depart, they do not tarry,
	'idaka la yattinā panīma	10	Then they set face
14.	^{c}*imma bin 'ili-mi mōti*	8	Toward the son of El, Mot,
	tōka qartihu hamriyya[17]	8	Into his city, Mire,

15.	*makki kussi'u*[17a] *ṯibtihu*	8	To Ooze, the throne he sits upon,
	ḫaḫḫi[17a] *'arṣu naḥlatihu*	8	Slime, the land of his possession.
16.	*tiššaʾā gāhumā wataṣīhā*	10	They raise their voices and cry,
	tuḥumu 'al'iyāni bin[18] *baᶜli*	10	Message of the valiant one, the son, Baal,
	hawatu 'al'iyi qarradīma	10	Word of the conqueror of heroes:
19.	*bahaṯa ⸢l⸣abinu*[19] *'ili-mi mōtu*	11	Be gracious, O son of El, Mot,
	ᶜabduka 'anā wadū ᶜālamika	11	Your slave am I and yours forever.
20.	*šamaḫa bin 'ili-mi mōtu*	9	The son of El, Mot, rejoiced,
	yiššaʾu gāhu wa⸢y⸣aṣīḥu[20]	9	He raises his voice and cries:
21.	*'īka yaṣīḥanna baᶜlu ᶜim 'aḫḫīya*	12	How offensive has Baal become with my brothers!
	'īka yiqra'unna haddu ᶜim 'aryīya	12	How unfortunate Haddu has become with my kin!

21

NOTES

Herdner 5, Col. I, lines 1-16; Col. II, lines 2-23

[1]The emendation is that of Albright and Gaster. See Herdner, p. 32, note 3. The fact that the couplet remains unbalanced by one syllable suggests that *kamā* may have been the original intention, i.e. *kamā rukusi 'ipadika*, nine syllables.

[2]The meaning and therefore vocalization and syllable count are unclear. The apparent shift of subject to the first person is likewise confusing.

[3]The *w* is to be deleted with the similar line in Herdner 2, line 19f.: *taba*^{c}*ā ġalmami lā yaṯibā*. The poet's dictation may have been altered by his change in the word order, since the parallel to the line from Herdner 2 is more precisely: *taba*^{c}*ā 'ilāmi lā yaṯibā* rather than what we find here in the text.

[4]The vocalization and meaning of this word are not certain.

[5]Omit *bn* from the text with the parallels, including Col. II, line 8f. The formula of which this word is a part has several similar forms which vary with it in different metrical contexts. It is thus especially subject to improper construal in oral dictation. Cf. Herdner, p. 33, note 1.

[6]The vocalization is tentative. Also possible is *napš* or the like.

[7]The placement of vowels is tentative.

[8]The text becomes obscure and broken here. Lines 27-35 are an exact reproduction of lines 1-8 and therefore not repeated.

[9]Insert *ya'riku* as the Ugaritic equivalent of the similar reading in Isaiah 57:4. The parallel has been noticed by both Cross and Ginsburg.

[10]*bapīhu* has been interchanged with *bakabidihu* in oral dictation. Consequently they should be transposed to their obviously proper order.

[11]See note 10.

[12]Such a word as *bl* could easily have been dropped from the text by haplography, and is thus speculatively restored here, at the suggestion of Professor Cross.

[13]The meaning of the triplet is not quite clear. Especially difficult is *ḥrr zt*, the translation of which is tentative.

[14]The first word in line 8 is obviously without parallel or membership in the surrounding lines. It is likely that extra-metrical phrases such as this were either spoken rather than sung, or sung as cadenzas, breaking the normal musical pattern.

[15]There are several variations on this couplet about the message and word of Baal, which serve varying metrical contexts. Cf. the triplets in Col. I, line 11f., and Col. II, line 16f.

[16]See note 3.

[17]Or a similar vocalization.

[17a]Or read the genitive form here, if the apposition is considered closely linked to its referent. Meter is, of course, unaffected.

[18]*bn* is here vocalized in the construct, on the analogy of Hebrew *bat ṣiyyōn*, Ugaritic *ṯōr 'ili*, etc.

[19]Insert the vocative *la* with the parallel in line 11.

[20]The text must be emended to the third person. Cf. Herdner, p. 34, note 4.

[21]At this point the text becomes too fragmentary for analysis.

CHAPTER III

EARLY HEBREW POETRY

Exodus 15: The Song of Miriam

Cross and Freedman have each completed recent studies of the Song of Miriam[1] which update their still basic work of 1950.[2] We tend to follow, though not in all respects, the moderate approach to meter and strophe developed by Cross in his study, "The Song of the Sea and Canaanite Myth."[3]

The poem has a remarkably well-preserved text in the MT, strongly supported by the versions. *Waw* as a conjunction before cola is almost never evidenced, as we would expect in the earliest strata of Israelite poetry.[4] The date, style, *Sitz im Leben*, and other salient features of Exodus 15 have been well discussed by Cross so recently that they would be unnecessarily repeated here in any detail.

The identification of strophes in Hebrew meter is conjectural and even somewhat arbitrary. No formal indication of strophe occurs in Old Testament poetry. Indeed, the concept, though a useful one, is borrowed from classical prosody where its function is understood. We do not divide poems into strophes in the following pages. It should be noted that many members of the Albright school, including Cross and Freedman, employ strophes for convenience, with the understanding that this is a subjective enterprise. In the case of Exodus 15 the reader may prefer to follow the strophic boundaries set by Cross.[5]

We differ by way of interpretation with Cross's recent study in a few significant particulars only: the need to emend the consonantal text of v. 1, the identification of v. 8 as a triplet, the identification of vv. 17a-17b and 17c-18 as couplets, etc.

It is our assumption that all pre-monarchic Old Testament poetry would have been either composed or preserved in the north owing to the location of the central sanctuary there prior to the time of David. Accordingly we vocalize most of the poems treated in this chapter according to a supposed early northern pronunciation. Most of this is theoretical and some quite problematic.[6] The general characteristics of vowels, and certainly of syllables, may, however, be understood.

Exodus 15 is interesting to the student of Hebrew prosody by reason of its strongly mixed meter. In no other early Old Testament poetry do we find more baroque variation between short and long meter, as well as between couplets and triplets.[7] Repetitive parallelism abounds, and other archaic indices are frequent.[8] Yet the overall unity and structure of the poem are remarkably clear.

The meter may be diagrammed as follows:

couplet	b:b::b:b	v. 1
triplet	b:b::b:b::b:b	v. 3-4
couplet	l:l	v. 5
couplet	b:b::b:b	v. 6
couplet	b:b::b:b	v. 7
triplet	l:l:l	v. 8
triplet	b:b::b:b::b:b	v. 9
couplet	b:b::b:b	v. 10
triplet	l:l:l	v. 11

Part II

triplet	b:b::b:b::b:b	v. 12-13
couplet	l:l	v. 14
triplet	b:b::b:b::b:b	v. 15
couplet	b:b::b:b	v. 16a
couplet	l:l	v. 16b
couplet	b:b::b:b[9]	v. 17a-b
couplet	b:b::b:b	v. 17c-18

Reconstructed Text[10]

Part I

v. 1	*'ašīr layahwē*	5	אשר ליהו[11]
	kī ga'ō ga'a	5	כ גא גא

	sus warōkēb	4	סס ורכב[12]
	rama bayam	4	רמ בימ [ ][13]
v. 3	*yahwē gibbōr*	4	יהו ⟨גבר⟩[14]
	yahwē šimō	4	יהו שמ
v. 4	{*mirkabt par^{c}ō* / *par^{c}ō waḥēl*}	4	[15]{מרכבת פרע / פרע וחל}
	yara bayam	4	יר בימ
	mibḥar šalīšēw	5	מבחר שלשו
	ṭubba^c bayam sup	5	טבע[16] בימ ספ
v. 5	*tihōmōt yakassiyūma yama*	10	תהמת יכסימ[17] ⟨ימ⟩[18]
	yaradū bamaṣōlōt kamō 'abn	10	ירד במצלת כמ אבנ
v. 6	*yamīneka yahwē*	6	ימנכ יהו
	ni'dar bakōḥ	4	נאדר[19] בכח
	yamīneka yahwē	6	ימנכ יהו
	tir^{c}aṣ 'ōyēb	4	תרעצ איב
v. 7	*barōb ga'ōneka*	6	ברב גאנכ
	tahrōs qamēka	5	תהרס קמכ
	tašallaḥ ḥarōneka	7	תשלח חרנכ
	yō'kilēmu kaqaš	6	יאכלמ כקש
v. 8	*baruḥ 'appēka ni^{c}ramū mēm*	9	ברח אפכ נערמ ממ
	niṣṣabū kamō nēd nōzilīm	9	נצב כמ נד נזלמ
	qapa'ū tihōmōt balēb yam	9	קפא תהמת בלב ימ[20]
v. 9	*'amar 'ōyēb*	4	אמר איב
	'erdōp 'aśśīg	4	ארדפ אשג

	'aḥallēq šalal	5		אחלק שלל
	timla'-ēm napšī	5		תמלא-מ[21] נפש
	'arīq ḥarbī	4		ארק חרב
	tōrīš-ēm yadī	5		תרש-מ[22] יד
v. 10	*našapta baruḥeka*	7	(11)	נשפת ברחכ[23]
	kissamu yam	4		כסמ ימ
	ṣalalū ka^{c}ōpart	6	(11)	צלל כעפרת
	bamēm 'addīrīm	5		בממ אדרמ
v. 11	*mī kamōka ba'ēlīm yahwē*	9		מ כמכ באלמ יהו[24]
	mī kamōka ni'dar baqudš	8		מ כמכ נאדר בקדש
	nōra' tahillōt ^{c}ōśē pil'	8		נרא תהלת עש פלא

Part II

v. 12	*naṭiṯa yamīneka*	7	[25]נטת ימנכ
	tibla^{c}ēmu 'arṣ	5	תבלעמ ארצ[26]
v. 13	*naḥita baḥasdeka*	7	נחת בחסדכ
	^{c}am zū ga'alta	5	עמ ז גאלת
	nihhalta ba^{c}uzzeka	7	נהלת בעזכ
	'el nawē qudšeka	6	אל נו[27] קדשכ
v. 14	*šama^{c}ū ^{c}ammīm yirgazūn*	8	שמע עממ ירגזנ
	ḥīl 'aḥaz yōšibē pališt	8	חל אחז ישב פלשת[28]
v. 15	*'az nibhalū*	4	[29]אז נבהל
	'allūpē 'edōm	5	אלפ אדמ[30]
	'ēlē mō'ab	4	אל מאב
	yō'ḥazēmu ra^{c}d	5	יאחזמ רעד

	namōgū kōl	4	נמג כל
	yōšibē kana^{c}n	5	ישב כנענ
v. 16	*tappīl ^{c}alēhim*	5	תפל עלהמ
	'ēmatā wapaḥd	5	אמת ופחד
	bagudl zarō^{c}eka	6	בגדל[31] זרעכ
	yiddamū ka'abn	5	ידמ כאבנ
	^{c}ad ya^{c}bōr ^{c}ammeka yahwē	8	עד יעבר עמכ יהו
	^{c}ad ya^{c}bōr ^{c}am zū qanita	8	עד יעבר עמ ז קנת
v. 17	*tabī'ēm tiṭṭa^{c}ēm*	6	תבאמ[32] ⌜⌝תטעמ[33]
	bahar naḥlateka	6	בהר נחלתכ
	makōn lašibteka	6	מכנ לשבתכ
	pa^{c}alta yahwē	5	פעלת יהו
	miqdaš yahwē	4	מקדש ‹יהו›[34]
	kōninū yadēka	6	כננ ידכ
v. 18	*yahwē yimlōk*	4	יהו ימלכ
	la^{c}ōlam wa^{c}ad	5	לעלמ ועד[35]

Translation

Part I

v. 1 I will sing to Yahweh
For he is highly exalted,

Horse and rider
He cast into the sea.

v. 3 Yahweh is a warrior,
Yahweh is his name.

v. 4 {The chariots of Pharoah
Pharoah and his army
He cast into the sea,

The elite of his troops
He drowned in the Reed Sea.

v. 6 Your right hand, Yahweh,
Is terrible in strength

Your right hand, Yahweh,
Shattered the enemy.

v. 7 In your great majesty
You smashed your foes,

You sent forth your fury,
It consumed them like stubble.

v. 8 At the blast of your nostrils the waters were heaped up,
The swells mounted up as a hill,[36]
The deeps churned in the heart of the sea.

v. 9 Said the enemy:
"I shall pursue, I shall overtake,

I shall divide the spoil,
My greed will be sated.

I shall bare my sword,
My hand will conquer."

v. 10 You blew with your breath,
The sea covered them.

They sank like a lead weight
In the dreadful waters.

v. 11 Who is like you among the gods, Yahweh?
Who is like you, terrible among the holy ones?[37]
Awesome in praiseworthy acts, wonder worker.

Part II

v. 12 You stretched out your right hand,
The underworld swallowed them.

v. 13 You led faithfully
The people whom you delivered,

You guided powerfully
To your holy encampment.

v. 15 Then were dismayed
The chieftans of Edom,

The nobles[38] of Moab
Were seized with trembling,

They melted utterly,
The enthroned[39] of Canaan.

v. 16 You brought down upon them
Terror and dread,

By your great power
They were struck dumb as a stone.

When your people passed over, Yahweh,
When the people whom you created passed over,

v. 17 You brought them, you planted them
In the mount of your possession.

The dais of your throne
You have made, Yahweh.

A sanctuary, Yahweh,
Your hands have created,

v. 18 Yahweh will reign
Forever and ever!

NOTES

Exodus 15: The Song of Miriam

[1]F. M. Cross, Jr., "The Song of the Sea and Canaanite Myth," *Journal for Theology and Church* 5 (1968), 1-25; D. N. Freedman, "Strophe and Meter in the Song of the Sea," *A Light Unto My Path: Old Testament Studies in Honor of J. M. Myers* (1974), 163-203.

[2]*Studies in Ancient Yahwistic Poetry* (hereafter *SAYP*), 45-65 = "The Song of Miriam," *JNES* 14 (1955), 237-250.

[3]See note 1.

[4]See *SAYP* 125-29 and the table in *SAYP* 161-68. *waw*, *kī*, *'et*, *'ăšer*, the article, and other prosaic or additional elements are commonly omitted from the texts of the poems reconstructed in this chapter. *kol* ("all") is likewise frequently deleted as an accretion to the text.

[5]See note 1. *SAYP* 45-65, although less recent, is more detailed.

[6]Among the theoretical problems are the following: The vocalization of *Yahweh* is treated in detail in Cross, "Yahweh and the God of the Patriarchs," *HTR* 55 (1962), 251-55. Cf. also M. Pope, *Job, the Anchor Bible*, Vol. 15, xiv, note 1. We assume it to have been pronounced *yahwē* (< **yahwī*) although this is uncertain. The energic verbal form was either *inna/in* or *anna/an*. Merely for convenience, we adopt the former vocalization with Barth, *Sprachwissenschaftliche Studien*, Leipzig, 1907, 1ff. The connecting element in Aramaic was *in*, in Arabic *an*. Hebrew *en* is perhaps allophonic for one of these; or else all of the three may be considered mutual allophones. A choice between the three is really quite arbitrary.

Seghol in pause before the second person suffix (*suseka*, *ḥasdeka*, etc.) is retained unreduced, with the MT, but in all positions rather than merely the pausal. According to classical models of vocalic change, the sound was originally either *a* (*-*aka*) or *i* (*-*ika*). It varied, however, with the shorter -*ak* form, just as we have side-by-side survivals of *ēka/ēk*, *ba/bamō*, *ᶜal/ᶜalē*, *lō/lahu*, *bām/bahim*, *'ēl/'elōh/'ĕlōhīm*. They were selected often by poets *metri causa* and must often be restored when suggested by meter. On some of these cases see Cross and Freedman, *Early Hebrew Orthography* (hereafter *EHO*), 65f. In some cases the shorter forms were more colloquial, but nevertheless available for use in poetry.

Especially problematic is the vocalization of the infinitive construct (*laquṭul/ liqṭōl/ laquṭl*-, etc.?) and the imperative in some forms (*šamaᶜū/ šamᶜū/ šimᶜū*, etc.?). We generally opt for the fuller forms, a position for which there is some evidence (cf. Sperber, *A Grammar of Masoretic Hebrew*, Copenhagen, 1959, pp. 64-65). It is quite possible that the vocalizations varied or at least *could be* varied in poetry (cf. English heaven/heav'n, etc.). Likewise some plurals and construct plurals are difficult (*ṣxdaqōt/ ṣidqōt, malkē/ malakē*, etc.). Where the MT is suspect but no certainty is forthcoming as to a vocalization we occasionally resort to the use of *x* to indicate the assumption of a vowel of completely uncertain quality.

The extent of tone lengthening is also unknown, as is all allophonic variation (e.g. *kul/kol, 'amīrē/'ămīrē/'ĕmīrē*, etc.). *Aleph* and *resh* commonly behave similarly in Hebrew. We assume here that they were not doubled in the early period in contrast to the other gutterals (which are less quiescent in both Biblical Hebrew and Biblical Aramaic), and that they colored vowels (e.g. *i>e*). This is entirely open to question, however. Vocalizational problems receive attention in A. Sperber's *Historical Grammar of Biblical Hebrew*, Leiden, 1966.

[7]A good deal of free variation between short and long meter does occur later, in poetry such as is found in the latter portions of II Isaiah. This poetry is generally *archaistic* rather than archaic. In it, there is little visibly meaningful relationship between "b" and "l" cola.

[8]On the isolation and interpretation of various archaic forms in the poetry of this chapter, see W. F. Albright, "Archaic Survivals in the Text of Canticles," *Hebrew and Semitic Studies submitted to Godfrey Rolles Driver*, ed., D. W. Thomas and W. D. McHardy, Oxford, 1963, 1-7; D. N. Freedman, "Archaic Forms in Early Hebrew Poetry," *ZAW* 72 (1960), 101-7; H. D. Hummel, "Enclitic *Mem* in Early Northwest Semitic, especially Hebrew," *JBL* 76 (1957), 85-107; M. Pope, "Ugaritic Enclitic -*m*," *JCS* 5 (1961), 123-28; N. Sarna, "Some Instances of the Enclitic -*m* in Job," *JJS* 6 (1955), 108-10. Note also that the perfect and imperfect forms of the verb vary as A and B words in parallelism, not precisely bound either to tense or aspect. Cf. Cross, "The Song of the Sea and Canaanite Myth," 15, note 55. On the ability of the imperfect to serve as past narrative in Hebrew, see F. R. Blake, *A Resurvey of Hebrew Tenses*, Rome, 1951.

[9]For vv. 17-18, Cross, "The Song of the Sea," construes a triplet and a short couplet, an equally satisfactory approach.

[10]Obviously prosaic particles or additions are deleted without discussion but are marked. This will be standard practice in the treatment of Hebrew poetry here.

[11]The exact original form of the word is uncertain. The versions differ as to reading. MT *'āšīrāh*, the cohortative, would have originally appeared as *'šr* in the older orthography. We therefore choose *'šr* and vocalize it as the l.c.s. imperfect. Cross, "The Song of the Sea," 13, note 41) emends to *šr* (*šīrū*) with the parallel in v. 21. Meter is unaffected.

[12]The vocalization *rōkēb*, i.e. the participle, is tentative. It is supported by the LXX, Vulgate, Old Latin, and Syro-hexapla. It refers to a chariot rider, not a horseman, since the poem would predate cavalry warfare. Also possible is *rikbō* or the like. Cf. *SAYP*, 54, note 2.

[13]Verse 2 is probably out of place in this setting. It is discussed at length by Cross and Freedman in *SAYP*, 54-56, note 3. They reconstruct (vocalization and meter are ours):

ᶜuzzī wazimratī yahwē	8	עז וזמרת יהו
yihyē liya layašuᶜā	8	יהי לי לישע
zē 'ēlī wa'arōmiminhu	9	ז אל ו›ארממנה‹
'elōhē 'abī wa'anwēhu	9	אלה אב ו›אנוה‹

This reconstruction assumes the reversal of formulae in dictation, but is otherwise the MT consonantal reading. The fact that these couplets are apparently inappropriate at this point is, however, no denial of their antiquity, as examination of the orthography of the MT demonstrates.

[14]Read *gibbōr* with the LXX and Samaritan. MT *'š mlḥmh* is an ancient variant, suitable for a different metrical context.

[15]We treat the text as preserving two variants, metrically equivalent, following this principle in *SAYP*, *ad loc*.

[16]Since *mbḥr* is singular, a singular verb is required.

[17]Reading the *Piel*. The consonantal text is ambiguous as to conjugation.

[18]Our restoration of *yama* assumes that it (or something like it) has been lost by haplography. The form would not be the locative but the adverbial. Note that *ym* is the exact form of the end of the preceding word. Also possible: *bayam*.

[19]We omit the *hireq compaginis* with the parallel word in verse 9 (which, however, has the *hireq* in the Samaritan text). If it is to be preserved, meter is not significantly affected. Cf. *SAYP*, 59, note 14.

[20]Cross, "The Song of the Sea," 12, continues the stichometry outlined in *SAYP*, analyzing v. 8a as a 5:4 couplet, part of a b:b::b:b::b:b triplet beginning in v. 7. Since each of its three cola describes the same thing, viz., the mounting up of the water, we suggest the arrangement here, an l:l:l triplet, for v. 8. *balēb yam* after *tihōmōt* shows that the missing formula in v. 5 may well involve *yam* in some form.

[21]Read the enclitic *mem*, with its presumed vocalization after a consonant, *-ēm*. This clears up an otherwise problematic reading.

[22]See note 21.

[23]While 7:4 is uncommon for short meter (usually no more than two syllables' imbalance is normal for short meter, and one syllable's imbalance for long meter) the 7:4::6:5 thus produced is 11:11 overall, fully balanced.

[24]A 9:8:8 triplet, while not entirely balanced, is quite acceptable. In Ugaritic, triplets sometimes show imbalance (by one syllable additional) in the last line. For the initial line to be longer is rare in Ugaritic poetry but not in Hebrew poetry.

[25]The b:b::b:b::b:b triplet in vv. 12-13 is roughly balanced overall, 12:12:13 as vocalized here. If all the forms with *-eka* here were vocalized with the short form, *-ak*, meter would be 6:5::6:5::6:5. Exactly how the poet might have vocalized the triplet is conjectural.

[26]We consider v. 12 to be the initial part of the triplet (vv. 12-13) although it does not describe exactly the same thought as do the following two bicola (v. 13). Yet it has similar meter and begins with a 2.m.s *Qal* perfect as they do. Similar reasons apply in the case of v. 18. The decision is somewhat arbitrary.

[27]MT *'l* is possibly secondary since it is not required for locative force in such a context, but its deletion would be highly conjectural and without textual demand.

[28]Another colon may have followed here originally, making the verse a triplet. The parallelism seems slightly incomplete, although *'ammīm* may be seen as further delineated by the listing of the various nations immediately following in v. 15.

[29]Note the pattern 4:5, etc. in vv. 15-16, followed by 5:5, as in II Samuel 1:21-22. An alternate, although highly conjectural stichometry for vv. 14-15 here would be:

šamaᶜū ᶜammīm yirgazūn	8
ḥīl 'aḥaz yōšibē pališt	8
⌜⌝*nibhalū 'allūpē 'edōm*	8
'ēlē mō'ab yō'ḥazēm raᶜd	8
namōgū ⌜⌝*yōšibē kanaᶜn*	8

[30]In the case of place names vocalization based on cuneiform transcriptions is commonly accepted (e.g. *pališt* in v. 14 above). For *'dm* Ugaritic has *'udm* (= *'udum* or the like), which would have served graphically for *'ᵉdōm* or *'udum* equally. For want of certainty, the late Hebrew vocalization is retained here.

[31]Reading the segholate *gudl* with the near parallel in Psalm 79:11.

[32]Read the short form of the object suffix. The longer form, *'ēmu* (MT *-ēmō*) while common in this chapter, need not be levelled through in every instance, as has been done.

[33]See note 32.

[34]Read *yahwē*, more likely original, with the Samaritan.

[35]Cross considers the bicolon in v. 18 to be a short couplet, self-contained, thus grouping the bicola in v. 17 into a b:b::b:b::b:b triplet.

[36]The translation of MT *nd* is problematic. "Hill" is a likely proposal. Cf. Cross, "The Song of the Sea and Canaanite Myth," 16, note 58.

[37]Read *qudš* as the collective, fully parallel to *'lm*.

[38]The reading of *'lm* (from *'ayil*) as "chieftans/nobles" or the like, fairly transparent in this context, is of great importance for the understanding of Judges 5:8, q.v.

[39]A translation such as "enthroned" is required by the context. Cf. Cross, "The Song of the Sea and Canaanite Myth," 15, note 53.

The Song of Heshbon: Numbers 21:27-30

This short song exhibits several interesting features including metrical regularity, balanced couplets, rhyme (vv. 27, 28), mixed meter, a triplet, and indications of very archaic orthography. Certain of the suggestions as to textual emendation made by Hanson[1] are incorporated here. Verse 30, too corrupt to present confidently in the text, is discussed in the notes.

The schematic structure may be diagrammed as follows:

couplet	1:1	v. 27
couplet	1:1	v. 28
couplet	1:1	
couplet	1:1	v. 29
triplet	1:1:1	
couplet (?)	b:b::b:b (?)	v. 30

The meter is largely composed of seven-beat cola: 7:7, 7:7, 7:7, 6:6, 7:7:7, (for the last couplet see note 5).

Reconstructed Text[2]

v. 27	*bō'ū tibbanē ḥešbōn*	7	בא תבנ חשבנ[3]
	tikkōninna ᶜīr sīḥōn	7	[4]⌜⌝תכננ ער סחנ
v. 28	*'ēš yaṣa'ā miḥḥešbōn*	7	⌜⌝אש יצא מחשבנ
	lahab min qiryat sīḥōn	7	להב ⌜⌝[4]מנ קרית סחנ
	'akalā ᶜarē mō'ab	7	אכל ער מאב
	balaᶜā bamōt 'arnōn	7	⟨בלע⟩[4] במת ארננ
v. 29	*'ōy laka malk mō'ab*	6	אי לכ ⟨מלכ⟩[4] מאב
	'abadta ᶜam kamōš	6	אבדת עמ כמש
	natan banēw palēṭīm	7	נתנ בנו פלטמ
	wabanōtēw bašabīt	7	ובנתו בשבת
	lamalk 'amōrī sīḥōn	7	למלכ אמר סחנ

v. 30 . . . .   - - - - - - - - - - -
. . . .   - - - - - - - - - - -

. . . .   - - - - - - - - - - -
. . . .   5- - - - - - - - - - -

Translation

v. 27 Come, let Heshbon be built,
Let be established the city of Sihon.

v. 28 Fire went out from Heshbon,
Flame from Sihon's city.

It devoured the cities of Moab,
It swallowed the high places of Arnon.

v. 29 Woe to you, king of Moab,
You have perished, people of Chemosh.

His sons are given captive
And his daughters in captivity
To the king of the Amorites, Sihon.

v. 30 . . . .
. . . .

. . . .
. . . .

NOTES

The Song of Heshbon: Numbers 21:27-30

[1]Paul Hanson, "The Song of Heshbon and David's *Nîr*," *Harvard Theological Review* 61 (1968), 297-320.

[2]Hanson (*ibid.*) reconstructs the poem with each couplet scanning 7:7. This contrasts with our own view that the song is written in mixed meter. Freedman (in private communication) has also argued that the meter is not uniform but mixed. The primary cause for disagreement is the uncertainty of use of case endings in the very early Hebrew period. We differ with Hanson in the analysis of the morphology of this period, seeing no reason to assume the widespread use of case endings from the older Canaanite period as he does. Generally his emendations are quite convincing, however, and their excellence is not diminished by this disagreement.

[3]We have provisionally reversed the order of the final two words of this line (*tibbanē* and *ḥešbōn*) since the following three cola each end with an *ōn* sound. The point of this colon, moreover, is to say, "Let Heshbon be built," rather than "Come to Heshbon." The parallelism confirms this. However, it may be that no tampering with word order is justified since the third couplet of the song, like the MT arrangement of the first couplet, ends its second line with an *ōn* sound but does not end its first line (*mō'ab*) this way. Meter is unaffected in any case. *tikkōninna* is an energic form; an equally possible vocalization is *tikkōnanna*.

[4]The emendations follow Hanson, *op. cit.*

[5]Hanson reconstructs v. 30 generally as follows (we delete case endings, however):

nīr mō'ab 'abad	(5)	נר מאב אבד
ḥešbōn ᶜadē daybōn	(6)	חשבנ עד דיבנ
našammā		נשמ -------
nōpḥ ᶜadē mēdaba'	(6)	נפח עד מדבא

"The yoke of Moab has perished,
From Heshbon to Dibon,

Destroyed is . . . . .
From Noph to Medeba."

Also possible (but only conjectural) are the following reconstructions of the difficult final half of this presumably b:b::b:b couplet:

našammā ᶜīr nōpḥ	*našammā mō'ab*	*našammā ᶜīr nopḥ*
waᶜīr mēdaba'	*nōpḥ ᶜadē mēdaba'*	*ba'ēš mēdaba'*

etc.

Lamech's Song to his Wives: Genesis 4:23-4

This prideful song of Lamech is of inexactly discernable early date.[1] Most of its prosodic features, including an analysis of its fixed pairs, have been well discussed by Gevirtz.[2] It is of simple structure and of regular, although mixed, meter. The stichometry may be outlined schematically as follows:

couplet	1:1	v. 23
couplet	1:1	
couplet	1:1	v. 24

v. 23	*ᶜadā waṣillā šamaᶜn qōlī*	9	עד[3] וצל[4] שמענ קל
	našē lamk ha'zēnna 'imratī	9	נש למכ האזנ אמרת
	'īš haragtī lapiṣᶜī	7	[5]אש הרגת לפצע
	wayald laḥabburatī	7	וילד לחברת
v. 24	*kī šibᶜatēm yuqqam qēn*	7	כ[6] שבעתמ יקמ קנ
	walamk šibᶜīm wašibᶜā	7	[7]ולמכ שבעמ ושבע

Translation

v. 23 Adah and Zillah, hear my voice,
Wives of Lamech, give ear to my speech.

A man have I slain for my wound,
Even a boy for my hurt

v. 24 If Cain be avenged sevenfold,
Then Lamech seventy and seven![8]

NOTES

Lamech's Song to his Wives: Genesis 4:23-4

[1]The arguments for date including style, proper names, literary genre, etc. are given by Stanley Gevirtz, *Patterns in the Early Poetry of Israel*, *Studies in Ancient Oriental Civilization*, No. 32, Chicago, University of Chicago Press, 1963, p. 25f.

[2]*Ibid.*, 25-34.

[3]The stichometry here follows the LXX rather than that of the *BH*. Gevirtz demonstrates that the legitimate parallel to *nāšē lamk* is *ᶜādā waṣillā*, citing numerous examples of proper names "in parallel formation with a descriptive or identifying word or epithet" from both Ugaritic and Old Testament poetry (*ibid.*, 26-27).

[4]*šamᶜan* is also a possible vocalization. MT *šamaᶜᵃn* represents a resolution of an earlier stage's *šamaᶜn*. This was a short form of the imperative which may have been employed by the composer *metri causa*.

[5]Omit MT *kī* as an explanatory prosaic interpolation.

[6]Retain *kī* here since it is the conditional particle, "If."

[7]It would be necessary to retain *waw* at the outset of this colon under any circumstances since it is a *waw* of apodosis in a conditional sentence. The *waw* at the outset of the second colon of the preceding couplet (*wayald lahabburatī*) is, however, a product of the discretion of the composer/reciter.

[8]For a discussion of the reason for the "unusual" parallelism of this verse (*seven* being paralleled by *eight* would be more normal for Hebrew poetry), see Gevirtz, *op. cit.*, 15-24, and 29-30.

Some Short Poems from Genesis and Judges

The following several pieces are taken from brief poetic inserts within narrative sections of Genesis and Judges. All are recast in northern vocalization and premonarchic orthography. A variety of metrical types is found: five 7:7 couplets, one 6:6 couplet, a 9:7 unbalanced couplet, a 5:5::5:5 couplet, and a 6:6::6:6::5:6 triplet.

Genesis 2:23

The pair of couplets in Genesis 2:23 which describe Adam's naming Eve a "woman" are 1:1, with balanced cola. The couplets contain several examples of assonance, and particularly *figura etymologica*. Although not recognized as poetry in the versions (along with Judges 15:16, etc.) its features of style, parallelism, syntax, and meter demonstrate this pericope's poetic nature.

Reconstructed Text

zō't pa^{c}*m* ^{c}*aṣm mi*^{cc}*aṣamay*	7	זאת"[1] פעם [2]עצם מעצמי
wabaśar mibbaśarī	7	ובשר מבשר
lū zō't yiqqarē 'iššā	7	ל זאת יקרא אש
kī mē'īš luqqaḥā zō't	7	כ מאש[3]לקח זאת

Translation

This now is (a) bone from my bones,
And flesh from my flesh.

Indeed this shall be called 'woman'
Because from man this was taken.

Genesis 25:23

Yahweh's announcement to Rebecca of the future fate of her twins is recognized as poetic in the versions. A slight change in stichometry from that of the received text produces a superior structure without essential change of meaning. The poem has two couplets, both of which are 1:1. A more bold textual emendation would yield a b:b::b:b couplet from this verse; this possibility is discussed in the notes. In either case the couplets are balanced and regular.

Reconstructed Text[4]

šanē gōyēm babiṭnēk	7	שנ[5] גימ בבטנכ
šanē lu'mēm mimmēᶜēk	7	⸢⸣[6]שנ לאממ ממעכ
yipparēdū lu'm millu'm	7	יפרד[7] ⸢⸣[8]לאמ מלאמ
yi'maṣ rab yaᶜbōd ṣaᶜīr	7	יאמצ ⸢⸣[9]רב יעבד צער

Translation

Two nations are in your womb;
Two peoples within your loins.

They shall divide, people from people;
The elder shall be strong, (yet) it shall serve the younger.

Three Couplets from Judges 14

In Judges 14 there appear three independent couplets from the Samson cycle, separated in the narrative by prose material. It is possible that they were once part of a poetic saga concerning Samson and have been excerpted from it for use in the story as it is found in the Hebrew Bible. All are simple 1:1 couplets.

Reconstructed Text, Judges 14:14[10]

mē'ōkēl yaṣa' ma'kal	7	מ⸢⸣אכל יצא מאכל
wamiᶜᶜaz yaṣa' matōq	7	ומעז יצא[11] מתק

Translation[12]

From the eater came something to eat,
And from the strong came something sweet.

Reconstructed Text, Judges 14:18a[13]

ma matōq middabaš	6	מ מתק מדבש
wama ᶜaz mē'ărī	6	ומ עז מאר[14]

Translation

What is sweeter than honey,
And what is stronger than a lion?

Reconstructed Text, Judges 14:18b[15]

lulēʾ ḥarašt̄im baᶜiglatī	9	ללא חרשתמ בעגלת
lōʾ maṣaʾtim ḥīdatī	7	לא מצאתמ חדת

Translation

If you had not plowed with my heifer,
You would not have found out my riddle.

Judges 15:16

Samson's boast of victory in battle is transparently poetic, as recognized in most of the versions in contrast to the MT. Its repetitive parallelism signals its early date; assonance is very strong. The meter is simple b:b::b:b, completely balanced.

Reconstructed Text

balǝḥī ḥimōr	5	בלח חמר
ḥamōr ḥamartīm	5	חמר חמרתמ[16]
balǝḥī ḥimōr	5	בלח חמר
hikkētī ʾalp ʾīš	5	הכת אלפ אש

Translation

With the jawbone of an ass,
I heaped them in a heap.

With the jawbone of an ass,
I slew a company[17] of men.

Judges 16:23-24

This Philistine taunt song against Samson is notable for its rhyme and simple repetitiveness, appropriate to the jeering of a crowd at a hated enemy as described in the immediate context. It may perhaps best be termed "doggerel" in light of its inelegant style. Schematically these verses comprise a triplet, b:b::b:b::b:b.

Reconstructed Text

natan bayadēnu	6	נתנ[18] [][19]בידנ
šimšōn 'ōyibēnu	6	⸢⸣[20]שמשנ איבנ
natan bayadēnu	6	נתנ[19] בידנ
šimšōn 'ōyibēnu	6	‹שמשנ›[21] איבנ
maḥrīb 'arṣēnu	5	⸢⸣[22]מחרב ארצנ
hirba ḥalalēnu	6	⸢⸣[23]הרב חללנ

Translation

Given into our hand is
Samson our enemy

Given into our hand is
Samson our enemy.

Ravager of our land,
Who multiplied our slain.

NOTES

Some Short Poems from Genesis and Judges

[1]The use of *zō't* rather than *hī'* in reference to Eve is not surprising. It may be a clue to the type of poem from which this short pair of couplets is taken, namely a poem in which is described Adam's naming of various animals as discussed in 2:19-20. In such a hypothetical poem Adam would use the words *zō't* and *zeh* (early *zī*) often as each animal was brought before him.

[2]The use of *paᶜm* ("now" or "at last") also suggests that these couplets were possibly part of a longer poem of which the naming of Eve might have been a final part. *paᶜm* in the sense of "now" or the like is attested in Prov. 7:12 without the article. The usual cliche with the article has caused the article to be added here where it does not belong in old poetry, sometime in the course of transmission.

[3]The Samaritan Pentateuch, LXX, and Targum Onkelos read *'īšāh*, "her man/husband." Speiser (*Genesis*, p. 15) correctly follows MT and the remainder of the versions, however, with the explanation that *'īš* is used in contrast to *'iššāh* rather than in similarity to it.

[4]Cross has noted the possibility of another arrangement of the text, which would yield a b:b::b:b couplet. It assumes that the *šny* of the MT is superfluous before a dual such as *gōyēm* would properly have been, and that *yprd* of the consonantal text might best read *yuprad*. This produces:

gōyēm babiṭnēk	5	גים בבטנכ
lu'mēm mimmeᶜēk	5	לאממ ממעכ
yuprad lu'm millu'm	5	יפרד לאמ מלאמ
rab yaᶜbōd ṣaᶜīr	5	רב יעבד צער

[5]Although *šny* is not technically needed here, since the dual of *gōyēm* and *luᶜmēm* would suffice (and would have been the original vocalization), it may well be that *šanē* was purposely used for emphasis (and/or *metri causa* ?). Therefore it is retained here.

[6]Omit *waw* consecutive here and at some points in following couplets as a typical accretion in course of transmission.

[7]The Qal passive singular *yuprad* is also possible. See note 4.

[8]This *waw* joined the text sometime after the stichometry had shifted to its present misarrangement in the MT, and is surely to be deleted.

[9]See note 8.

[10]Here LXX A follows the MT. LXX B, however, reads: τί βρωτὸν ʼεξῆλθεν ʼεκ βιβρώσκοντας;, "What edible came from the eater?" This reflects an original consonantal text exactly the same as reconstructed here but pointed as follows: *māh 'okl yaṣa' me'ōkēl*. Since the particle *ma* would have appeared written with the final *mater heh* (מה) in the LXX Hebrew *Vorlage*, the absence in the Greek of a reflex for the Hebrew article is explained.

[11]LXX B omits *ys'* in the second colon, probably by simple haplography. LXX A retains it.

[12]The translation reflects, imperfectly, the assonance of the couplet.

[13]Recognized as poetic in the versions, this couplet also embodies considerable assonance, especially in *m* sounds.

[14]The word for lion, from a theoretical proto-Semitic **'aryu* had by the time of Amorite Mari resolved into *'ărī* or the like, with two syllables, and would surely have resolved in Hebrew as well at an early date. The final vowel would not appear orthographically.

[15]The poetic response of Samson to the solution of his riddle by the Philistines contains a rhyme scheme: ABC DBC. The assonance of the couplet is magnified by the similar initial *l* sounds of the two cola. The MT has preserved the original form of the couplet, as the versions suggest. This feature of rhyme in Hebrew poetry is not infrequent; cf. Genesis 4:23-4, 49:3; Numbers 21:27f; Judges 16:24; Amos 5:12, etc.

[16]Read *ḥamartīm* with LXX, Old Latin, and Vulgate; the first bicolon requires a verb. Although meter is affected by the change (for the better), the consonantal text is unaffected. Assonance continues strong.

[17]"Company" is superior to "thousand" since *'lp* is clearly a political or military unit in many Old Testament contexts. Cf. G. Mendenhall, "The Census Lists of Numbers 1 and 26." *JBL* 77 (1958), 52-66.

[18]MT *ntn* may have originally been intended as a Qal passive, and was understood as active later in transmission. A crowd chant, however, is based on common knowledge, and is usually short and catchy. Therefore the active sense is possible, with the subject (Dagan or the like) understood but not expressed, or expressed in a part of the poem not used by the collector of the materials.

[19]MT *'ĕlōhēnû* seems inappropriate in the speech of Philistines. One would expect *Dagan*, unless the poem were composed by an Israelite with strong prejudice against mentioning the name of a foreign deity. Such prejudices are later developments, however, so it is unlikely that *'ĕlōhēnû* was original

in any case. If the Qal passive of *ntn* was original but subsequently misunderstood, the supply of an appropriate subject is understandable.

[20]Omit *'et* here and at other points in the song as prosaic.

[21]Since this line constitutes the people's repetition of the tyrants' taunt, *šimšōn* must be restored as most commentators suggest.

[22]Omission of the conjunction here, required by sound prosody, is supported by LXX B, and the Vulgate.

[23]Omission of the conjunction here is supported by LXX A. Since conjunctions (especially *waw*) were used in early poetry, one may never delete them automatically. Yet the evidence of the versions is chaotic, showing that one must delete them at least often. Cf. Cross and Freedman, *Studies in Ancient Yahwistic Poetry*, 161-68.

The Oracles of Balaam: Numbers 23:7-10; 18-24; 24:3-9; 15-19

The Oracles of Balaam are to be dated not later than 1000 B.C. This date is based on the defective orthography of the received text in comparison with Phoenician and Hebrew inscriptions of early date as well as certain features of content.[1] The nature of the orthography suggests that the poem circulated in written form as early as or prior to the Gezer Calendar and Phoenician royal inscriptions dated to the tenth century. Further, some features of the parallelism, especially the relative paucity of repetitive parallelism, suggest a date somewhat later than Exodus 15.[2]

Interesting for our study of meter are the many similarities between the second and third oracles, which are of roughly the same length and contain many of the same patterns in the same order. Perhaps the melodies were nearly the same for each section of these two oracles. This may be supported by the equivalence of 23:22 and 24:8, identical possibly because they were suggested by a similar melody and meter.

The meter is repetitious, mostly 1:1 couplets with only three triplets in all four oracles. No short meter is found at all. Counts of 7:7 and 8:8 predominate except in the case of the second oracle, where 6:6 is found once. The meter is mixed in normal, unpredictable fashion.

The prosodic structure of the respective oracles may be diagrammed as follows:

The First Oracle: Numbers 23:7-10

couplet	1:1	23:7
couplet	1:1	
couplet	1:1	23:8
couplet	1:1	23:9
couplet	1:1	
couplet	1:1	23:10
couplet	1:1	

The Second Oracle: Numbers 23:18-24

couplet	1:1	23:18
couplet	1:1	23:19
couplet	1:1	
couplet	1:1	23:20

couplet	1:1	23:21
couplet	1:1	
couplet	1:1	23:22
couplet	1:1	23:23a
couplet	1:1	23:23b
couplet	1:1	23:24
couplet	1:1	

The Third Oracle: Numbers 24:3-9

triplet	1:1:1	24:3-4a
couplet	1:1	24:4b
couplet	1:1	24:5
couplet	1:1	24:6
couplet	1:1	
couplet	1:1	24:7
couplet	1:1	
couplet	1:1	24:8
couplet	1:1	
couplet	1:1	24:9
couplet	1:1	

The Fourth Oracle: Numbers 24:15-19

triplet	1:1:1	24:15-16a
couplet	1:1	24:16b
couplet	1:1	24:17
couplet	1:1	
couplet	1:1	
triplet	1:1:1	24:18
couplet	1:1	

The First Oracle, Reconstructed Text: Numbers 23:7-10[3]

23:7	*min 'aram yanḥēnī balaq*	8	מנ ארמ ינחנ בלק
	malk mō'ab mihhararē qadm	8	מלכ מאב מהרר קדמ
	lika 'urra lī ya^{c}qōb	7	לכ אר לי[4] יעקב
	lika zu^{c}ma yiśra'ēl	7	⸢י⸣לכ זעמ ישראל
23:8	*ma 'eqqōb lō' qabbō yahwē*	8	מ אקב לא קב ⟨יהו⟩[5]
	wama 'ez^{c}ōm lō' za^{c}am 'ēl	8	ומ אזעמ לא זעמ ⟨אל⟩[5]

23:9	*kī mērō'š ṣurīm 'er'innu*	8	כ מראש צרמ אראנ
	miggibaᶜōt 'ašūrinnu	8	⸢מגבעת אשרנ
	hinnē ᶜam labadad yiškōn	8	הנ עמ לבדד ישכנ
	wabagōyīm lō' yitḥaššab	8	ובגימ לא יתחשב
23:10	*mī mana ᶜapar yaᶜqōb*	7	מי[6] מנ עפר יעקב
	mī sapar robᶜ yiśra'ēl	7	מי ספר ⸢רבע⸣[7] ישראל
	tamōt napšī mōt yašarīm	8	תמת נפש מת ישרמ
	tᵉhī 'aḥritī kamōhu	8	תה אחרת כמה

Translation

23:7 From Aram Balak brought me
The king of Moab from the mountains of the East.

"Come, curse for me Jacob,
Come, denounce Israel."

23:8 How can I curse whom Yahweh has not cursed,
And how can I denounce whom Yahweh has not denounced?

23:9 For from the top of the mountains I see him
From the hills I behold him

Behold, the people dwells alone,
And among the nations does not consider itself.

23:10 Who can count the dust of Jacob,
Who can number a fourth of Israel?

Let my own death be the death of the righteous,
Let my end be like his.

The Second Oracle: Numbers 23:18-24

23:18	*quma balaq wašamaᶜa*	8	קמ[8] בלק ושמע[8]
	ha'zīna ᶜēdī bin ṣippōr	8	האזנ עד[9] בנ[10] צפר

23:19	*lō' 'īš 'ēl wayakazzēb*	7	לא אש אל ויכזב
	bin 'adam wayitnaḥḥam	7	⌜⌝בנ אדמ ויתנחמ
	hahū' 'amar walō' ya^{c}śē	8	ההא אמר ולא יעש
	wadibbēr walō' yaqīmin	8	ודבר ולא יקמנ[11]
23:20	*hinnē barōk luqqaḥtī*	7	הנ ברכ[12] לקחת
	barōk walō' 'ašībin	7	⌜⌝ברכ ולא אשבנ[13]
23:21	*lō' hibbīṭ 'ōn bayiśra'ēl*	8	לא הבט אנ ב⟨ישראל⟩[14]
	lō' ra'a ^{c}amal baya^{c}qōb	8	⌜⌝לא רא עמל ב⟨יעקב⟩
	yahwē 'elōhēw ^{c}immō	7	יהו אלהו עמ
	watōra^{c}at malkō bō	7	ותרעת[15] מלכ[16] ב
23:22	*'ēl mōṣi'ō mimmiṣrēm*	7	אל מצא[17] ממצרמ
	katō^{c}apōt rē'm lahu	7	כתעפת ראמ לה[18]
23:23	*kī lō' naḥš baya^{c}qōb*	6	כ לא נחש ביעקב
	lō' qasm bayiśra'ēl	6	⌜⌝לא קסמ בישראל
	ka^{c}ēt yē'amēr laya^{c}qōb	8	כעת יאמר ליעקב
	layiśra'ēl ma pa^{c}al 'ēl	8	⌜⌝לישראל מ פעל[19] אל
23:24	*hēn ^{c}am kalabī' yaqūm*	7	הנ עמ כלבא יקמ
	waka'ărī yitnaśśa'	7	וכאר יתנשא
	lō'yiškab ^{c}ad yō'kal ṭarp	7	לא ישכב עד יאכל טרפ
	wadam ḥalalīm yištē	7	ודמ חללמ ישת

Translation

23:18 Rise, Balak, and hear,
Give ear to my witness, son of Zippor.

23:19 Not a man is God that he should lie,
Nor a son of man that he should change his mind.

Has he spoken and will he not do?
Or said and will he not fulfill?

23:20 Behold to bless I was brought,
To bless and I can not demur.

23:21 He has not beheld misfortune in Israel,
He has not seen trouble in Jacob.

Yahweh his god is with him,
And the shout of his king is with him.

23:22 It is God who brought him out of Egypt;
He has as it were the horns of a wild ass.

23:23 For there is not enchantment against Jacob,
No divination against Israel.

Now let it be said of Jacob,
Of Israel, 'What has God done!'

23:24 Behold, the people like a lion rises up,
And like a lion lifts itself.

It will not lie down until it has eaten the prey,
And the blood of the slain has drunk.

The Third Oracle: Numbers 24:3-9

24:3	*nu'm bil^{c}am binu bx^{c}ōr*	7	נאם בלעם בנ[20] באר
	nu'm gabr ša tūmā ^{c}ēnō	7	⸢נאם⸣ גבר ש תמ[21] ענ
24:4	*nu'm šōmē^{c} 'amīrē 'ēl*	7	נאם שמע אמר אל
	ša maḥzē šadday yiḥzē	7	⟨ש⟩[22]מחז שדי יחז
	nōpēl wagalūy ^{c}ēnēm	7	נפל וגלי ענמ
24:5	*ṭōbū 'ohalēka ya^{c}qōb*	8	⸢⸣טב[23] אהלכ יעקב
	miškanōtēka yiśra'ēl	8	משכנתכ ישראל
24:6	*kanaḥalīm niṭṭayū*	7	כנחלמ נטי
	kagannōt ^{c}alē nahar	7	כגנת על נהר

	ka'ahalīm niṭṭaᶜū	7	כאהלמ נטע [ ] [24]
	ka'arazīm ᶜalē mēm	7	כארזמ על ממ
24:7	*yizzal mēm middalayēw*	7	יזל ממ מדליו
	wazarᶜō bamēm rabbīm	7	וזרע בממ רבמ
	yarūm mē'agag malkō	7	⌜ירמ מאגג מלכ
	watinnaśśē' malkutō	7	ותנשא מלכת
24:8	*'ēl mōṣi'ō mimmiṣrēm*	7	אל מצא ממצרמ
	katōᶜapōt rē'm lahu	7	כתעפת ראמ ל ⟨ה⟩[25]
	yō'kal gōyīm ṣarēhu	7	יאכל גימ צר ⟨ה⟩[26]
	ᶜaṣmōtēhim yagarrēm	7	⌜עצמתהמ יגרמ [ ] [27]
24:9	*karaᶜ šakab kalabī'ā*	8	כרע שכב כ ⟨לבא⟩[28]
	kalabī' mī yaqīminnu	8	כלבא מ יקמנ[29]
	mubarrikēka bārūk	7	מברככ ברכ
	wa'ōrirēka 'arūr	7	וארככ ארר

Translation

24:3 Oracle of Balaam, son of Beor,
Oracle of the man whose eye is true,
24:4 Oracle of him who hears the words of God.

Who sees the vision of Shaddai,
Falling down with uncovered eyes.

24:5 Good are your tents, O Jacob,
Your tabernacles, O Israel.

24:6 Like wadis they stretch,
Like plantations beside a river.

Like aloes they are planted,
Like cedars by the water.

24:7 Water shall flow from his buckets,
And his seed in many waters.

His king shall be higher than Agag,
And his kingdom shall be exalted.

24:8 It is God who brought him out of Egypt,
He has as it were the horns of a wild ox.

He shall devour the nations who are his adversaries,
Their bones shall he break.

24:9 He crouched, lay down like a lioness,
Like a she-lion; who will raise him up?

May those who bless you be blessed,
And those who curse you be cursed.

The Fourth Oracle: Numbers 24:15-19

24:15	*nu'm bil^{c}am binu bx^{c}ōr*	7	נאם בלעם בנ באר
	nu'm gabr ša tumā ^{c}ēnō	7	⌜נאם ⌜גבר ש תמ ענ
24:6	*nu'm šōmē^c 'amīrē 'ēl*	7	נאם שמע אמר אל [ ][30]
	ša maḥzē šadday yiḥzē	7	⟨ש⟩[31]מחז שדי יחז
	nōpēl wagalūy ^{c}ēnēm	7	נפל רגלי ענמ
24:17	*'er'innu walō' ^{c}atta*	7	אראנ ולא עת
	'ašūrin walō' qarōb	7	אשרנ[32] ולא קרב
	darak kōkab miyya^{c}qōb	7	דרכ ככב מיעקב
	waqam šibṭ miyyiśra'ēl	7	וקמ שבט מישראל
	maḥaṣ pa^{c}atē mō'ab	7	⌜מחצ פעת מאב
	waqodqod kol banē šūt	7	וקדקד כל בנ שת[33]
24:18	*yihyē 'edōm yarēšā*	7	⟨י⟩[34]הי אדמ ירש
	yihyē yarēšā śē^{c}īr	7	⟨י⟩הי ירש שער [ ][35]
	wayiśra'ēl ^{c}ōśē ḥēl	7	וישראל עש חל

yirdēm ya^{c}qōb 'ōyibēw	7	ירדמ[36] יעקב איבו[37]
wahi'bīd śarīd mi^{cc}īr	7	והאבד שרד מער

Translation

24:15 Oracle of Balaam, son of Beor,
Oracle of the man whose eye is true,
24:16 Oracle of him who hears the words of God.

Who sees the vision of Shaddai,
Falling down with uncovered eyes.

24:17 I see him but not now,
I behold but not near.

A host[38] shall march out of Jacob,
And a tribe shall arise out of Israel.

It shall crush the temples of Moab,
And the head of all the sons of Shut.

24:18 Edom shall be a possession,
Seir shall be a possession,
When Israel does valiantly.

Jacob shall bring low his enemies,
And shall destroy him who flees a city.

NOTES

The Oracles of Balaam: Numbers 23:7-10; 18-24; 24:3-9; 15-19

[1]For a review of the arguments for an early date, see Albright, *Yahweh and the Gods of Canaan*, p. 15, note 38 and p. 29-30, note 68; also "The Oracles of Balaam," *JBL* 63 (1944), 207-9.

[2]See Albright, *Yahweh and the Gods of Canaan*, 14f.

[3]Prosaic features are regularly deleted here at various points. Many instances of *waw* consecutive surely were original to early poems and many are retained here. In the course of transmission, however, *waw* has been appended almost mechanically to far too many cola. Many *waws* must therefore be deleted. Cf. Cross and Freedman, *Studies in Ancient Yahwistic Poetry*, 161-68.

[4]Albright has suggested a vocalization, *liya*, (see *Yahweh and the Gods of Canaan*, p. 11-12, note 31) which is supported by the orthographies of early Phoenician and Ugaritic inscriptions. The received text is not helpful in determining the original vocalization. Words such as (MT) *mî* and *lî* probably varied in pronunciation in early periods (e.g. *lī* vs. *liya*); the composer's choice would often have been *metri causa*.

[5]The inversion of these two divine names follows the more original order, preserved in the Old Greek. Against Albright, *Yahweh and the Gods of Canaan*, p. 33, we suspect that Numbers 23-4 is not "essentially E."

[6]If the vocalization were *mīya* the meter would adjust to 8:8, a quite acceptable count. *mī* seems to be the correct vocalization of the word at most points in the oracles. Cf. also note 4.

[7]Omit *'et* as prosaic, a later addition by a copyist. Albright's suggested emendation to *turba*^{c}*at* is not convincing.

[8]Read the long form of the imperatives in this verse, with the Samaritan Pentateuch. The early orthography was ambiguous, and it is likely that only a tradition of oral pronunciation alive among the Samaritans would have preserved the fuller forms. Later a fuller orthography fixed the tradition.

[9]MT ^{c}*aday* is unlikely. Read ^{c}*ēdī* with the Old Greek and the Samaritan Pentateuch.

[10]*binu* (MT *b*^{e}*nô*) is the composer's choice *metri causa* in 24:3 and 24:15, where it is required for balance. It does not belong here but was added mechanically in typical expansionist fashion from its use in those contexts.

[11]Here the *nun* is probably the *nun energicum* rather than a part of the object suffix. The Parallelism indicates that an object suffix is superfluous. The *heh* of the MT is a later addition.

[12]The Qal infinitive absolute of *brk* here and in the complementing colon is the most reasonable and conservative reading of the consonantal text.

[13]The *nun* is *energicum* rather than part of the object suffix. See note 11.

[14]The reversal of *Israel* and *Jacob* in this couplet as the MT preserves it unbalances the meter to an unusual (though not impossible) 7:9. Such a reversal would be a typical dictation error in oral poetry, but may also have been a simple copy error in textual transmission. At any rate the desirable "A" word is apparently *Israel*, and the "B" word is *Jacob*. The opposite is the case in v. 23.

[15]The emendation of MT to *tōra*^{c}*at* (not a change of the consonantal text) is from Albright, *JBL* 63 (1944), 215, n. 43.

[16]The vocalization of the suffix here, ambiguous in the early orthography, is attested by the Syriac and Targum Onkelos.

[17]Omit *mem* with the exact parallel in 24:8 and read the 3.m.s. suffix. The *mem* was probably a dittography of the initial *mem*s in ממצרם following.

[18]We assume that the alternate (longer) form of the 3.m.s. suffix was used here by the composer *metri causa*. If not, reduce the count to 7:6.

[19]The participle would also be possible here.

[20]The vocalization *binu* is the form of this word with case ending preserved by the composer *metri causa*. The MT *b*^{e}*nô* represents the only reasonable resolution of the consonantal text available to the Masoretes, who had no memory of the case endings.

[21]Wellhausen (*Die Composition des Hexateuchs*) was the first to construe the MT consonants as *ša tumā*, and this happy emendation has much improved the text.

[22]Substitute the archaic relative *ša* for MT *'ăšer* which is a late, prosaic word, and highly unlikely in early poetry. See also note 21 above.

[23]Omit MT *mā(h)* ("How") as the result of dittography from the *mem* at the end of ^{c}*ēnēm* in v. 4 immediately above. If it is retained, count 9:8.

[24]Omit MT *yhwh* which is certainly inappropriate, and read *nṭ*^{c} as a niphal 3 pl. in parallel with the previous couplet. *yhwh* of the MT was built up in transmission from *yw* of *nṭyw* in the previous colon, confused with *nṭ*^{c}*w* here, etc.

[25]See note 18.

[26]See note 18.

[27]MT *wḥṣyw ymḥṣ* probably represents an ancient variant colon, which would be read *waḥiṣṣēhu yimḥaṣ* or the like in the early periods, before orthographic revisions.

[28]Read *labī'ā* with the Samaritan Pentateuch, a good witness in these chapters. MT *'ărī* was probably inserted here from the similar couplet in 23:24 by a copyist who suspected dittography. This is understandable since at an early stage the orthography would have been simply *lb'* for both forms of "lioness." Another possibility is that *labī'a* varied with *'ărī* in alternate versions of this couplet.

[29]Also possible for this line is the vocalization: *wakalabī'-mi yaqūmin* ("And like a lion he rises.").

[30]MT *wyd*^{c} *d*^{c}*t* ^{c}*lywn* may well represent the remnants of an ancient variant to the third line of the triplet. Its original form might have been: *nu'm yōdē*^{c} *dē*^{c}*ōt* ^{c}*elyōn* or the like.

[31]See note 22.

[32]The *nun* is best understood as the *nun energicum*. Cf. notes 11, 13.

[33]For this vocalization and a discussion of *šūt/Sutu*, see Albright, *Yahweh and the Gods of Canaan*, 46f.

[34]Restore the *yodh* and take the form as the imperfect. A future sense is required, and the *waw* conversive with *hāyāh* so common in the later periods could have easily been read into the context since it requires only the substitution of *waw* for the graphically similar *yodh*.

[35]Transpose *'ybw* to the end of the following couplet where it produces both better sense and more likely meter.

[36]The *mem* is a "mi" particle attached without vocalic value to *yrd*, and not the preposition with *y*^{c}*qb*. The sense of the couplet is much improved in this way.

[37]See note 35.

[38]For *kōkab* as "host" see S. Gevirtz, "A New Look at an Old Crux, Amos 5:26," *JBL* 87 (1968), 267-76.

The Song of Deborah: Judges 5:2-30

One of the longest early Yahwistic poems, the Song of Deborah divides with some consistency into five parts. The predominating meter is 1:1, with occasional b:b::b:b and other combinations.

Interesting metrical patterns include the possible variations of stichometry in v. 2, and a b:b::l couplet (7:6::13) in v. 12. The latter is in effect the equivalent of a b:b::b:b couplet except that a melodic cesura must be made arbitrarily in the middle of the l colon. A similar couplet (l::b:b) is found at II Samuel 1:23. These would not have been problems for the singer of the songs, and should not be a problem for the analyst.

Several relatively long couplets (e.g. 10:10 and 11:11) appear in the song. These are reminiscent of Ugaritic couplets in terms of length. The song abounds with chiasm, *figura etymologica*, and repetitive parallelism, now better seen in several new emendations proposed by Cross and adopted in our reconstruction. Many of the prosodic features of the song have already been discussed by Cross and Freedman.

To avoid needless overcrowding of the text and notes obvious emendations (of prose particles, etc.) and those proposed and defended by Cross and Freedman are marked but not annotated in the reconstructed text.

The structure of the song may be diagrammed as follows:

Introduction		
couplet	l:l	v. 2
Part I (Background)		
triplet	b:b::b:b::b:b	v. 3
couplet	l:l	v. 4
couplet	b:b::b:b	
couplet	b:b::b:b	v. 5
couplet	b:b	v. 6
triplet	b:b:b	
triplet	l:l:l	v. 7
couplet	l:l	v. 8
couplet	l:l	
triplet	l:l:l	v. 9-10a
couplet	(l:l)	v. 10b, c

triplet	(l:l:l)	v. 11
couplet	(l:l)	
couplet	b:b::l	v. 12
couplet	l:l	v. 13
Part II (The Tribes)		
couplet	l:l	v. 14
couplet	l:l	
triplet	l:l:l	v. 15
couplet	l:l	
couplet	l:l	v. 16
couplet	l:l	v. 17
couplet	l:l	
couplet	l:l	v. 18
Part III (The Battle)		
triplet	l:l:l	v. 19
couplet	l:(l)	
couplet	l:l	v. 20
couplet	l:l	v. 21a, b
triplet	l:l:l	v. 21c-22
couplet	l:l	v. 23
couplet	l:l	
Part IV (Jael and Sisera)		
couplet	l:l	v. 24
couplet	b:b::b:b	v. 25
couplet	l:l	v. 26
couplet	b:b::b:b	
triplet	l:l:l	v. 27
Part V (The Ladies' Conversation)		
couplet	l:l	v. 28
couplet	b:b::b:b	
couplet	l:l	v. 29
couplet	b:b::b:b	v. 30
triplet	l:l:l	

Reconstructed Text

Part I

Introduction[1]

v. 2	*bapuru^c para^{c}ōt bayiśra'ēl*	10	בפרע פרעת בישראל
	bahitnaddēb ^{c}am barūkē yahwē	10	בהתנדב עמ ברכ יהו[2]
v. 3	*šama^{c}ū malakīm*	6	שמע מלכמ
	ha'zīnū rōzinīm	6	האזנ רזנמ
	'anōkī layahwē	6	אנכ ליהו
	'anōkī 'ašīra	6	אנכ אשר
	'azammēr layahwē	6	אזמר ליהו
	'elōhē yiśra'ēl	6	אלה ישראל
v. 4	*yahwē baṣē'tak miśśē^{c}īr*	8	יהו בצאתכ משער
	baṣa^{c}dak miśśadē 'edōm	8	בצעדכ משד אדמ
	'arṣ ra^{c}ašā	4	ארצ רעש
	gam šamēm naṭapū	6	גמ שממ נטפ
	^{c}abīm naṭapū	5	[3]עבמ נטפ [ ][4]
v. 5	*harrīm nazollū*	5	הרמ נזל
	mippanē yahwē	5	מפנ יהו
	mippanē zē sinay	6	⟨מפנ⟩[5] ז סני
	mippanē yahwē	5	מפנ יהו
	'elōhē yiśra'ēl	6	אלה ישראל
v. 6	*bayamē šamgar*	5	בימ שמגר [ ][6]
	bayamē ya^{c}ēl	5	בימ יעל

	ḥadilū 'ōriḥīm	6	חדל ארח‹מ›
	hōlikē natibōt	6	הלכ נתבת
	'ōriḥōt ᶜaqalqalōt	7	⌜⌝[7]ארחת עקלקלת
v. 7	*ḥadal pxrazōn bayiśra'ēl*	9	חדל פרזנ בישראל
	ḥadal ᶜad šaqamti dabōrā	9	חדל עד שקמת דבר
	ᶜad šaqamti 'ēm bayiśra'ēl	9	‹עד›[8] שקמת אמ בישראל
v. 8	*yibḥarū 'ēlīm ḥadašīm*	8	[9]יבחר אלמ חדשמ
	'azē laqaḥūm śaᶜīrim	8	אז לקחמ שערמ
	magēn 'im yēra'ē warōmḥ	8	מגנ אמ ירא ורמח
	ba'arbaᶜīm 'alp bayiśra'ēl	9	בארבעמ אלפ בישראל
v. 9	*libbī laḥōqiqē yiśra'ēl*	9	לב לחקק ישראל
	mitnaddibīm barūkē yahwē	9	⌜⌝מתנדבמ ⌜⌝[10]ברכ יהו
v. 10	*rōkibē 'atōnōt ṣaḥōrōt*	9	רכב אתנת צחרת
v. 10	. . . .		- - - - - - - - -[11]
v. 11	. . . .		- - - - - - - - -[12]
v. 12	*ᶜurī ᶜurī dabōrā*	7	ער ער דבר
	ᶜurī dabbirī šīr	6	ער דבר שר
	qum baraq wašxbē šōbēka bin 'abīnoᶜm	13	קמ ברק ושב שבכ בנ אבנעמ
v. 13	*'azē šōridū la'addīrīm*	9	אז שרד[13] לאדרמ
	ᶜam yahwē yarad lagibbōrīm	9	עמ יהו ירד ל⌜⌝[14]גברמ

Part II

v. 14	*minni 'eprēm šōridū-mi ba*^{c}*imq*	10	מנ אפרמ שר⟨ד⟩-מ[15] בעמ⌜ק[16]
	'aḥrēka binyamīn ba^c*amamēk*	10	אחרכ בנימנ בעממכ
	minni makir yaradū muḥōqiqīm	11	מנ מכר ירד מחקקמ
	mizzubulūn mōšikīm bašibṭ sōpēr	11	⌜מזבלנ משכמ בשבט ספר
v. 15	*śarrē yiśśakar* ^{c}*im dabōrā*	9	⌜שר ⌜ישש[17]כר עמ דבר
	wayiśśakar kēn baraq	7	וישש כר כנ ברק
	ba^c*imq šalaḥ baraglēw*	7	בעמק של[18]ח ברגלו
	bapalaggōt ru'bēn	6	בפלגת ראבנ
	gadōlīm ḥōqiqīm	6	גדלמ חקק⟨מ⟩[19]
v. 16	*limma yašabta bēn mišpatēm*	9	למ[20] ישבת בנ ⌜משפתמ
	lašumu^c *šariqōt* ^{c}*adarīm*	9	לשמע שרקת עדרמ [ ][21]
v. 17	*gil*^{c}*ad ba*^{c}*ibr yardēn šakēn*	8	[22]גלעד בעבר ⌜ירדנ שכנ
	dan limma yagūr 'aniyōt	8	דנ למ יגר אנית
	'ašēr yašab laḥōp yammīm	8	אשר ישב לחפ יממ
	wa^c*alē miprašēw yiškōn*	8	ועל מפרצו ישכנ
v. 18	*zubulūn* ^{c}*am ḥērēp napšō lamūt*	10	זבלנ עמ חרפ נפש למת
	naptalī ^{c}*ala marōmē šadē*	10	נפתל על מרמ שד

Part III

v. 19	*ba'ū malakīm nilḥamū*	8	בא מלכמ נלחמ
	nilḥamū malakē kana^c*n*	8	⌜נלחמ[23] מלכ כנענ
	bata^c*nak* ^{c}*al mē magiddō*	8	בתענכ על מ מגד

	biṣ^{c} kasp lō' laqaḥū	6	בצע כספ לא לקח
	. . . .		[24]_ _ _ _ _ _ _ _
v. 20	*min šamēm nilḥamū kōkabīm*	9	מנ שממ נלחמ ככבמ
	mimmazzalōtām ^{c}im sisrā'	9	ממ⌜ז⌝לתמ ⌜⌝[25]עמ סרא
v. 21	*naḥl qišōn garapām*	6	נחל קשנ גרפמ
	{*qiddimām naḥl qišōn* / *naḥl qišōn qiddimam*}	6	{קדממ נחל קשנ / נחל קשנ קדממ}[26]
	tidrakūna parašē ^{c}uzzō	9	תדרכנ פ⟨ר⟩[27]ש עז
v. 22	*'az halamū ^{c}iqqibē susīm*	9	אז הלמ עקב סס⟨מ⟩[28]
	daharū daharōt 'abbīrēw	9	דהר ⌜⌝[29]דהרת אברו
v. 23	*'orū 'arōr mērōz*	6	אר ⟨ארר⟩[30] מרז [ ][31]
	'orū 'arōr yōšibā	7	אר ארר ישב
	kī lō' ba'ū la^{c}izrat yahwē	9	כ לא בא לעזרת יהו
	la^{c}izrat yahwē bagibbōrīm	9	לעזרת יהו בגברמ

Part IV

v. 24	*taborrak minnašīm ya^{c}ēl*	8	תברכ מנשמ יעל [ ][32]
	minnašīm ba'ohl taborrak	8	מנשמ באהל תברכ
v. 25	*mēm ša'al*	3	ממ שאל
	ḥalab natanā	5	חלב נתנ
	basipl 'addīrīm	5	בספל אדרמ
	hiqrībā ḥim'ā	5	הקרב חמא
v. 26	*yadā layatēd tišlaḥinna*	9	יד ליתד תשלחנ
	yamīna lahalmut ^{c}amēlīm	9	ימנ להלמת עמלמ

	halamā sisxra	6	הלמ סםרא
	maḥaqā rō'šō	5	מחק ראש
	maḥaṣā sisxrā	6	מחצ ⟨סםרא⟩[33]
	ḥalapā raqqatō	6	חלפ רקת
v. 27	*bēn raglēha kara^{c} šakab*	8	בנ רגלה כרע ⸢שכב[34]
	bēn raglēha kara^{c} napal	8	בנ רגלה כרע נפל
	šam kara^{c} napal šadūd	7	[35]⸢שמ ⟨כרע⟩ נפל שדד

Part V

v. 28	*ba^{c}d ḥalōn nišqapā 'ēm sisxrā'*	10	בעד ⸢חלנ נשקפ ⟨אמ סםרא⟩[36]
	tayabbēb 'ēm sisxrā' ba^{c}d 'išnab	10	תיבב אמ סםרא בעד אשנב
	madu^{c} bōšēš	4	מדע בשש
	rikbō labō'	4	רכב לבא
	madu^{c} 'iḥḥar	4	מדע אחר
	pa^{c}m markabtō	4	[37]פעמ מרכבת
v. 29	*ḥakmat śarōtēha ta^{c}ninna*	9	[38]חכמת שרתה תעננ
	'ap hī' tašīb 'xmarēha lā	9	אפ הא תשב אמרה ל
v. 30	*halō' yimṣa'ū*	5	הלא ימצא
	yaḥalliqū šalal	6	יחלק שלל
	raḥm raḥmatēm	4	רחמ רחמתמ
	larō'š gibbōr	4	לראש גבר
	šalal ṣib^{c} lasisxrā'	7	[39]שלל צבע ⸢לסםרא
	šalal ṣib^{c}ē-mi riqmā	7	שלל צבע-מ רקמ
	ṣib^{c} riqmatēm laṣaw'ar	7	צבע רקמתמ לצואר [ ]

Translation

Part I

Introduction

v. 2 When locks were long in Israel,
When volunteered the people, the consecrated of Yahweh.

v. 3 Hear, O Kings,
Give ear, O princes,

I to Yahweh,
Even I will sing.

I will sing to Yahweh
The God of Israel.

v. 4 Yahweh, when you went forth from Seir,
When you marched from Edom's field,

The earth trembled,
Even the heavens dripped;

The clouds dripped,
v. 5 The mountains quaked

Before Yahweh
Before the One of Sinai,

Before Yahweh
The God of Israel.

v. 6 In the days of Shamgar,
In the days of Jael,

The travellers ceased,
Those who walk the roads,
The twisting paths.

v. 7 The peasantry ceased in Israel,
It ceased until you arose, Deborah,
Until you arose, a mother in Israel.

v. 8 They chose new chiefs,
Indeed they took for themselves champions.

Was not spear and shield to be seen
Among forty thousand in Israel?

v. 9 My heart is with the commanders of Israel
Who volunteered, the consecrated of Yahweh,
v. 10 Riding upon tawny asses.

v. 10 b,c . . . .

v. 11 . . . .

v. 12 Awake, awake, Deborah,
Awake, utter a song!

Arise, Barak, and capture your captors, son of Abinoam!

v. 13 Then bring them down, O mighty ones,
Let the host of Yahweh come down, O warriors!

Part II

v. 14 From Ephraim bring them down into the valley;
After you, Benjamin, among your kinsmen.

From Machir descended the commanders,
From Zebulun those who wield the marshall's staff.

v. 15 The princes of Issachar were with Deborah,
And Issachar, faithful to Barak,
In the valley rushed at his heels.

In the clans of Reuben
Great are the commanders.

v. 16 Indeed you dwell among the sheepfolds
To hear the piping for the flocks.

. . . .

v. 17 Gilead tents across the Jordan;
Dan indeed sojourns on ships.

Asher dwells at the seashore
And by its inlets he encamps.

v. 18 Zebulun is a people who scorned its life to die;
Naphtali mounted the heights of the field.

Part III

v. 19 The kings came, they fought,
They fought, the kings of Canaan,
At Taanach, by the waters of Megiddo.

Spoil of silver they did not take,
. . . .

v. 20 From the heavens the stars fought,
From their stations, with Sisera.

v. 21 Wadi Kishon swept them away,
Wadi Kishon overwhelmed them.

His mighty chargers pounded
v. 22 Yes, hammered the hoofs of the horses,
Raced chariot-races his stallions.

v. 23 Bitterly curse Meroz
Bitterly curse her inhabitant

For they came not to Yahweh's aid,
To Yahweh's aid with warriors.

Part IV

v. 24 Blessed above women be Jael,
Above women of the tent let her be blessed.

v. 25 Water he asked,
Milk she gave;

In a majestic bowl
She brought ghee.

v. 26 Her hand to a tent-pin she put,
Her right hand to a workmen's wedge.

She smote Sisera,
She smashed his head;

She struck Sisera,
She pierced his temple.

v. 27 At her feet he sank, he lay down flat,
At her feet he sank, he fell down.
There he sank, he fell down slain.

Part V

v. 28 Through a window peered Sisera's mother,
Sisera's mother cried out through a lattice.

Why tarries
His chariotry in coming?

Why delay
The hoofs of his chariot-(horses)?

v. 29 The wisest of her ladies answers her,
Yes, she returns words to her.

v. 30 Have they not found,
Divided the booty?

A maid, or two
For each warrior.

Booty of dyed cloth for Sisera,
Booty of dyed cloths, embroidered,
A dyed cloth, embroidered, for the neck.

NOTES

The Song of Deborah: Judges 5:2-30

[1]It is preferable to title the first couplet an introduction to the poem rather than the first part of the poem since it has very little relation to the couplets which begin at v. 3.

[2]More than one vocalization and stichometry may be imagined for this couplet:

a.	*bapuru*^{c} *para*^{c}*ōt bayiśra'ēl*	10	בפרע פרעת בישראל
	bahitnaddibū nadībē ^{c}*am*	9	בהתנדב נדב עם
	barrikū yahwē	(extra-metrical)	ברכ יהו

"When locks were long in Israel,
When volunteered the great-hearted of the people,
Bless Yahweh!"

b.	*bapuru*^{c} *para*^{c}*ōt bayiśra'ēl*	10	בפרע פרעת בישראל
	bahitnaddēb ^{c}*am barrikū yahwē*	10 etc.	בהתנדב עם ברכ יהו
c.	*bapuru*^{c} *para*^{c}*ōt bayiśra'ēl*	10	בפרע פרעת בישראל
	bahitnaddēb ^{c}*am*	5	בהתנדב עם
	barrikū yahwē	5	ברכ יהו

etc.

There is no certain basis for choosing between these possibilities. Cross and Freedman (*SAYP*, 13f. adopted reading "a" with equal justification to that for the reading adopted here.

[3]Omit MT *gam* as dittography.

[4]*mem* here is suspect but not clearly superfluous. Perhaps it entered the text through a misunderstanding of the parallelism.

[5]The repetitive parallelism requires *mippanē* here.

[6]The biographical note on Shamgar is likely an interpolation.

[7]MT *yēl*^{e}*kū* may be a partial dittography from *hōlikē* above or an explanatory expansion; it breaks the parallelism of the triplet.

[8]Restore ^{c}*ad* here to complete the parallelism, which is complex and lovely.

[9]Commentators generally regard this first couplet in the MT as very unusual. The textual emendations adopted here are relatively conservative yet result in a finally sensible text. Neither gods nor gates intervene properly here, but rather the text deals with the choosing of military leaders, as Cross has pointed out. Cf. the "chiefs of Moab" in Ex. 15:15 (MT *'êlê mō'ab*).

[10]Omit *ba*^{c}*am* as inappropriate here. The association of ^{c}*am* with the *Hithpael* of *ndb* elsewhere in the poem probably contributed to its interpolation here.

[11]This couplet is too corrupt to restore at present. The versions offer no clear help.

[12]There is almost (but not quite) enough information in the MT and versions to reconstruct the full text of this verse. The word written *mḥṣṣym* in the MT is obscure and possibly very far from what originally stood in its place. The couplet at the end of this verse must be somewhat similar to v. 13, although this raises the possibility of dittography. We suggest tentatively the following:

miqqōl maḥṣōṣrīm bēn maš'abbīm	9	מקל מחצצרם בנ משאבמ
šam yittinū ṣidaqōt yahwē	9	שמ יענ צדקת יהו
ṣidaqōt pirzōnō bayiśra'ēl	10	צדקת פרזנ בישראל
'azē yaradū laśa^{c}*īrīm*	9	אז ירד לשערמ
yarad la'addīrīm ^{c}*am yahwē*	9	ירד לאדרמ עמ יהו

"At the sound of the trumpeters at the watering places,
There they give the triumphs of Yahweh,
The triumphs of his peasantry in Israel.

Then let them descend, O champions,
Let descend, O mighty ones, the host of Yahweh."

[13]MT (consonantal) *yrd* and *šrd* suggest to Cross a *š*-causative of *yrd*, eventually misunderstood and corrupted. It is conceivable that an imperfect could be seen as the source of this, e.g. *yšrd* (*yašawrid*>*yašōrid*). This would be a conservative appraisal, and would suggest a northern provenance for the poem. Our adoption of MT (consonantal) *šrd* simply omits *yrd*, still conservatively reflecting a northern orthography (*šawrid* > *šōrid*). Beyond the historical evidence that the north was the site of preservation and creation of pre-monarchical traditions in Israel, there is much orthographic evidence in a

poem such as this to suggest a northern origin. However, we must be careful not to base theories of provenance on textually difficult passages.

[14] Omit MT *ba* as an interpolation to smooth out the reading of the line after corruption had set in.

[15] The emendation to a *š*-causative of *yrd* is again reasonable although not certain.

[16] Read ^{c}*mq*, "valley," rather than the generally suspect ^{c}*mlq*, "Amalek."

[17] Omit *ba* as an interpolation (cf. note 14). A parallel line, now lost, may once have followed this one.

[18] The MT pointing (a *Pual*) is suspect. The Qal active is preferable, and is adopted here.

[19] This couplet, like those before and after it, deals with a description of a tribe relative to war. Reuben's existential anxiety ("great were the searchings of heart") is not very likely to be discussed in such a context. Accordingly, we emend to "commanders," the *Qal* participle, which varies with the *Piel/Polel* participle in the poem. A possible *Sitz im Leben* for these blessings is the review of the troops prior to battle.

[20] This particle, of common use in Ugaritic, is probably from *lu + *himma>limma. Both particles, *lu* and *himma* are attested separately as well in Ugaritic, as are their cognates in Hebrew. *lumma* or the like is also a possible vocalization.

[21] The second colon of v. 16 is very likely a dittography of the second colon of v. 15 and thus may be omitted.

[22] For verses 17 and 18 Cross and Freedman offer a different stichometry, with tribal names considered extra-metrical, e.g.:

gil^{c}*ad*
ba^{c}*ibr yardēn šakēn*   6

dan
limma yagūr 'aniyōt   7

etc.

There is in fact no reason not to include the tribal names within the meter, although either approach makes sense of the text.

[23] One may also retain ^{c}*az* here and vocalize *mlk* as *malkē*.

[24] The second colon (or first colon, possibly) of this couplet has apparently disappeared through haplography. This statement of faithfulness to the demands of holy war is entirely appropriate, and the second colon would presumably have completed the image.

[25]The MT is corrupt. A form of *mzl* is preferable to the received text's *msl*, and *nilḥamū* may be deleted as vertical dittography.

[26]This colon is conflate in the MT. The solution is from *SAYP*, 17, note h.

[27]Cf. *SAYP*, 18, note j.

[28]The plural is correct, following LXX (A). The *mem* belongs after *ss* rather than before *dhr* of the following line.

[29]For this reconstruction we follow Albright, "The Song of Deborah in the Light of Archaeology," *BASOR* 62 (1936), p. 30.

[30]Haplography has caused *'rr* to drop from the text, and it should be restored, with *SAYP*, 18, note m.

[31]Omit *'āmar mal'ak yahwēh* as a commentary statement.

[32]Family detail about Jael is marginal, and should be omitted.

[33]The parallelism requires the name *sisxra* or the like at this point.

[34]Omit MT *npl* as verticle dittography.

[35]*ba'ăšer* is prosaic. Its insertion into the text has resulted in the displacement of *šam*.

[36]Reading the expansion with LXX (A). Cf. *SAYP*, 19, note v.

[37]Singulars are better read in this line than the MT plurals; the consonantal text is unaffected.

[38]Read singulars here as well; no change in the consonantal text is necessary.

[39]Our reconstruction involves climactic parallelism plus chiasm. This triplet is difficult in the MT and versions. While little different from the consonantal text, our reconstruction is conjectural. It is nevertheless to be preferred to the awkward reading of the received text.

The Blessing of Jacob: Genesis 49:1-27

The Blessing of Jacob is a collection of tribal blessings, a genre also found in Deuteronomy 33, Judges 5:14-18, and Psalm 68:28. The blessings were probably first circulated in oral form as individual blessings and eventually gathered for preservation together in writing.

Most of the problematic features of the poems that comprise the Blessing of Jacob have been discussed by Cross and Freedman,[1] and more recently, although in less detail, by Speiser.[2] Except in isolated instances no serious question has been raised against the relatively early date of the blessings. The many examples of archaic orthography throughout the chapter suggest that the poem assumed written form at least by the outset of the monarchy. The collection in its present form is probably not later than the late period of the Judges.

While there are specific textual and stichometric problems at some points, the overall metrical pattern of the poem is clearly visible. There is no short (b:b::b:b) meter whatsoever. Long (l:l) couplets predominate, with a generous sprinkling of triplets (l:l:l). Only a few cases of unbalanced meter may be found, and these are but a syllable from being fully even (6:7, 8:7:7, etc.).

Although the text is as corrupt as that of Judges 5, much can now be made of it that is both sensible and artful poetry. Only vv. 4 and 22 remain obscure in parts. The metrical scheme may be diagrammed as follows:

Introduction	triplet	l:l:l	v. 1b-2
Reuben	triplet	l:l:l	v. 3
	triplet	l:l:l	v. 4
Simeon and Levi	couplet	l:l	v. 5
	couplet	l:l	v. 6
	couplet	l:l	
	couplet	l:l	v. 7
	couplet	l:l	

Judah	triplet	1:1:1	v. 8
	couplet	1:1	v. 9
	couplet	1:1	
	couplet	1:1	v. 10
	couplet	1:1	
	couplet	1:1	v. 11
	couplet	1:1	
	couplet	1:1	v. 12
Zebulun	couplet	1:1	v. 13
	couplet	1:1	
Issachar	couplet	1:1	v. 14
	couplet	1:1	v. 15
	couplet	1:1	
Dan	couplet	1:1	v. 16
	couplet	1:1	v. 17
	couplet	1:1	
Gad	couplet	1:1	v. 19
Asher	couplet	1:1	v. 20
Naphtali	couplet	1:1	v. 21
Joseph	triplet	1:1:1	v. 22
	couplet	1:1	v. 23
	couplet	1:1	v. 24
	couplet	1:1	
	couplet	1:1	v. 25
	couplet	1:1	
	couplet	1:1	v. 25c-26a
	couplet	1:1	v. 26
	couplet	1:1	
Benjamin	triplet	1:1:1	v. 27

Reconstructed Text

Introduction[3]

v. 1b	*hē'asipū wa'aggīda lakim*	10	האספ ואגד לכמ ⌜י⌝[4]
	hiqqabiṣū šimᶜū banē yaᶜqōb	10	הקבצ ⌜י⌝[5]שמע בנ יעקב
	wašimᶜū 'el yiśra'ēl 'abīkim	10	ושמע אל ישראל אבכמ

Reuben

v. 3	*ru'bēn bakōrī 'atta*	7	ראבנ בכר את
	koḥī warē'šit 'ōnī	7	כח וראשת אנ
	yitr śi'tī wayitr ᶜuzzī	7	יתר שאת ויתר עז
v. 4	. . . .	(9?)	[6]--------------
	kī ᶜalita ᶜalē miškabī	9	כ עלת ⟨על⟩[7] משכב ⌜י⌝[8]
	'āz ḥillalta yaṣūᶜ 'abīka	9	אז חללת יצע ⟨אבכ⟩[9]

Simeon and Levi

v. 5	*šimᶜōn walēwī 'aḥḥīm*	7	שמענ ולו אחמ
	kilyē ḥamas mxkrōtām	7	כלי חמס מכרתמ[10]
v. 6	*baqahalām 'al tabō' napšī*	9	ב⟨קהלמ⟩[11] אל תבא נפש
	basōdām 'al tiḥḥad kabēdī	9	ב⟨סדמ⟩ אל תחד כבד[12]
	kī ba'appām haragū 'īš	8	כ באפמ הרג אש
	baraṣōnām ᶜiqqarū šōr	8	⌜י⌝ברצנמ עקר שר
v. 7	*'arūr 'appām kī ᶜaz*	6	ארר אפמ כ עז
	ᶜibratām kī qašā	6	⌜י⌝עברתמ כ קש[13]
	'aḥalliqēm bayaᶜqōb	7	אחלקמ ביעקב
	'apīṣēm bayiśra'ēl	7	⌜י⌝אפצמ בישראל

Judah

v. 8	*yahudā yōdūka 'aḥḥēka*	9	יהד⌜⌝[14] ידכ אחכ
	yadēka ba^{c}urp 'ōyibēka	9	ידכ בערפ איבכ
	yištaḥwū lak banē 'abīka	9	ישתחו לכ בנ אבכ[15]
v. 9	*gur 'aryē yahudā*	6	גר ארי יהד
	miṭṭarp binī ^{c}alita	7	מטרפ בנ עלת[16]
	karā^{c} rabaṣ kalabī'ā	8	כרע רבצ כ⟨לבא⟩[17]
	kalabī' mī yaqīminnu	8	⌜⌝כלבא מ יקמנ
v. 10	*lō' yasūr šōpēṭ miyyahudā*	9	לא יסר ש⟨פ⟩[18]ט מיחד
	wamuḥōqēq mibbēn dagalēw	9	ומחקק מבנ ⟨ד⟩[19]גלו
	^{c}ad kī yuba' šay lō	6	עד כ יבא שי ל[20]
	walō yiqhat ^{c}ammīm	6	ול יקהת עממ
v. 11	*'asōrī lagapnō ^{c}ērō*	8	אסר לגפנ ער[21]
	laśōrēqō bin 'atōnō	8	לשרק[22] בנ[23] אתנ
	kibbēs bayēn labušō	7	כבס בינ לבש
	badam ^{c}anabīm sutō	7	⌜⌝בדמ ענבמ סת
v. 12	*ḥaklīlī ^{c}ēnēm miyyēn*	7	חכלל ענמ[24] מינ
	laban šinnēm miḥḥalab	7	⌜⌝לבנ שנמ מחלב

Zebulun

v. 13	*zubulūn*		זבלנ[25]
	laḥōp yammīm yašab	6	לחפ ימם ישב
	^{c}al mipraṣēw yiškōn	6	על מפרצו ישכנ
	hū'a lōpēp 'aniyōt	7	הא[26] ל⟨פ⟩[27]פ אנית
	yirkab ^{c}al ṣiyyē ṣidōn	7	ירכ⟨ב⟩[28] על ⟨צי⟩[29] צדנ

Issachar

v. 14	*yiśśakar ḥimōr garm*	6	יששכר חמר גרמ .
	rōbēṣ bēn mišpatēm	6	רבצ ⌝בנ ⌝משפתמ[30]
v. 15	*yir'ē manuḥō kī ṭōb*	7	ירא מנח כ טב
	yabbīṭ 'arṣ kī naᶜēmā	7	⟨יבט⟩[31] ארצ כ נעמ
	yiṭṭē šikmō lasubul	7	⌝יט[32] שכמ לסבל[33]
	wayᵉhī lamas ᶜōbēd	7	ויה למס עבד

Dan

v. 16	*dan yadīn dīn ᶜammō*	6	דנ ידנ ⟨דנ⟩[34] עמ
	ka'aḥd šibṭ yiśra'ēl	6	כאחד שבט ישראל
v. 17	*dan naḥaš ᶜalē dark*	6	⌝דנ[35] נחש על דרכ
	šapipōn ᶜalē 'orḥ	6	⌝שפפנ על ארח
	hanōšēk ᶜiqqibē sus	7	הנשכ עקב סס
	yippōl rokibō 'aḥōr	7	יפל רכב אחר
v. 18	. . . .		[36]_ _ _ _ _ _ _ _ _

Gad

v. 19	*gad gadūd yagūdinna*	7	גד גדד יגדנ[37]
	wahū' yagūd ᶜaqibam	7	והא יגד עקב⟨מ⟩[38]

Asher

v. 20	*'ašēr šamēnā* {*laḥmō* / *'arṣo*}	7	⌝אשר שמנ {לחמ[39] / ארצ}
	hū' yittēn maᶜdannē malk	7	הא יתנ מעדנ מלכ

Naphtali[40]

v. 21	*naptalī 'ēlā šilliḥā*	8	נפתל אל שלח
	hanatanā 'amīrē šapr	8	הנתנ אמר שפר

Joseph

v. 22	. . . .		- - - - - - - - -
	. . . .		- - - - - - - - -
	. . . .		[41]- - - - - - - - -
v. 23	*wayamarrirēhu rab*	7	וימררה[42] רב
	yiśṭōmēhu baᶜl ḥiṣṣīm	7	ישטמה בעל חצמ
v. 24	*watiššabēr ba'ētān qaštō*	9	ותשב⟨ר⟩ באתנ קשת
	yippazirū gīdē zarōᶜēw	9	⌜י⌝יפז⟨ר גד⟩ זרער
	miyyadē 'abīr yaᶜqōb	7	מיד אבר יעקב
	{*miššōmēr 'ibn yiśra'ēl* {*merōᶜē*	7	{משמר אבנ[43] ישראל {מרע
v. 25	*mē'ēl 'abīka yaᶜzōrak*	9	מאל אבכ[44] ⌜י⌝יעזרכ
	wa'ēl šadday yabarrikikka	9	רא⟨ל⟩[45] שדי[46] ⌜י⌝יברככ
	bxrakōt šamēm miᶜᶜal	7	ברכת שממ[47] מעל
	bxrakōt tihōm mittaḥt	7	ברכת תהמ[48]⌜י⌝ ⟨⟩[49]מתחת
	bxrakōt šadēm waraḥm	7	ברכת שדמ ורחמ
v. 26	*bxrakōt 'ab wa'ēm*	6	ברכת אב ואמ[50]
	bxrakōt gabr waᶜul	6	ברכת גבר ועל
	bxrakōt hararē ᶜad	7	ברכת ה⟨ר⟩ר[51] עד
	bxrakōt gibᶜōt ᶜōlam	7	⟨ברכת⟩[52]גבעת עלמ
	tihyēna larō'š yōsēp	7	תהינ לראש יספ
	laqodqod nazīr 'aḥḥēw	7	⌜י⌝לקדקד נזר אחו

Benjamin

v. 27	*binyamīn zi'b yiṭrap*	6	בנימנ זאב יטרפ
	baboqr yō'kal ᶜadō	6	בבקר יאכל עד[53]
	laᶜarb yaḥallēq šalal	7	לערב יחלק שלל

Translation

Introduction

v. 1b Gather that I may inform you,
v. 2 Approach and listen, sons of Jacob,
Listen to Israel your father.

Reuben

v. 3 Reuben, my first-born are you,
My strength and the prime of my manhood,
The best of my pride and the best of my strength.

v. 4 . . . .
For you went up upon my bed,
Yes, you profaned the couch of your father.

Simeon and Levi

v. 5 Simeon and Levi are two brothers,
Weapons of violence are their merchandise.

v. 6 Into their assembly do not enter, O my soul,
In their counsel do not join, O my heart.

For in their anger they slew a man,
At their whim they maimed an ox.

v. 7 Cursed be their fury so strong,
Their wrath so harsh.

I will disperse them in Jacob,
I will scatter them throughout Israel.

Judah

v. 8 Judah, your enemies shall praise you,
Your hands shall be on the neck of your enemies,
The sons of your father shall bow down to you.

v. 9 A lion's whelp is Judah,
From the prey, my son, you have gone up.

He crouches, he couches like a lioness,
Like a she-lion; who dares rouse him?

v. 10 There shall not fail a judge from Judah,
Nor a commander from among his standards,

Until tribute is brought to him,
And to him the allegiance of the nations.

v. 11 He is one who tethers his donkey foal to his vine,
To his choice vine his she-ass's colt.

He washes in wine his clothes,
In the blood of grapes his robe.

v. 12 Darker are his eyes than wine,
Whiter his teeth than milk.

Zebulun

v. 13 Zebulun:
At the shore of the seas he settles,
At its inlets he encamps.

He fares on ships,
He rides the vessels of Sidon.

Issachar

v. 14 Issachar is a bony ass,
Crouching between the saddlebags.

v. 15 He sees for himself a resting place so good,
He observes a land so pleasant.

He bends his shoulder to bear burdens,
So has become a corvee slave.

Dan

v. 16 Dan judges the cause of his people,
United, a tribe of Israel.

v. 17 Dan is a serpent on the road,
A viper on the path,

Who snaps at the heels of a horse,
So its rider falls backward.

Gad

v. 19 Gad is a band that raids,
But he raids from the rear.

Asher

v. 20 As for Asher, [his food is rich / his land is fertile],
He produces royal delicacies.

Naphtali

v. 21 Naphtali is a spreading terebinth,
Which sends forth lovely foliage.

Joseph

v. 22 . . . .
. . . .
. . . .

v. 23 And a shooter confronted him,
An archer attacked him,

v. 24 But his bow was broken forever,
The sinews of his arms were disjointed.

From the hands of the champion of Jacob,
From the [keeper / shepherd] of the sons of Israel,

v. 25 From the God of your father who helps you,
And El Shaddai who blesses you,

Blessings of heaven above,
Blessings of the deep beneath,
Blessings of breasts and womb,

v. 26 Blessings of father and mother,
Blessings of man and child,

Blessings of the mountains of old,
Blessings of the eternal hills,

Let them be upon the head of Joseph,
On the crown of the one set apart from his brothers.

Benjamin

v. 27 Benjamin is a wolf who preys.
In the morning he devours his prey,
In the evening he divides the spoil.

NOTES

The Blessing of Jacob: Genesis 49:1-27

[1]*Studies in Ancient Yahwistic Poetry* (hereafter *SAYP*), 69-93.

[2]E. A. Speiser, *Genesis*, *The Anchor Bible*, Vol. I, 361-372.

[3]Obvious prosaic or expansionist (e.g. some *waws* at the outset of cola) elements are omitted without annotation.

[4]Omit the rest of verse one as a prosaic, explanatory expansion. See *SAYP*, 77, n. 1.

[5]Also possible is a vocalization of *wašama*^{c}*ū* or the like. The number of syllables in the imperative and infinitive construct is not certain in every case, and may well have been variable. The construct plural of some nouns (e.g. *malkē*, or *malakē*) is uncertain and probably was of only two syllables in the case of most segholates. But this is uncertain as well.

[6]The meaning of the first line of the triplet is so obscure as to make any morphological reconstruction uncertain. Something like the following (but cf. *SAYP*, 77, n. 7) is sound metrically but its semantic relation to the rest of the triplet is problematic:

paḥazta kamēm 'al tōtar 9 פחזת כממ אל תתר

The LXX and Targum Onkelos reflect a text at least close to this, although the versions are all reading an already corrupt text.

[7]Cf. *SAYP*, 78, n. 8.

[8]Transpose MT *'ābîkā* to the end of the next line. Cf. *SAYP*, 78, n. 11.

[9]See note 8.

[10]The vocalization of this word is unknown; it may have one or two more syllables than the three it is given here. The short form of the 3 pl. suffix is assumed rather than MT -*ēhem*. Both forms varied together from early periods and appear randomly distributed in the MT. If the suffix is the dual, which is possible but not necessary grammatically, vocalize -*ēm* or the like.

[11]*qahalām* and *sōdām* are best transposed within the couplet. *qahal* is far more likely as an A word in the poetry. The reversal of these nouns is a typical dictation error in oral poetry.

[12]This vocalization follows the LXX.

[13]The adjective *qašā* is appropriately parallel to ^{c}*az* above, as MT *qāšātā* is not.

[14]MT *'attā* is an explanatory expansion in this position. The independent pronouns do indeed occur frequently in blessings, however.

[15]Cross and Freedman (*SAYP*, 73; 81, notes 22-25a) offer a different stichometry, which entails considerably more textual emendation and the reading *'ibēka* for "enemies" as in Ugaritic in order to be metrically as likely:

yahudā hodī 'atta	7	יהד הד את
yadak ba^{c}*urp 'ibēka*	7	ידכ בערפ אבכ
yahudā yōdūka 'aḥḥēka	9	יהד ידכ אחכ
yištaḥwū lak banē 'abīka	9	ישתחו לכ בנ אבכ

Such a reconstruction produces excellent poetry, however, and may be considered as a strong alternative to the reconstruction adopted here.

[16]Also very possible is the third person form ^{c}*alā* (MT ^{c}*ālāh*) which evens the meter to 6:6.

[17]Read *lābi'ā* for MT *'aryēh*. Cf. Numbers 24:9 above. There is considerable confusion in some formulae between the two words since they are both very frequent and close in meaning. The early orthography made no distinction between לבא (*labī'*) and לבא (*labī'ā*) which may have confused the formulae very early in the course of transmission.

[18]Cf. *SAYP*, 82, n. 31.

[19]Cf. *SAYP*, 82-83, n. 33.

[20]A convincing explanation of this couplet was finally offered by W. Moran, "Genesis 49:10 and its Use in Ezekiel 21:32," *Biblica* 39 (1958), 405-25.

[21]This first line of the couplet may now be understood. For the meaning and form of *'asōrī*, see Moran, *BANE*, p. 60. *lgpn* is best vocalized with the suffix in parallel to *lśrq* of the next line. The emphasis is not on Judah's ownership of a donkey foal, but on his ownership of a vineyard. ^{c}*ēr* (MT ^{c}*āyir*) has now been thoroughly defined by M. Held in "Philological Notes on Mari Covenant Rituals," *BASOR* 200 (1970), 32-40.

[22]The *heh* of MT *lśrqh* is best taken as a *mater* for the sound -*ō* rather than the feminine morph. This removes a *hapax legomenon* from the Old Testament and does not affect the meaning of *śrq*, "choice vine." The reference is to his (Judah's) choice vine rather than to any general vine.

[23]The first person suffix of the MT is meaningless here. While it may be a case ending of some sort, it is likely to be nothing more than a copy error.

[24]F. Anderson, "Orthography in Repetitive Parallelism," 89 (1970), 343, suggests reading the archaic suffix here (*ᶜēnēmō*, and presumably *šinnēmō* below).

[25]Reconstruct the first couplet with the parallel in Judges 5:17. Cf. *SAYP*, 85, n. 47.

[26]The long form of the independent pronoun varied with the shorter form from early times, and occurs frequently although not exclusively in early poetry. The MT, from what may be a Babylonian tradition (see Cross, *ALQ*, *passim*) preserves only *hū'*. Qumran, however, preserving the Palestinian tradition, reads *hū'a* regularly. Either is possible at any point in the old poetry and a decision between the forms is sometimes best indicated by meter.

[27]This happy emendation is original with Albright; cf. *SAYP*, 85, n. 48.

[28]Cf. *SAYP*, 85, n. 49.

[29]*Ibid.*

[30]This couplet is discussed in *SAYP*, 86, nn. 50-52. MT *gārem* (early *garm*) is emended there to *gīdīm*, "sinewy." Here it is left unchanged even though the meaning "bony" is questionable. The image is still somewhat obscure.

[31]*yabbīṭ* or the like is required as a parallel to *yir'ē* above. It may have been lost originally because of its visual similarity with the *bet* and *ṭet* of *ṭōb* before it.

[32]Omit the conjunction with LXX and read the imperfect as elsewhere in the blessings.

[33]The vocalization of the infinitive construct is uncertain, and it was possibly variable in pronunciation. Also possible are *lasbol*, *lasbul*, or even *lasobl*, *lasubl*. The placement of the vowel may have been determined by accentual features of the constructs in which it was used.

[34]Insert *dīn*, "cause," probably lost by haplography. Many parallels (including v. 19 below) suggest that strong *figura etymologica* of this type is to be expected in blessings. See *SAYP*, 87, n. 59.

[35]MT *yᵉhî*, not used elsewhere in the poem in this way, disturbs the meaning and is to be omitted. It belongs at Dt. 33:22.

[36]Verse 18 is obviously an interjection of some sort, possibly liturgical, and not part of the poem proper.

[37]Read the energic form rather than the suffix. The vocalization was either *inna* or *anna*. Either form is possible on the evidence of MT vocalizations. The former is the vocalization suggested by the Aramaic tradition, but the latter is supported by the usual form -*anna* in Arabic. The short form *in* or *an* is frequently employed and could possibly be read here as well. The various forms are allophonic rather than phonemic. See p. 87, n. 6.

[38]The *mem* restored here after *ʿqb* is from the *mem* which is found awkwardly before *'šr* at the beginning of the following couplet. Note also that the pointing of *ʿqb* here differs from its pointing in v. 17 above. These two forms probably existed side by side and should be left substantially as they appear in the received text.

[39]The MT conflates two alternate parts of the formula. See *SAYP*, 89, n. 70.

[40]The reconstruction of this blessing follows the LXX and involves no change from the consonantal received text. See *SAYP*, 89, n. 73 which is almost the same reconstruction.

[41]There are many problems with v. 22. Cross has suggested taking MT *prt* as the f.s. noun with case ending, "of a cow" in the sense of "of a countess," and *ʿly ʿyn* of the MT as *ʿēlī ʿēn*, "haughty eyed" or the like. *bnt ṣʿd ʿl šr* of the original orthography could then be read *binī tiṣʿad ʿēlī šūr*, "My son you strut haughty of sight," or the like. This results in:

bin parati yōsēp	6	בנ פרת יספ
bin parati ʿēlī ʿēn	7	בנ פרת על ענ
binī tiṣʿad ʿēlī šūr	7	בנ תצעד על שר

Also possible is to take *ʿl šr* of the final line as "young of an ox," or the like in parallel with *bnt ṣʿd*, "young of a . . . . ." But a convincing reconstruction is still lacking.

[42]This verb and those immediately following may well be read as singulars, because of the singular pronouns in v. 24. The sense is thus improved. The relation of these verses (23 and 24) to v. 22 remains unclear.

[43]The collective *'ibn*, "sons," is better here than MT *'abn*, "stone." The latter is unusual when an epithet (either *šōmēr* or *rōʿē*) has already been used. However, the divine epithet *'bn* is attested elsewhere and cannot be ruled out.

[44]Omit *waw* as unnecessary and perhaps even awkward.

[45]*'ēl* is probable, rather than MT *'et*, a copy error.

[46]See note 44.

[47]The vocalization of *brkt* is uncertain. It was either *birkōt*, *b^e rakōt*, or *bærakōt*. In the following couplets where it occurs regularly, the balance of the meter is unaffected in any case.

[48]MT *rbṣt* is a harmonization with Deuteronomy 33:13, which lacks *brkt* to allow for *rbṣt* metrically. It therefore is secondary here.

[49]The preposition is required here in parallel with its use directly above (*mi^{cc}al*).

[50]The text has conflated two cola and dropped the initial word *bærakōt* from one of them. The meter produced by this reconstruction suggests that the bicolon is now complete (but cf. *SAYP*, 92, n. 81).

[51]*hrr* is an obvious emendation in parallel with *gb^c t* below.

[52]Insert *brkt* to complete the parallelism well established in the previous couplets.

[53]The suffix may be restored from the *waw* at the outset of the following line.

The Blessing of Moses: Deuteronomy 33

The Blessing of Moses was written down or circulated in writing by the tenth century.[1] In addition to orthographic archaisms, a number of other archaic features are to be found in the poem, particularly in areas of diction and structure.[2]

Certain sections of the poem (e.g. vv. 8b-9b, 24, 27) continue to evade sure analysis, although the overall structure and meter may now be reconstructed with some certainty.

No short (b:b::b:b) meter is found, as is the case in the Blessing of Jacob in Genesis 49, and the tribal blessings of the Song of Deborah in Judges 5. Triplets are quite frequent and appear, as usual, in no predictable order. The length of various blessings varies with the prominence of the tribe in question. Haplography at a few points has affected our ability to reconstruct the complete metrical pattern, yet every tribe is represented by what seems to be an adequate and appropriate blessing.

The meter is freely mixed yet rarely unbalanced. Imbalance when it occurs does not exceed one syllable. Some prose material occurs, particularly in v. 8 and v. 9, and at the introductions to the individual blessings ("And to X he said,").

The metrical structure of the chapter may be diagrammed as follows:

Introduction	triplet	1:1:1	v. 2
	couplet	1:1	
	couplet	1:1	v. 3
	couplet	1:1	
	couplet	1:1	v. 4
	triplet	1:1:1	v. 5
Reuben	couplet	1:1	v. 6
Judah	couplet	1:1	v. 7
	couplet	1:1	
Levi	couplet	1:1	v. 8a
	. . . .[3]		v. 8b-9b
	couplet	1:1	v. 9c
	couplet	1:1	v. 10

	couplet	1:1	
	couplet	1:1	v. 11
	couplet	1:1	
Benjamin	triplet	1:1:1	v. 12
Joseph	(couplet)	1:(1)	v. 13
	couplet	1:1	
	couplet	1:1	v. 14
	couplet	1:1	v. 15
	couplet	1:1	v. 16
	couplet	1:1	
	couplet	1:1	v. 17
	couplet	1:1	
	couplet	1:1	
Zebulun	couplet	1:1	v. 18
	couplet	1:1	v. 19
	couplet	1:1	
Gad	(couplet)	1:(1)	v. 20
	couplet	1:1	
	couplet	1:1	v. 21
	triplet	1:1:1	
Dan	couplet	1:1	v. 22
Naphtali	triplet	1:1:1	v. 23
Asher	triplet	1:1:1	v. 24
	(couplet)	1:(1)	v. 25
	(couplet)	1:(1)	
General Blessing	triplet	1:1:1	v. 26
	couplet	1:1	v. 27
	couplet	1:1	
	couplet	1:1	v. 28
	couplet	1:1	
	couplet	1:1	v. 29
	couplet	1:1	
	couplet	1:1	

Reconstructed Text

Introduction[4]

v. 2	*yahwē missinay ba'*	6	יהו מסני בא
	wazaraḥ miśśēᶜīr	6	וזרח משער ⸣[5]
	hōpīᶜ mēhar pa'rān	6	הפע מהר פארנ
	'ittō-mi ribabōt qōdašīm	9	⸢אתמ רבבת קדש⟨מ⟩[6]
	miyyamīnō 'ašarū 'ēlīm	9	מימנ אש⟨ר א⟩[7]למ
v. 3	*'ap ḥōbibē ᶜammīm*	6	אפ חבב עממ
	kol qudš bayadeka	6	כל קדש[8] בידכ
	himtakkū laraglēka	7	⸢המתכ[9] לרגלכ
	yiśśa'ū-m dabarōtēk	7	ישאמ דברתכ[10]
v. 4	*tōrā ṣiwwa lanu mōšē*	8	תר צו לנ מש
	mōrašat qxhillat yaᶜqōb	8	מרש⟨ת⟩[11] קהלת יעקב
v. 5	*yahwē bayašurūn malk*	7	⸢יה⟨ו⟩[12] בישרנ מלכ
	bahit'assēp ra'šē ᶜam	7	בהתאספ ראש עמ
	yaḥdēw šibtē yiśra'ēl	7	יחד⟨ו⟩[13] שבט ישראל

Reuben

v. 6	*yᵉḥī ru'bēn 'al yamot*	7	יח ראבנ[14] ⸢אל ימת
	wayihyū matēw mispar	7	ויהי מתו מספר

Judah

v. 7	*šamaᶜ yahwē qōl yahudā*	8	שמע יהו קל יהד
	wa'el ᶜammō tabō'inna	8	ואל עמ תבאנ
	bayadēka tarīb lō	7	[15]⟨ב⟩יד⟨כ ת⟩רב ל
	waᶜizr miṣṣarēw tihyē	7	ועזר מצרו תהי

Levi

v. 8a	*habū lalēwī tummēka*	8	⟨הב ללו⟩[16] תמכ
	'urrēka la'īš ḥasdeka	8	⌜ארכ לאש חסדכ[17]
	. . . .		[18]_ _ _ _ _ _ _ _ _
v. 9c	*šamarū 'imratēka*	7	⌜שמר אמרתכ
	b^{e}rīteka yinṣōrū	7	ברתכ ינצר
v. 10	*yōrū mišpaṭēka laya^{c}qōb*	9	יר משפטכ[19] ליעקב
	watōrōteka layiśra'ēl	9	ותרתכ לישראל
	yaśīmū qxṭort ba'appeka	9	ישמ קטר⟨ת⟩[20] באפכ
	wakalīl ^{c}alē mizbiḥeka	9	וכלל על מזבחכ[21]
v. 11	*barrēk yahwē ḥēlō*	6	ברכ יהו חל
	wapo^{c}l yadēw tirṣē	6	ופעל ידו תרצ
	maḥaṣ motnē-mi qamēw	7	מחצ מתנמ קמו
	muśanni'ēw man yaqūm	7	⌜משנאו מנ יקמ⌝[22]

Benjamin

v. 12	*yadīd yahwē yiškōn labaṭḥ*	8	ידד יהו ישכנ לבטח
	^{c}ēlī ḥōpēp ^{c}alēw kol yōm	8	על חפפ עלו כל ⌜ימ
	wabēn katēpēw šakēn	7	ובנ כתפו שכנ

Joseph

v. 13	*maburrakt yahwē 'arṣō*	7	מברכת יהו ארצ
	. . . .		[23]_ _ _ _ _ _ _ _
	mimmagd šamēm mi^{cc}al	6	ממגד שממ מ⟨ע⟩ל[24]
	mittihōm rōbiṣt taḥt	6	⌜מתהמ רבצת תחת

v. 14	*mimmagd tabū'at šamš*	6	˹י˺ממגד תבאת [25]שמש
	mimmagd garšē yarīḥ	6	˹י˺ממגד גרש [26]ירח ˹י˺[27]
v. 15	*mērō'š hararē qadm*	6	˹י˺מראש הרר קדמ
	mērō'š gibᶜōt ᶜōlam	6	˹י˺מ⟨ראש⟩[28] גבעת עלמ
v. 16	*mimmagd 'arṣ wamxlō'ā*	7	˹י˺ממגד ארצ ומלא
	raṣōn šōkinī sīnay	7	˹י˺רצנ שכנ [29]סני
	tihyēna larō'š yōsēp	7	תה⟨ינ⟩[30] לראש יספ
	laqodqod nazīr 'aḥḥēw	7	לקדקד נזר אחו
v. 17	*bakōr šōr hadar lō*	6	בכר שר[31] הדר ל
	waqarnē rē'm qarnēw	6	וקרנ ראמ קרנו
	bām ᶜammīm yanaggaḥ	6	ב˹י˺מ[32] עממ ינגח
	yiddaḥū 'apsē 'arṣ	6	י⟨דח⟩[33] אפס ארצ
	hēm rxbabōt 'eprēm	6	˹י˺המ רבבת אפרמ
	hēm 'alpē manaśśē	6	˹י˺המ אלפ מנש
	Zebulun		
v. 18	*śamaḥ zubulūn baṣē'teka*	9	שמח זבלנ בצאתכ
	wayiśśakar ba'ohalēka	9	וישׂשכר באהלכ
v. 19	*ᶜam mihhar yiqqarē'ū*	7	עמ[34] מהר יקרא
	šām yizbaḥū zibḥē ṣidq	7	שמ יזבח זבח צדק
	kī šapᶜ yammīm yīnaqū	7	כ שפע יממ ינק
	ṣapūnē ṭamūne ḥōl	7	˹י˺⟨צ⟩[35]פנ טמנ חל
	Gad		
v. 20	*barūk mirḥabē gad*	6	ברכ מרחב[36] גד
	. . . .		[37]- - - - - - - - - -

	gad kalabī'ā šakēn	7	⟨גד⟩[38] כלבא שכנ
	ṭarap zarō^{c} 'ap qodqod	7	⌜טרפ זרע אפ קדקד
v. 21	*kī yir'ē rē'šit lahu*	7	⟨כ⟩[39] ירא ראשת ל⟨ה⟩[40]
	yiššōm ḥilqat muḥōqēq	7	⌜ישמ חלקת מחקק⌝[41]
	yit'assēpūn ra'šē ^{c}am	7	[42]⌜יתא ⟨ספנ⟩[43] ראש עמ
	ṣxdaqōt yahwē ^{c}aśū	7	צדקת[44] יהו עש
	mišpaṭēw ^{c}im yiśra'ēl	7	משפטו עמ ישראל

Dan

v. 22	*dan gur 'arye y^{e}hī*	6	דנ גר ארי ⟨יה⟩[45]
	yazannēq mibbašan	6	יזנק מ⌝בשנ

Naphtali

v. 23	*naptali śab^{c} raṣōn*	6	נפתל שבע רצנ
	malē' birkat yahwē	6	מלא ברכת[46] יהו
	yam wadarōm yīraš	6	ימ ודרמ ירש⌝[47]

Asher

v. 24	*barūk mibbanīm 'ašēr*	7	ברכ מבנמ אשר
	yihyē raṣūy 'aḥḥēw	6	יהי[48] רצי אחו
	ṭabal bašamn raglēw	6	⌜טבל[49] בשמנ רגלו
v. 25	*barzil wanaḥušt man^{c}ulēka*	9	ברזל ונחשת מנעלכ
	. . . .		[50]_ _ _ _ _ _ _ _ _
	. . . .		[51]_ _ _ _ _ _ _ _ _
	wakayōmēka dob'eka	8	וכימכ דבאכ

General Blessing

v. 26	*'ēn ka'ēl yašurūn*	6	אנ כאל ישרנ
	rōkēb šamēm ba^{c}az	6	רכב שממ בעז⌝[52]
	bagē'ūt šaḥaqīm	6	⌜בגאת שחקמ

v. 27	*ma^{c}ōnō 'elōhē qadm*	7	מענ אלה קדמ
	mittaḥt zarō^{c}ōt ^{c}ōlam	7	⌜⌝מתחת זרעת עלמ
	yagarrēš mippanēka 'ōyēb	9	⌜⌝יגרש מפנכ איב
	wašōnē' mippanēka hašmīd	9	ו⟨שנא מפנכ⟩[53] השמד
v. 28	*yiškōn yiśra'ēl baṭḥ*	6	⌜⌝ישכנ ישראל בטח
	badad ya^{c}ūn ya^{c}qōb	6	בדד ⟨י⟩[54]ענ יעקב
	'el 'arṣ dagan watirōš	7	אל ארצ דגנ ותרש
	'ap šamēw ya^{c}rōpū ṭal	7	אפ שמו יערפ טל
v. 29	*'ašrēka yiśra'ēl*	6	אשרכ ישראל [ ][55]
	^{c}am nōša^{c} bayahwē	6	עמ נשע ביהו
	'ašrē magēn ^{c}izreka	7	⟨אשר⟩[56] מגנ עזרכ
	'ašrē ḥarb ga'wateka	7	⌜⌝אשר[57] חרב גאותכ
	yikkaḥēšū 'ōyibēka laka	10	⌜⌝יכחש איבכ לכ
	wa'atta ^{c}al bamōtēmu tidrōk	10	ואת על במתמ תדרכ

Translation

v. 2 Yahweh from Sinai came,
And beamed from Seir,
He shone from Paran.

With him were myriads of holy ones,
At his right hand proceeded the mighty ones,

v. 3 Indeed, the guardians of the peoples,
All the holy are at your hand.

They prostrate themselves at your feet,
They carry out your words.

v. 4 Moses commanded to us a law,
An inheritance of the assembly of Jacob.

v. 5 Yahweh is king in Jeshurun,
At the gathering of the heads of the people,
Together the tribes of Israel.

Reuben

v. 6 Let Reuben live and not die,
Although his men are few.

Judah

v. 7 Hear, Yahweh, the voice of Judah,
And to his people come.

With your own hands contend for him,
And be a help from his foes.

Levi

v. 8a Give to Levi your Thummim,
Your Urrim to your loyal man.

v. 8b-9b . . . .

v. 9c They observed your words,
And your covenant they kept.

v. 10 They teach your ordinances to Jacob,
And your laws to Israel.

They put incense before you,
And whole burnt offering upon your altar.

v. 11 Bless, Yahweh, his substance,
And the work of his hands accept.

Smite the loins of his foes,
His haters, whoever shall arise.

Benjamin

v. 12 The beloved of Yahweh encamps in safety,
The exalted one hovers over him all day,
And between his shoulders he tents.

Joseph

v. 13 Blessed of Yahweh is his land,
. . . .

From the abundance of the heavens above,
From the deep crouching beneath;

v. 14 From the abundance of the produce of the sun,
From the abundance of the yields of the moon;

v. 15 From the top of the ancient mountains,
From the top of the eternal hills;

v. 16 From the abundance of the earth and its fullness,
The favor of the one who tents on Sinai,

May they be on the head of Joseph,
On the brow of the leader of his brothers.

v. 17 The first-born of the Bull, majesty is his,
And the horns of the wild bull are his horns.

With them the nations he gores,
The ends of the earth are attacked.

Behold the myriads of Ephraim,
Behold the thousands of Manasseh!

Zebulun and Issachar

v. 18 Exult, Zebulun, in your going forth,
And Issachar, in your tents.

v. 19 The people from the mountains are called,
There they sacrifice righteous sacrifices.

For the affluence of the seas they suck,
The hidden treasures of the sand.

Gad

v. 20 Blessed be the broad lands of Gad,
. . . .

Gad as a lioness lies in wait,
He rips the arm, and the head as well.

v. 21 Indeed he seeks out the finest for himself,
He pants after a commander's share.

The heads of the people gathered,
The righteousness of Yahweh they performed,
His justices with Israel.

Dan

v. 22 Dan is a lion's whelp,
Who shies away from a viper.

Naphtali

v. 23 Naphtali is satisfied with favor,
Full of the blessing of Yahweh
West and south he inherits.

Asher

v. 24 Most blessed of the sons is Asher,
He is the favorite of his brothers,
He dips his feet in oil.

v. 25 Iron and bronze are your bolts,
. . . .

. . . .
And as your days, so is your strength.

General Blessing

v. 26 There is none like the God of Jeshurun,
Who rides the heavens in might,
In glory the clouds.

v. 27 His refuge is the God of old,
Beneath are the arms of the Eternal.

He drove out before you the enemy,
And your foe before you he destroyed.

v. 28 Israel encamps in safety,
Aloof dwells Jacob.

In a land of grain and wine,
Indeed, his heavens drip dew.

v. 29 Blessed are you, Israel,
A people who found safety in Yahweh.

Blessed is the shield which helps you,
Blessed your glorious sword.

Your enemies fawn upon you,
But you tread upon their backs.

NOTES

The Blessing of Moses: Deuteronomy 33

[1] Cf. Cross and Freedman, *SAYP*, 97. The tenth century would be the *terminus ad quem.*

[2] For various points of view see T. H. Gaster, "An Ancient Eulogy on Israel: Deuteronomy 33:3-5, 26-29," *JBL* 66 (1947), 53-62; R. Gordia, "The Text and Meaning of Deuteronomy 33:27," *JBL* 67 (1948), 69-72; J. W. Pythian-Adams, "On the Date of the 'Blessing of Moses'," *JPOS* 3 (1923), 158-66.

[3] See note 17.

[4] Prosaic elements are deleted throughout, without annotation when they are obvious and minor. More detail on minor textual emendations is given in *SAYP*, 97-122.

[5] MT *lmw* is to be omitted as vertical dittography from *lmw* (also corrupt) three cola below. It makes no sense at all here.

[6] Supply the *mem*, lost by similarity with the initial *mem* of the following word. Although the collective, *qudš*, is used below in v. 3, it would be awkward here with *rbbt*, "myriads," which fairly requires a plural to follow. This obviates MT *w'th mrbbt* at the outset of the couplet. Our reading is with *SAYP*, 105f., n. 8.

[7] The MT here is quite unsatisfactory. Our reading follows *SAYP*, 106, n. 11. For an alternate approach (reading *'sd 'lm*), see P. D. Miller, "Two Critical Notes on Psalm 68 and Deuteronomy 33," *HTR* 57 (1964), 240-43.

[8] No suffix is required either by parallelism or grammar. The MT suffix is secondary. For *qudš* as a collective in a similar context, see Exodus 15:11.

[9] The verbs and nouns in this couplet are best taken as plurals. We read here the consonantal MT without change.

[10] The form as pointed in the MT suggests a singular of *dabbéret* (דַּבֶּרֶת) which is *hapax* in the Old Testament. It is fine metrically, however.

[11] The construct form is required by the grammar.

[12] Until the time of the monarchy, surely it is Yahweh who is king, and this verse is a reference to that fact. An election or the like is not described, but rather a ceremony of recognition.

[13] Restoration of this suffix improves the sense vastly. Here we have an alternate word to that in the almost identical formula in Genesis 49:16.

[14]The vocalization *ru'bēn* represents the original form of the word which resolved in the speech of the Masoretes to *r^{e}'ûbēn*.

[15]The emendation proposed here for this line is conjectural; it at least results in an appropriate parallelism both of sense and meter.

[16]The restoration of the first two words is made from the text of Deuteronomy at Qumran, and the LXX.

[17]This form is superior to MT *ḥăsîdĕka* in sense and grammar.

[18]Vv. 8b-9b, although somewhat parallelistic, are rightly prose and were not original to the material here.

[19]It is possible although not probable that the *lamedh* here and in the line below could be taken as the vocative morpheme.

[20]MT *q^{e}ṭôrāh* is a *hapax* and suspect, since the normal and frequent form is *q^{e}ṭōret*, a resolution of older *qxṭort*, as here.

[21]The exact vocalization of *mzbḥk* is difficult. As a form for the place of doing something, an original **mazbiḥ*...or *mazbaḥ*...would be expected, but MT *mizbē^{a}ḥ* reflects *mizbiḥ*... which we retain here.

[22]The plural in -*ūn* is certainly secondary. It arose after *mn* was misunderstood as the preposition rather than the singular relative pronoun. The preposition, of course, makes little sense in the context.

[23]A colon has been lost here, judging from the parallelism. The meter does not necessarily reflect this since a difference of one syllable only is involved.

[24]Read *$m^{c}l$* with Genesis 49:25, Targum Onkelos, and 2 MSS.

[25]The singular of the word is preferable semantically. No change in meter or consonantal text is involved.

[26]The singular of *grš* would also be possible here as with *tb't* above. The consonantal text is, of course, ambiguous as to plurality.

[27]MT consonantal *yrḥm* in parallel with *šmš*, "sun," must refer to a singular. The form could be interpreted as a genitive with *mi*-particle, employed by the poet *metri causa*. However, the *mem* may as well be omitted, as a dittography of the *mem* immediately following.

[28]*rō'š* is better read here than MT *meged* (*magd*) only because of the parallelism within the couplet. Vertical dittography would produce the MT reading. Meter is unaffected.

[29]The *hireq compaginis* with *škn* is either a remnant of the case ending (cf. *SAYP*, 116, n. 53) or of a very different old morpheme (see Moran, "The Hebrew Language in its Northwest Semitic Background," p. 60). It is presumably employed here by the poet *metri causa*, but must have had a certain semantic value above that of the mi-particle, for example, judging from its use with participles in Amarna Canaanite.

[30]The MT here conflates two forms, *t^e hî* and *tabō'*, neither of which is as satisfactory as the f. pl. *tihyēna* supplied from the parallel in Genesis 49:26.

[31]The possessive pronoun is to be omitted with the Greek, Samaritan Pentateuch, Syriac, and Vulgate. *šōr* refers to Jacob; it is an old patriarchal noble title, parallel to the possible form **parati* (of a cow/countess) in Genesis 49:22 (q.v.).

[32]In the process of leveling through certain forms, the Masoretes and compilers before them often eliminated the free interchange of various alternate forms used in poetry (cf. Cross and Freedman, *EHO*, Excursus: "Orthographic Problems in the Masoretic Text," 65-70). Thus *bahem*, which varied with *bām*, may well be secondary here; the shorter form, which we have chosen to reconstruct, is suggested, but not required, by the meter.

[33]Reading the niphal of *dhy*. Cp. *SAYP*, 117, n. 60.

[34]To take the consonantal text's *^c mm* as the construct plural plus the *mi*-particle would be another acceptable reading of the text. Eissfeldt has linked this reading with Mt. Tabor ("Der Gott Tabor," *Archiv für Religionswissenschaft* 31 (1934), 14-41), although the text does not imply any specific locale or cult. The meaning would be similar to that of *'am mihhar*.

[35]MT is obscure. The emendation to *ṣpn* is conservative yet acceptable semantically and metrically.

[36]MT *marḥîb* would imply erroneously that the blessing applies to Yahweh rather than Gad. *mirḥabē*, "broad lands," is preferable.

[37]It is likely that a colon (or more) has fallen out of the text by haplography, judging from the parallelism.

[38]The tribal name belongs at the beginning of this couplet, as generally recognized.

[39]Transpose *kī* to this position from its secondary placement at the outset of the next colon.

[40]It is not certain that the longer alternate form of the preposition plus suffix is original here. If *lō* is to be read, adjust the meter accordingly to *6*.

[41]MT *spn* belongs with *yt'* of the following word.

[42]This triplet is now understood, but may not have been original to this context, since it seems generally to deal with the tribes as a whole rather than with Gad.

[43]*yit'assēpūn* is precisely the substitute formula we would expect for *bahit'assēp* of v. 5. It is metrically equivalent; the remainder of the colon is identical to its counterpart in v. 5. The MT consonantal text has the consonants necessary for the word, but in jumbled order.

[44]Also possible is the pronunciation *ṣidqōt*, as often in the MT.

[45]*y*^{e}*hī* or the like was lost by haplography, by reason of *homoioteleuton*. In any period after the tenth century the line would have appeared thus: דן גר אריה יהי. The *yodh* and *heh* of *'aryēh* were repeated in the *yodh* and *heh* of *y*^{e}*hī*. In Genesis 49:17, the word *y*^{e}*hī* occurs in a blessing of Dan where it does *not* belong. This would represent the result of a typical dictation error in oral poetry: the transposition of an element of one formula to the context of another. Such errors occur when the poet is dictating for a scribe, or when a scribe who knows the poem gets his formulae (or whole couplets) confused. Absence of the music and the slow speed of the dictation or copying distorts the meter and allows words that do not belong in a given couplet to be included. At any rate, *y*^{e}*hī* does belong to a blessing of Dan, but the one in v. 22 here rather than Genesis 49:17. *yihyē* is also possible since its consonants (*yhy*) in the early period are overlapped by the *yodh* and *heh* of *'aryēh* and the initial *yodh* of *yazannēq* immediately following. *yihyē* does occur in blessings contexts; for example, in connection with Asher (v. 24).

[46]Or vocalize *bərakat* or the like.

[47]A verb is expected here, thus *yīraš*. MT *y*^{e}*rāšāh* is not as appropriate.

[48]Or read *y*^{e}*hī*. Cf. note 45.

[49]The perfect is superior to the metrically equivalent participle.

[50]A colon or more has apparently fallen out through haplography.

[51]If the *waw* before *kayōmēka* is original it would suggest even more haplography since a *waw* at the outset of a colon is almost always original only to a second (or third) colon in a triplet or couplet. The lines of v. 25 as they appear in the received text are hardly a couplet.

[52]Omit MT *rk* after *b*^{c}*z* as unsatisfactory semantically. They may represent the first two letters of *rkb*, either from an aborted recopying of the same line, or a mistaken repeat of *rkb* at the outset of the following line.

[53]The first two words of this line are filled out according to the parallelism. MT *'ămōrî* is suspicious in the context, although not impossible.

[54]Read *yaᶜūn* with von Hoonacker, "La benediction de Moise," *Le Museon*, 42 (1929), p. 59.

[55]*yiśra'ēl mī kamōka* is an alternate formula which could as well be employed here. Cf. *SAYP*, 121, n. 90.

[56]Insert *'šr* which is preserved in the parallel line in the incorrect vocalization, that of the relative.

[57]*'šr* of the MT stands for *'ašrē*, "happy, blessed." If *'šr* were to be deleted, read *magēnō ᶜizreka / ḥarbō ga'wateka* (6:6) or the like, for the needed sense.

II Samuel 22=Psalm 18

This royal song of thanksgiving is especially instructive to the student of Hebrew meter since no other poem of comparable length appears in parallel in the Old Testament. The frequent and sometimes significant discrepancies between the two texts help to determine those features of the early poetry that were fixed as compared to those that could be varied, substituted for, or added to. One may see in the two poems the operation of oral composition and transmission. These are manifest in the interchangeability of cliches and metrically equivalent phrases (formulae) as well as the inconsistent representation of various conjunctions, especially *waw*, before cola.

The poem has been studied in detail by Cross and Freedman in *Studies in Ancient Yahwistic Poetry*,[1] including a table of "The Evidence for the Use of the Conjunction at the Beginning of Cola, in the Hebrew Text and the Principal Versions,"[2] The treatment by Cross and Freedman includes ample discussion of date, text, style, orthography, provenance, etc.

It may be said, in agreement with Cross and Freedman, that Psalm 18 represents a Judahite version of the poem, whereas II Samuel is Israelite.[3] We have arbitrarily chosen to represent the poem in the northern vocalization in this study. Largely because of the resolution of diphthongs in the north, the northern orthography is less committed to secondary interpretations. For example, the northern *yrd* could be read *yōrīd* or *yarad*, etc. In the south the Hiphil would be written *ywrd*, for *yawrīd*. In later periods, however, the northern *yrd* would have been taken invariably to designate *yarad*, which could then be normalized in both texts, possibly obscuring the original meaning. By following the northern orthography we may occasionally escape an erroneous reading already inherent in the secondarily vocalized texts.

Although the exact date of the composition and subsequent inscription of the poem cannot be proved, we shall reconstruct the text according to northern tenth century norms, the tenth century being the *terminus a quo* of the poem.[4] Metrical syllabic count would remain unchanged even if the poem were in fact composed somewhat later than this early date.

No short meter (b:b::b:b, etc.) occurs in the poem. This is in striking contrast to the contemporaneous Lament of David, which, except for its refrains, is written exclusively in short meter. Triplets are not abundant (there are six triplets as opposed to forty-six couplets), and occur in typically unpredictable order. Meter is mixed and rarely the same for more than two couplets in succession. An unusual metrical pattern (7:9, 9:7) is found in vv. 20-21. It is rare to discover couplets whose cola are not evenly balanced. Rarer still is this sort of pattern, which reminds one of the b:l::l:b, etc. of Qinah. In vv. 39-40 a similar pattern (9:7, 9:7) is found. No specific reason for these unusually unbalanced couplets is forthcoming. The verses in question are textually and poetically sound. They could reflect poetic license in the division of the lines (i.e. the cesura was made so that they could be sung as if 8:8), but such an explanation is questionable. At any rate, these patterns are clear exceptions to the normal patterns in the remainder of the song, and must be noted as such.

The overall metrical structure may be diagrammed as follows:

Part I

couplet	1:1	v. 5
couplet	1:1	v. 6
couplet	1:1	v. 7
couplet	1:1	
triplet	1:1:1	v. 8
triplet	1:1:1	v. 9
couplet	1:1	v. 10
couplet	1:1	v. 11
couplet	1:1	v. 12
couplet	1:1	v. 13
couplet	1:1	v. 14
couplet	1:1	v. 15
couplet	1:1	v. 16
couplet	1:1	

couplet	1:1	v. 17
couplet	1:1	v. 18
couplet	1:1	v. 19
couplet	1:1	v. 20
couplet	1:1	v. 21
couplet	1:1	v. 22
couplet	1:1	v. 23
couplet	1:1	v. 24
couplet	1:1	v. 25
couplet	1:1	v. 26
couplet	1:1	v. 27
couplet	1:1	v. 28
couplet	1:1	v. 29
couplet	1:1	v. 30
triplet	1:1:1	v. 31

Part II

couplet	1:1	v. 32
triplet	1:1:1	v. 33-4
couplet	1:1	v. 35
triplet	1:1:1	v. 36
couplet	1:1	v. 37
couplet	1:1	v. 38
couplet	1:1	v. 39
couplet	1:1	v. 40
couplet	1:1	v. 41
couplet	1:1	v. 42
couplet	1:1	v. 43
couplet	1:1	v. 44
couplet	1:1	v. 44c-45a
couplet	1:1	v. 45b-46b

couplet	1:1	v. 47
triplet	1:1:1	v. 48-49a
couplet	1:1	v. 49b
couplet	1:1	v. 50
couplet	1:1	v. 51

Reconstructed Text[5]

Part I

	. . . .		[6]- - - - - - - - - -
v. 5	*'apapūnī ḥablē b^{e}līya^{c}l*	9	אפפנ חבל 〈בליעל〉
	wanaḥlē mōt yaba^{cc}itūnī	9	ונחל 〈מת〉 יבעתנ[7]
v. 6	*ḥablē šx'ōl sababūnī*	8	חבל שאל סבבנ
	qiddimūnī mōqišē mōt	8	קדמנ מקש מת
v. 7	*baṣar lī 'eqra' yahwē*	7	בצר ל אקרא יהו
	'el 'elōhay 'ašawwē^c	7	⸢אל אלהי אשוע
	yišma^c mihhēkalō qōlī	8	ישמע מהכל קל
	šaw^{c}atī {tabō' ba'uznēw / lapanēw tabō'	8	שועת [8]{תבא באזנו / לפנו תבא
v. 8	*taga^{cc}aš watir^{c}aš 'arṣ*	7	⸢תגעש[9] ותרעש ארצ
	mōsadē harrīm yirgazū	8	מסד הרמ ירגז
	yitga^{cc}ašū kī ḥara lō	8	יתגעש כ חר ל[10]
v. 9	*^{c}ala ^{c}ašan ba'appēw*	7	על עשנ באפו[11]
	wa'ēš mippīhu tō'kēl	7	ראש מפ〈ה〉[12] תאכל
	gaḥalīm ba^{c}arū minnu	8	גחלמ בער[13] ⸢מנ
v. 10	*yiṭṭē šamēm wayarad*	7	⸢יט[14] שממ[15] וירד
	wa^{c}arapil taḥt raglēw	7	וערפל תחת רגלו

v. 11	*yirkab ^{c}alē karūbīm*	7	⌜ירכב על כרב⟨מ⟩[16]
	yid'ē ^{c}alē kanpē ruḥ *ya^{c}ōp*		⌜ידא[17] על כנפ רח יעפ
v. 12	*yašīt ḥušk sabībōtēw*	7	ישת חשכ סבבתו
	sukkatō ḥxšxrat mēm	7	סכת חשרת[18] ממ
v. 13	*^{c}abē šaḥaqīm nagdō* *nagdo ^{c}abīm ^{c}abarū*	7	[19]עב שחקמ נגד נגד עבמ עבר
	barad wagaḥalē 'ēs	7	ברד וגחל אש
v. 14	*yar^{c}ēm bašamēm yahwē*	7	ירעמ בשממ יהו
	wa^{c}ilyōn yittēn qōlō	7	ועלינ יתנ קל
v. 15	*yišlaḥ ḥiṣṣīm wayapīṣēm*	8	⌜ישלח חצמ ויפצמ
	yibrōq baraq wayahummēm	8	⟨י⟩[20]ברק ברק ויהממ
v. 16	*yēra'ū 'apīqē-mi yam*	8	ירא אפקמ[21] ימ
	yiggalū mōsadōt tēbēl	8	יגל מסדת תבל
	baga'wateka yahwē	7	בגאותכ יהו
	minnišmat ruḥ 'appēka	7	מנשמת רח אפכ
v. 17	*yišlaḥ yadō mimmarōm* *mimmarōm yiqqaḥēni*	7	[22]ישלח יד ממרם ממרם יקחנ
	yamšēnī mimmēm rabbīm	7	ימשנ מממ רבמ
v. 18	*yaṣṣīlēnī me'ōyibay kī ^{c}azzū*	11	יצלנ מאיבי ⟨כ⟩[23] עז[24]
	miśśōni'ay kī 'amaṣū mimminnī	11	משנאי כ אמצ ממנ
v. 19	*yaqaddimūnī bayōm 'ēdī*	9	יקדמנ בימ אד
	way^{e}hī yahwē lamiš^{c}an lī	9	ויה יהו למשענ ל
v. 20	*yōṣi'ēnī lamirḥab*	7	⌜יצאנ למרחב
	yaḥalliṣēnī kī ḥapēṣ bī	9	יחלצנ כ חפצ ב

v. 21	*yigmōlēnī yahwē kaṣidqī*	9	יגמלנ יהו כצדק
	kabōr yaday yašīb lī	7	כבר ידי ישב ל[25]
v. 22	*kī šamartī darkē yahwē*	8	כ [26]שמרת דרכ יהו
	lō' paša^{c}*tī mē'elōhay*	8	⌜⌝לא ⟨פ⟩[27]שעת מאלהי
v. 23	*kī kol mišpaṭēw lanagdī*	8	כ כל משפטו לנגד
	ḥuqqatēw lō' 'asūr minnī	8	⌜⌝חקתו לא אסר ⌜⌝[28]מנ
v. 24	*'ehyē tamīm* ^{c}*immō*	6	⌜⌝אהי תממ עמ
	'eštammēr mi^{cc}*awōn*	6	⌜⌝אשתמר מעונ
v. 25	. . . .		[29]_ _ _ _ _ _ _ _
v. 26	^{c}*im ḥasīd titḥassad*	6	עמ חסד תתחסד
	^{c}*im tamīm tittammam*	6	עמ⌜⌝[30] תממ תתממ
v. 27	^{c}*im nabar titbarrar*	6	עמ נבר תתברר
	^{c}*im* ^{c}*iqqēš titpattal*	6	⌜⌝עמ עקש תתפתל[31]
v. 28	*'atta* ^{c}*am* ^{c}*anī tōšī*^{c}	7	את עמענ תשע
	wa^{c}*ēnēm ramōt tašpīl*	7	ועינמ [32] רמת תשפל
v. 29	*kī 'atta nērī yahwē*	7	כ את נר יהו
	'elōhay yaggīḥ ḥuškī	7	אלהי יגה חשכ
v. 30	. . . .		_ _ _ _ _ _ _ _
	. . . .		[33]_ _ _ _ _ _ _ _
v. 31	*ha'ēl tamīm darakēw*	7	האל תממ דרכו[34]
	'imrat yahwē ṣarūpā	7	אמרת יהו צרפ
	magēn hū' laḥōsīm bō	7	מגנ הא לחסמ ב

Part II

v. 32	*mī 'elōh mibbalᶜadē yahwē*	9	⸢⸣מ אלה[35]מבלעד יהו
	mī ṣur zulati 'elōhēnu	9	⸢⸣מ צר זלת אלהנ
v. 33	. . . .		[36]- - - - - - - -
v. 34	*mušawwē raglay ka'ayyalōt*	9	משו רגלי כאילת
	ᶜal bamōtē mōt yaᶜmīdēnī	9	⸢⸣על במת ⟨מת⟩[37] יעמדנ
v. 35	*mulammēd yaday limilḥamā*	9	מלמד ידי למלחמ
	niḥḥēt qašt naḥušt zarōᶜōtay	9	נחת[38] קשת נחש⟨ת⟩[39] זרעתי
v. 36	*tittēn lī magēn yišᶜeka*	8	תתנ ל מגנ ישעכ
	yamīneka tisᶜadēnī	8	ימנכ תסעדנ
	waᶜizrateka tarbēnī	8	וע⟨זר⟩[40]תכ תרבנ
v. 37	*tarḥīb ṣaᶜaday taḥtēnī*	8	תרחב צעדי תחתנ
	walō' maᶜadū qarsulay	8	ולא מעד קרסלי
v. 38	*'erdōp 'ōyibay* { *wa'ašmīdēm* / *'aśśīgēm* }	9	ארדפ איבי { ואשמדמ / ואשגמ }[41]
	walō' 'ašūb ᶜadē kallōtām	9	ולא אשב עד כלתמ
v. 39	{ *'akallēm* / *'emḥaṣēm* } *walō'* { *yaqūmūna* / *yakōlū qūm* }	9	⸢⸣ { אכלמ / אמחצמ } ולא { יקמנ / יכל קמ }[42]
	wayippōlū taḥt raglay	7	ויפל תחת רגלי
v. 40	*ta'zzirēnī ḥēl lamilḥamā*	9	⸢⸣תאזרנ[43] חל למלחמ
	takrīᶜ qamay taḥtēnī	7	תכרע קמי תחתנ
v. 41	*'ōyibay natatta lī ᶜurp*	8	⸢⸣איבי נתת ל ערפ
	muśanni'ay 'aṣammitēm	8	⸢⸣משנאי אצמתמ[44]
v. 42	*yašawwiᶜū wa'ēn mōšīᶜ*	8	ישוע ואנ משע
	'el yahwē walō' ᶜanamu	8	אל יהו ולא ענמ[45]

v. 43	*'ešḥaqēm ka^{c}apar 'arṣ*	7	אשחקמ כעפר ארצ
	kaṭīṭ ḥuṣōt 'adīqqēm	7	כטט חצת אדקמ
v. 44	*tapalliṭēnī mērībē ^{c}am*	9	⌜⌝תפלטנ מרב עמ
	wataśīmēnī larō'š gōyīm	9	ותשמנ לראש גימ
v. 44c	*^{c}am lō' yada^{c}tī ya^{c}bōdūnī*	9	עמ לא ידעת יעבדנ
v. 45a	*banē nēkar yitkaḥḥišū lī*	9	בנ נכר יתכחש ל
v. 45b	*lašmu^{c} 'uzn yiššami^{c}ū lī*	8	לשמע אזנ ישמע ל [ ][46]
v. 46b	*yaḥrōgū-mi misgarōtām*	8	יהרגמ מסגרתמ[47]
v. 47	*ḥay yahwē barūk ṣurī*	7	חי יהו ברכ צר
	yarūm 'elōhē yiš^{c}ī	7	⌜⌝ירמ אלה ישע
v. 48	*'ēl nōtēn naqamōt lī*	7	אל נתנ נקמת ל
	mōrīd ^{c}ammīm taḥtēnī	7	מרד עממ תחתנ
v. 49a	*mōṣi'ī mē'ōyibay*	7	מצא מאיבי
v. 49b	*miqqamay tarōmimēnī*	8	מקמי תרממנ
	mē'īš ḥamas taṣṣīlēnī	8	מאש חמס תצלנ[48]
v. 50	*^{c}alkēn 'ōdēka bagōyīm*	8	עלכנ אדכ בגימ
	yahwē lašimak 'azammēr	8	יהו לשמכ אזמר
v. 51	*magdīl yašu^{c}ōt malkō*	7	מגדל ישעת מלכ
	^{c}ōśē ḥasd lamašīḥō	7	⌜⌝עש חסד למשח

Translation

Part I

. . . .

v. 5 The chords of Belial surrounded me,
And the torrents of Death overwhelmed me.

v. 6 The chords of Sheol surrounded me,
The traps of Death confronted me.

v. 7 When I was in trouble I called, "Yahweh!"
To my God I cried for help.

From his palace he heard my voice,
My cry reached [his ears.
him.]

v. 8 The nether world quaked and shook,
The foundations of the hills shuddered,
They quaked when he was angry.

v. 9 Smoke rose from his nostrils,
And fire from his mouth devoured,
Coals flamed forth from him.

v. 10 He spread apart the heavens and descended,
With a storm cloud under his feet.

v. 11 He rode upon the Cherubim,
He flew upon the wings of the wind.

v. 12 He set darkness about him,
His pavilion is the raincloud.

v. 13 Banks of clouds were before him,
Before him clouds passed by,
Hail and lightning bolts.

v. 14 From the heavens Yahweh thundered,
And the most high gave forth his voice.

v. 15 He shot arrows and scattered them,
He flashed lightning and discomfited them.

v. 16 The sources of the sea were exposed,
The foundations of the world were laid bare,

At your roar, Yahweh,
At the blast of your nostrils.

v. 17 He stretched forth his hand from on high,
From on high he took me.
He drew me from the deep waters.

v. 18 He rescued me from my enemies though strong,
From my foes though mightier than I.

v. 19 They attacked me on the day of my disaster,
But Yahweh became my staff.

v. 20 He brought me out into an open place,
He liberated me because he was pleased with me.

v. 21 Yahweh rewarded me according to my righteousness,
According to my innocent hands he repaid me.

v. 22 For I have kept the ways of Yahweh,
I have not rebelled against my God.

v. 23 For all his judgments are before me,
His statutes I have not put aside from me.

v. 24 I have been honest with him,
I have kept myself from iniquity.

v. 25 . . . .
. . . .

v. 26 With the faithful you are faithful,
With the honest you are honest,

v. 27 With the sincere you are sincere,
With the cunning you are crafty.

v. 28 You will deliver a lowly people,
But haughty eyes you will humble.

v. 29 For you are my lamp, Yahweh.
My God illumines my darkness.

v. 30 . . . .
. . . .

v. 31 This is the God whose ways are perfect,
The word of Yahweh is tested,
He is a shield to those who trust in him.

Part II

v. 32 Who is God except Yahweh?
Who is the Rock but our God?

v. 33 . . . .
v. 34 Who makes my feet like does,
Who makes me stand upon the back of Death.

v. 35 Who trains my hands for the fight,
My fingers in bending the bronze bow.

v. 36 You give me your victory shield,
Your right hand upholds me,
And your help makes me great.

v. 37 You have lengthened my strides beneath me,
And my ankles do not give way.

v. 38 I pursue my enemies and I [destroy / overtake] them,
And I do not turn back until they are annihilated.

v. 39 I [annihilate / smite] them so that they [do not / cannot] rise,
So that they fall beneath my feet.

v. 40 You girded me with strength for battle,
You felled my adversaries beneath me.

v. 41 You gave me the neck of my enemies,
My foes I exterminate.

v. 42 They cried out but there was no savior,
To Yahweh, but he did not answer them.

v. 43 I pulverize them like the dust of the earth,
Like the dirt of the streets I crush them.

v. 44 You delivered me from the strife of the people,
And you placed me at the head of nations.

v. 44c A people whom I did not know serve me,
v. 45a Foreigners cringe before me.

v. 45b Upon hearing, they are obedient to me,
v. 46b Their hearts are seized with anguish.

v. 47 As Yahweh lives, blessed is my Rock,
Exalted be the God of my salvation.

v. 48 God gives victory to me,
Makes nations subject to me,
v. 49a Delivers me from my enemies.

v. 49b Over my adversaries you have exalted me,
From the violent man you have delivered me.

v. 50 Therefore I will praise you among the nations,
Yahweh, your name I will celebrate in song.

v. 51 Who magnifies the victories of his king,
Who shows loyalty to his anointed.

NOTES

II Samuel 22=Psalm 18

[1]*SAYP*, 125-58. Published also as "A Royal Psalm of Thanksgiving: II Samuel 22=Psalm 18," *JBL* 72 (1953), 15-34.

[2]*Ibid*, 161-68.

[3]*Ibid.*, 125-29.

[4]See *ibid.*, 128-29.

[5]Obviously prosaic elements and additions such as conjunctions are marked as omitted although not discussed. A reading is not considered an emendation unless it is found in neither poem.

[6]The introductory section (vv. 1-4) is impossible to reconstruct simply since it diverged greatly between north and south. There are really two theoretical original versions between which any harmonizations would fall, and they are reconstructed by Cross and Freedman in *SAYP*, 140-41. An objection to one part of this reconstruction is raised by Michael Fishbane: "Additional Remarks on *Rḥmyw* (Amos 1:11)," *JBL* 91 (1972), 391-393.

[7]Using the text of the Psalm, one may reconstruct the original form of this verse by reversing the formulae *mōt* and *bᵉlīyaᶜl*. The present text of the verse is the result of an oral dictation reversal or the like.

[8]Two ancient variant formulae are preserved between the two texts; both have five syllables and are thus completely interchangeable.

[9]The MT mixed pointing is ambiguous. Read the *Piel*.

[10]This triplet is slightly uneven (7:8:8) but otherwise sound. The majority of triplets in both Hebrew and Ugaritic are entirely even. See also note 13.

[11]The plural, "nostrils," is superior to the singular. Meter is unaffected.

[12]The longer form of the suffix, adopted here, would have been a normal variant available to the poet. Several such alternate forms vary between Psalm 18 and II Samuel 22.

[13]Read the unreduplicated form of the preposition and suffix, in the manner of *minnī* (vs. *mimminnī*). Later systematic revision of *minnu* to *mimminnu* and *mimminnī* to *minnī* has obscured the original variation. Note that this triplet, like that of v. 8, is unbalanced in one line (7:7:8). Here the

imbalance appears in the final colon in the manner most typical of Ugaritic unbalanced triplets.

[14]The normal imperfect without the *waw* conversive is probably original. Meter is unaffected.

[15]This *waw* is not the *waw* conversive nor may it be deleted as a needless conjunction, as frequently at the outset of cola.

[16]The plural is required by the parallelism and common usage in the Old Testament.

[17]*yd'* and *y*^{c}*p* represent variant formulae, metrically equivalent.

[18]*ḥšrt* is a *hapax legomenon*, thus uncertain. On the meaning, see *SAYP*, 146, note 33.

[19]Here the entire colon varied in ancient oral tradition, and must be resolved, as here by Cross and Freedman, into two metrically equivalent cola.

[20]Both texts are corrupt, but Cross and Freedman resolve the reading by this happy emendation.

[21]The *mi*-particle is preserved in the text of the Psalm. Note that it has been deleted in transmission (or purposeful revision) in the text of II Samuel.

[22]Here again variant lines have been jumbled and confused in the two texts. Cross and Freedman delete *yqḥn*, which is unnecessary.

[23]Insert *kī* with the parallel line. The meaning is "when" or the like, and is required.

[24]^c*z* must be made plural to parallel *'mṣ* below.

[25]Vv. 20-21 are unusual in meter, yet sound in other ways. Here syllabic meter may be less convincing to some than traditional or semantic parallelism meter. Since each couplet adds to a full sixteen syllables, its is possible that the cesura was made in such a way as to produce a count of 8:8 in each case.

[26]Note that *kī* is to be retained here as well as at the beginning of the following couplet. All the versions are in rare agreement in preserving it.

[27]Cross and Freedman suggest this emendation, which improves the sense without affecting meter.

[28]The shorter form of the preposition and suffix may well have been original here, *metri causa*. Cf. note 13.

[29]Omit v. 25 as either a near doublet of v. 21, or else corrupted by it. Without the conjunction at the beginning of the verse, meter would be 9:7, as in v. 21.

[30]MT *gbr* is suspect, since it destroys the parallelism. At any rate, *gibbōr* would have to be emended to *gabr* or the like.

[31]We may have here the form of an old gnomic quatrain (vv. 26-27).

[32]Or read the construct with enclitic *mem* (*ᶜênê-mi*/*ᶜênê-m*), which is, however, more difficult semantically.

[33]The meaning of v. 30 is obscure and has resisted all attempts at solution including that of Dahood, *Psalms I*, *The Anchor Bible*, Vol. 16, 114, note 30. It is best omitted from metrical consideration.

[34]Read the plural of *drkw*. The MT consonantal text is ambiguous as to plurality.

[35]Reading *'lh* with the Psalm. Note that an ancient poet could choose between *'ēl*, *'elōh*, and *'elōhîm*, giving himself considerable metrical freedom. None of the three forms is late, all three occurring in pre-exilic poetry, and commonly in Job.

[36]Verse 33 is too corrupt to restore convincingly. The MT of Psalm 18:33a has nine syllables if vocalized in the ancient manner, but the uncertainty of its integrity is too great for inclusion here.

[37]*mōt* must be inserted here, with Cross and Freedman, following the Biblical cliché, isolated by Albright from Job 9:8 and restored by him in Habakkuk 3:19. Simple haplography has caused the loss of *mt* after *bmt*.

[38]Cross notes that *nḥt* is to be understood as having reference to the *bending* or *stretching* of a bow as in Ugaritic (texts 19 and 23).

[39]The segholate *nḥšt* is far more common than the form *naḥušā*, although either is theoretically possible here. The former better fits the assonance of the line.

[40]Reading *ᶜzrtk* with the Qumran text. MT *ᶜnwtk* reflects the *r/w* confusion common in third and fourth century orthography, and subsequent correction with *n*. Meter is unaffected. Dahood's labored etymology (*Psalms I*, 115-6) is thus rendered unnecessary.

[41]These two formulae are metrically interchangeable as isolated by Cross and Freedman.

[42]Here four formulae vary around *walō'*. Either of the first two is correct, and either of the second two is correct. In all, four different lines are possible. Apparently the poet composed his line in metrical blocks of three, two and four beats, respectively but we do not know whether he himself viewed his composition in that manner. The 9:7 couplet is unusual meter, but not suspect otherwise, as may be said for v. 40 as well.

[43]The vocalization of *t'zrn* with four syllables, assuming the quiescence of the *aleph* is based on the northern orthography of II Samuel 22, where the *aleph* is in fact omitted entirely. The pronunciation may have varied regionally.

[44]Reading the *Piel*, without the conjunction, according to the consonantal text of the Psalm.

[45]Reading the fuller form of the suffix. The consonantal text is ambiguous as to the form of the suffix.

[46]Verse 46a is a doublet of verse 45a and should be omitted here.

[47]Note that the Psalm has the fuller form of the suffix (-*ēhim*) which either lengthened the line to nine syllables (45b may have been read with nine syllables in the south), or was compensated for by reading *yaḥrōgū-m*, or is merely a typical scribal revision. The latter is most likely.

[48]Cross and Freedman omit this colon and combine v. 49b with v. 50 to form a triplet. It is sound metrically and otherwise, however, so is retained here.

The Lament of David: II Samuel 1:19-27

This hymnic lament for Israel's war heros, Saul and Jonathan, exhibits much metrical regularity. Cross and Freedman's original study in 1950, though not primarily based upon the metrical factors elucidated here, went far toward reconstructing the form of the original song. From that, with several additions now possible, we may discern almost completely the pattern of the full poem as it might have appeared ca. 1000 B.C.

Especially interesting metrically are the many "b" couplets and triplets in the lament. Except for the three refrains, and the unusually sophisticated b:b::l::b:b triplet (equivalent to a b:b::b:b::b:b triplet) in v. 23, the entire poem is composed in short meter. This would seem to represent the highest concentration of short meter in our corpus of early Hebrew poetry.

The metrical structure may be diagrammed as follows:

Refrain	triplet	l:l:l	v. 19
	couplet	b:b::b:b	v. 20
	couplet	b:b::b:b	
	couplet	b:b::b:b	v. 21
	couplet	b:b::b:b	
	triplet	b:b::b:b::b:b	v. 22
	triplet	b:b::l::b:b	v. 23
	(triplet)	(b:b::b:b::b:b)	v. 24
	triplet	l:l:l	v. 25
	triplet	b:b::b:b::b:b	v. 26
Refrain	triplet	l:l:l	v. 27

Reconstructed Text

	Refrain		
v. 19	*hōy ṣxbī yiśra'ēl ša'ūl*	8	⟨הי⟩[1] צב[2] ישראל ⟨שאל⟩[3]
	ᶜalay bamōtēka ḥalal	8	עלי במתכ חלל
	'ēka napalū gibbōrīm	8	אכ נפל גברמ
v. 20	*'al taggīdū*	4	אל תגד
	baḥuṣōt 'ašqalōn	5	⟨בחצת אשקלנ⟩
	'al tabaśśirū	5	אל תבשר
	baraḥōbōt gat	6	⟨ב⟨רחבת⟩ גת⟩[4]
	pin tiśmaḥna	4	פנ תשמחנ
	banōt palištīm	5	בנת ⸢פלשתמ
	pin taᶜlozna	4	פנ תעלזנ
	banōt ᶜarēlīm	5	בנת ⸢ערלמ
v. 21	*harrē gilbōᶜ*	4	הר ⸢[5]גלבע
	'al ṭal 'al maṭar	5	אל טל ⸢אל מטר
	'al ᶜalēkim	4	⟨אל⟩[6] עליכמ[7]
	šaraᶜ tihōmōt	5	⸢ש⟨ר⟩ע ת⟨ה⟩מת[8]
	kī šam nigᶜal	4	כ שמ נגעל
	magēn gibbōrīm	5	מגנ גברמ
	magēn ša'ūl	4	מגנ שאל
	bal mašūḥ bašamn	5	בל משח בשמנ
v. 22	*middam ḥalalīm*	5	מדמ חללמ
	miḥḥilb gibbōrīm	5	מחלב גברמ

	qašt yōnatan	4	קשת ינתנ[9]
	lō' naśag 'aḥōr	5	לא נשג אחר
	waḥarb ša'ūl	4	וחרב שאל
	lō' tašūb rēqam	5	לא תשב רקם
v. 23	*ša'ūl wayōnatan*	6	שאל וינתנ
	ni'habīm na^{c}īmīm	6	נאהבמ נעממ
	baḥayyēhim wabamōtām lō' nipradū	12	[10]בחיהם ובמתמ לא נפרד
	minnašarīm qallū	6	מנשרמ קל
	mē'arayōt gabērū	7	מארית גבר
v. 24	. . . .		- - - - - - - -
	. . . .		[11]- - - - - - - -
	Refrain		
v. 25	*'ēka napalū gibbōrīm*	8	אכ נפל גברמ
	batawk milḥamā yōnatan	8	בתוכ מלחמ ינתנ
	^{c}alay bamōtēka ḥalal	8	עלי במתכ חלל
v. 26	*ṣar lī ^{c}alayka*	5	צר ל עליכ
	'aḥī yōnatan	5	אח ינתנ
	na^{c}amta lī ma'ōd	6	נעמת ל מאד
	nipla' 'atta	4	נפלא ⟨א⟩ת[12]
	'ahbateka lī	5	אהבתכ ל
	mē'ahbat našīm	5	מאהבת נשמ
	Refrain		
v. 27	*'ēka napalū gibbōrīm*	8	אכ נפל גברמ
	^{c}alay bamōtēka ḥalal	8	⟨עלי במתכ חלל⟩[13] [14]
	yō'bidū kilyē milḥamā	8	יאבד כלי מלחמ

Translation

v. 19 Woe! Gazelle of Israel, Saul,
Slain upon your high places;
How the mighty have fallen!

v. 20 Tell it not
In the squares of Gath,

Proclaim it not
In the streets of Ashkelon,

Lest they rejoice,
The Philistine maidens,

Lest they exult,
The daughters of the uncircumcised.

v. 21 O mountains of Gilboa,
Neither dew nor rain
(let there be),

Nor upon thee
The upswellings of the deeps.

For there was defiled
The shield of the warriors,

The shield of Saul,
Not anointed with oil,

v. 22 From the blood of the slain
From the bowels of the warriors,

The bow of Jonathan
Did not turn back,

And the sword of Saul
Did not return empty.

v. 23 Saul and Jonathan,
Beloved, gracious,

In their life and death they were not parted.

They were swifter than eagles,
They were stronger than lions.

v. 24 . . . .
. . . .

v. 25 How the mighty have fallen!
In the midst of battle, Jonathan,
Slain upon your high places.

v. 26 I am grieved over you,
My brother Jonathan;

You delighted me greatly,
You were wonderful.

To love you was for me
Greater than to love women.

v. 27 How the mighty have fallen!
Slain upon your high places--
The tools of war have perished.

NOTES

The Lament of David: II Samuel 1:19-27

[1]The restoration of *hōy* by separating the *he* of the MT article and interpolating a *yodh* is commonly proposed by commentators.

[2]We have no idea of the shading of this first vowel. Quite possibly it was, in effect, a vocal *shewa* with corresponding pronunciation. We do know that original final *y* and final *w* were resolved in Northwest Semitic speech as early as the Mari period, e.g. **piryu* > *piry* > *pxrī* (*p*^{e}*rī* or *pĭrī* or the like in pronunciation).

[3]Supply *ša'ūl*; it is lacking as the apposition to *ṣxbī yiśra'ēl*.

[4]While the received text seems to contain a haplography, the bones of the verse are present. The reconstruction adopted here involves supplying a parallel for *bahuṣōt* and the reversal of the formulae in the second half of each bicolon. The bicola then have ten syllables each, yet are composed in the short meter we expect to find in this lament.

[5]Any of the following combinations is theoretically possible: *harrē gilbō*^{c}, *har bagilbō*^{c}, *bahar gilbō*^{c}. The plural personal suffix of the text in the following couplet suggests that a plural is necessary here, as shown in the text. See also note 7.

[6]Since we now know of the Ugaritic parallel to this image,

bal ṭalla bal rabība

bal šara^{c} *tihāmtēmi* (7:7)

from I Aqhat 44-45 (thanks to H. L. Ginsberg, *JBL* 57 (1938), p. 213), we may reasonably suggest that the third *'al* be restored in parallel to the three occurrences of *bal* in the Ugaritic.

[7]If the original reading here were a singular, as LXX (L) and Vulgate suggest, emendation would be required of the MT consonantal *km* to *k* (*kim* to *ka*). There is a remote possibility that at a later stage of the orthography of the language, i.e. sometime later than the seventh century B.C., the three letters *caph*, *mem*, and *waw*, which occur in close order here (עליכמ ו) could have stood for the word *kamō*, "like." In this case the original could have read:

'al ṭal 'al maṭar	6	אל טל אל מטר
^{c}*alayka kamō*	5	עליכ כמ
šara^{c} *tihōmōt*	5	שרע תהמת

(Neither dew nor rain let there be upon thee, like the upswellings of the deeps.") This involves unusual stichometry, however, and the Ugaritic parallel strongly suggests the arrangement adopted above in the reconstructed text.

[8]The change of *daleth* to *resh* to *resh* to *heh* in these two words is a conservative emendation with felicitous semantic results. See note 6.

[9]*yōnatan* (<**yahwnatan*) is the appropriate eleventh-century pronunciation of this northern name.

[10]Unique to the poem is the balancing of b:b couplets (6:6 and 6:7) with an l colon (12). Yet this balance is perfect quantitatively without any change of the consonantal MT. Cf. Judges 5:12.

[11]The text of this verse is uncertain, although a reconstruction which is at least sensible may be conjectured:

banōt yiśra'ēl	5	בנת ישראל
'el ša'ūl bakīna	6	אל שאל בכנ
malbiškin šanī	5	⌜⌝מלבשכנ שנ
ᶜimmi ᶜadanīm	5	עמ עדנמ
maᶜlī ᶜxdī zahab	6	⌜⌝מעל עד זהב
ᶜalay labuškin	6	עלי לבשכנ

Translation:

O daughters of Israel,
Weep for Saul,

Who clothed you with scarlet,
As well as dainties,

Who put gold ornaments
Upon your dress.

[12]This welcome emendation originated with Cross and Freedman, *SAYP*, p. 26, n. k.

[13]The loss of *ᶜalay bamotēka ḥalal*, which appears in the two other occurrences of the refrain, is not due to any obvious type of haplography here. It would also be possible to restore another of the eight-syllable lines. Each of the refrains exhibits interchangeability both in the positioning of lines, and in the case of one line in each triplet, substitution. In the first refrain the unique line (*hōy ṣxbī yiśra'ēl ša'ūl*) refers to Saul, who indeed is the person mentioned first in order and primarily in the section immediately following. The second refrain has a unique line (*batōk milḥamā yōnatan*) in reference

to Jonathan since the verse immediately following concerns him. This final verse (v. 27) is a summation and thus mentions the more general fact that the tools of war have perished (*yō'bidū kilyē milḥamā*), also unique in the song.

[14]A translation such as "stabbed through your back(s)" or "slain, (and lying) on your back(s)" would be grammatically possible according to the consonantal MT. The usual translation, "slain upon your high places" or the like has always seemed slightly awkward semantically, because of the presence of the possessive pronoun, which has no unambiguous antecedent.

The Poetry of Amos

The position of the oracles of Amos at the outset of classical prophecy makes them a natural choice for metrical examination. Amos stands at the beginning of a new era of poetic composition, an era worth our study both for its own sake and for purposes of comparison with the earlier period. The poetry of Amos is chronologically the latest poetry with which we shall deal.[1]

Less than a fourth of the book is clearly metrical poetry.[2] Most of Amos is constituted by prose oracles which exhibit neither meter nor consistent parallelism. Occasional oracles might be classified as semi-poetic or the like since they contain either some repetitiousness which may be metrically quantified, or are generally parallelistic. They do not, however, display any of the usual types of syllabic meter visible elsewhere in Hebrew poetry.

There remain some passages whose categorization as prose or poetry is elusive. The contrast between prose and poetry in the ancient--like the modern--world is not always rigidly definable. Here a familiarity with and feeling for the material at hand is ultimately the means of delineation between prose and poetry.

Occasionally in the poetry of Amos there are hints of repetitive parallelism.[3] These remnants, although considerably removed from the full-blown early types and styles, are an aspect of the continuity between the poetry of the "writing prophets" and the older epic poetry of the league and early monarchy. In volume, however, the later poetry contains only a minute percentage of the repetitive parallelism of the early poetry. This we would expect.[4]

Throughout Amos the strong hand of the editor[5] is visible, largely in the connective and explanatory material between oracles. This necessitates the isolation and study of each pericope apart from the skillful editorial transitional material, so as to avoid treating either introductory or summary material as part of the original poetry. We discuss exegetical matters only where this information is in some way essential to the sense or discernment of structural features of the poem in question.

While some freedom has been exercised in the selection of oracles included in this section, the bulk of the poetry of Amos is treated. In any case there appears here a representative sampling of the various genres of meter found in the book.

Textual criticism in our treatment of Amos has been a valuable tool. It may be noted that in Amos the Targum is, as with all the prophets, expansionistic. The other versions are generally rather conservative, the Vulgate and the Syriac tending to reflect the MT, with the LXX differing more often.

Inasmuch as Amos was a southerner, his oracles are reconstructed in an approximated eighth century Judahite pronunciation. There are no differences between the poetry of this period and the period of the league and early monarchy that are so great as to affect syllable count. The orthography of Hebrew had indeed changed, however, and final vowels are now marked by *matres lectionis*.[6]

Similar principles of textual reconstruction and emendation apply to Amos as to the earlier poetry. Prosaic elements, and conjunctive elements at the outset of cola, are generally suspect. Prosaic elements are as common in the poetry of Amos as they are in moderately corrupted early texts such as II Samuel 22=Psalm 18, or The Song of Deborah. They are the semantic *matres lectionis* of a later age. Emendations in general are always to be made *ad sensum* rather than *metri causa*.[7]

No poem (unless 1:3-2:7 is judged fully poetic) in Amos is long enough to contain strophes, so the question of their existence is irrelevant here. Most of Amos' poetry is comprised of mixed 1:1 couplets. Two triplets are found (5:5-6) and one case of b:b::b:b meter occurs (3:8). Purposely unbalanced meter is attested (5:10, 5:12, 5:16) in close proximity, although this arrangement may be entirely accidental. Unbalanced 1:1 couplets are as a rule rare in the early poetry. An imbalance of one or, infrequently, two syllables between the cola of a couplet is nevertheless possible. It is not possible to see any trend toward imbalance developing in the poetry of Amos, however.

Evidence of the emergence of purposely uneven meter (Qinah) is found in Amos only in 3:3-6 and 5:12, although in exquisite form at those points. Qinah, sometimes called "prophetic" meter because of its use by the classical prophets, is not really an unbalanced meter, even though the length of individual cola always vary in a pattern in this style. Rather, the balance is to be found between couplets or bicola rather than between individual cola. In this way Qinah resembles short or b:b::b:b meter. Triplets may occur in this style (l:b::l:b::l:b, etc.) just as in the short meter (b:b::b:b::b:b). One such triplet may be seen in 3:4-5a.

The primary difference between the poetry of Amos and that of the earlier period is in length. Most of the prophet's metrical oracles were apparently quite short as compared, for example, to those of Balaam. The oracle in 1:3-2:7, which does not scan well by any system of meter, is a possible but solitary exception. Amos' oracles do have great impact and are superbly composed regardless of their length. Moreover, his oracles are cast in the three major styles of Hebrew poetry (l:l, b:b::b:b, and l:b::l:b), demonstrating his mastery of poetic skills.

Aside from the Qinah meter of 3:3-6, we meet no really new or surprising poetic meter in Amos. We may move immediately to the individual oracles themselves:

Amos 3:3-6

The seven bicola that comprise Amos 3:3-6 are so arranged that their combined effect is to saturate the reader or hearer with the impression that "if A then B." The entire movement of these bicola and their combinations has as its goal the effectiveness of the punchline constituted by v. 6b.[8] The overall intent of the poetic oracle is thus to convince the prophet's audience that some misfortune that has taken or will take place in a city is not unplanned or accidental, but is the doing of Yahweh. Verse 3, apparently a separate couplet (not combined into a fuller l:b::l:b or l:b::l:b::l:b couplet or triplet, at least metrically) begins the progression. Verse 6b, also a separate couplet, finishes it. The intervening couplets are perhaps best combined into a full l:b::l:b::l:b triplet and l:b::l:b couplet, although this grouping is somewhat arbitrary.

The text of the MT is relatively well preserved in comparison to our reconstructed original, especially in regard to conjunctions at the beginning of cola. The meter, beautifully patterned, may be outlined as follows:

couplet	1:b	v. 3
triplet	1:b::1:b::1:b	v. 4-5a
couplet	1:b::1:b	v. 5b-6a
couplet	1:b	v. 6b

Reconstructed Text: 3:3-6

v. 3	*hayēlikū šinaym yaḥdāw*	8	הילכו שנים יחדו
	bilti 'im nawdaᶜū	6	בלתי אם נודעו
v. 4	*hayišʼag 'aryē bayaᶜr*	7	הישאג אריה ביער
	bilti 'im ṭarp lō	5	⟨בלתי אם⟩[9] טרף לה
	hayittēn kapīr qōlō	7	היתנ כפר קלה [ ][10]
	bilti 'im lakad	5	בלתי אם לכד
v. 5	*hatippōl ṣippōr ᶜal 'arṣ*	7	התפל צפר על [11]״ארץ
	wamōqēš 'ēn lā	5	ומקש אנ לה
	hayaᶜlē paḥ min 'adamā	8	היעלה פח מנ ״אדמה
	walakōd lō' yilkōd	6	ולכד לא ילכד
v. 6	*'im yittaqaᶜ šōpar baᶜīr*	8	אם יתקע שפר בער
	waᶜam lō' yiḥradū	6	ועם לא יחרדו
	'im tihyē raᶜā baᶜīr	7	אם תהיה רעה בער
	wayahwē lō' ᶜaśa	6	ויהוה לא עשה

Translation

v. 3 Do two walk together
Unless they have met by appointment?

v. 4 Does a lion roar in the forest
Unless he has prey?

Does a young lion cry out
Unless he has taken something?

v. 5 Does a bird fall to the earth
When there is no trap for it?

Does a snare spring up from the ground
When it has taken nothing at all?

v. 6 Is a trumpet blown in the city
And the people are not afraid?

Does evil take place in a city
And Yahweh has not done it?

Amos 3:8

This short poem is unconnected to either the preceding or following material in the third chapter of Amos. It consists of a single couplet which may be diagrammed as follows:

couplet b:b::b:b

The poem has some relation in type to that of 3:3-6 in that it is also of the "if A then B" genre, although much shorter in duration and of clearly different meter.

Reconstructed Text

3:8	*'aryē ša'ag*	4	אריה שאג
	mī lō' yīra'	4	מי לא ירא
	yahwē dibbēr	4	⌜⌝יהוה דבר[12]
	mī lō' yinnabē'	5	מי לא ינבא

Translation

3:8 A lion has roared.
Who is not afraid?

Yahweh has spoken.
Who cannot prophesy?

Amos 5:5 and 5:6-7

The two brief poems contained in these distinct pericopes appear to exhibit remarkable regularity of meter and simplicity of construction. Each is composed of a triplet followed by a couplet. In the case of the first poem, a warning against worship at illegal sanctuaries, the meter may be outlined as follows:

triplet	1:1:1
couplet	1:1

The second poem, a call to repentance, may be analyzed similarly:

triplet	1:1:1
couplet	1:1

A common feature of the two poems may account for the juxtaposition in which we find them in the received text: they both begin with a form of the verb *drš*.[13] Clearly, however, the poems are basically independent of one another. The first of the two is especially noteworthy for its assonance, a device well-developed in the earlier poetry.

Reconstructed Text: 5:5

5:5	*'al tidrōšū bayt'ēl*	6	⌜⌝אל תדרשו ביתאל
	gilgal lō' tabō'ū	6	⌜⌝גלגל לא תבאו
	bi'r šib^c lō' ta^cbōrū	6	⌜⌝באר שבע לא תעברו
	gilgal galō yiglē	6	⌜⌝גלגל גלה יגלה
	bayt'ēl yihyē la'awn	6	⌜⌝ביתאל יהיה לאונ[14]

Reconstructed Text: 5:6-7

v. 6	*durušū yahwē waḥayū*	9	דרשו יהוה וחיו
	pin yiṣlaḥ ka'ēš babayt yōsēp	9	פנ יצלח כאש ⟨ב⟩[15]בית יספ
	wa'akalā wa'ayn mukabbē	9	ואכלה ואינ מכבה [ ][16]
v. 7	*hahōpikīm lala^cnā mišpaṭ*	9	ההפכמ ללענה משפט
	waṣadaqā la'arṣ hinnīḥū	9	וצדקה לארצ הנחו

Translation: 5:5

Do not seek Bethel,
To Gilgal do not go,
To Beer-sheba do not pass through.

Gilgal shall surely go into exile,
Bethel shall come to nought.

Translation: 5:6-7

v. 6 Seek Yahweh and live
Lest he break out like fire in[17] the house of Joseph,
And devour it with none to quench,

v. 7 O you who turn justice into wormwood,
And cast righteousness down to the earth.

Amos 5:10-11

This oracle depicts the corruption of Israel's legal system and the resultant economic disaster, perhaps exile, that would serve as punishment. The two verses form a unit, no couplet being independent of the greater poem. The meter may be outlined as follows:

couplet	1:1	v. 10
couplet	1:1	v. 11
couplet	1:1	
couplet	1:1	

Reconstructed Text: 5:10-11

v. 10	*śana'ū baša^{c}r mawkīḥ*	7	שנאו בשער מוכח
	dōbēr tamīm yata^{cc}ibū	8	⌜⌝דבר תממ יתעבו
v. 11	*lakēn ya^{c}n buskim ^{c}al dal*	7	לכנ יענ בסכמ על דל
	maś'ōt bar tiqqaḥū minnu	8	משאת בר תקחו ⌜⌝מנ[18]
	battē gazīt banitim	7	בתי גזת בנתמ
	walō' tayšibū bahim	7	ולא תישבו ב⟨ה⟩מ[18a]

karmē ḥamd naṭa^{c}*tim*	6	כרמי חמד נטעתמ
walō' tištū yaynām	6	ולא תשתו יינמ

Translation

v. 10 They hate correction at the gate,
Him who speaks the truth they despise,

v. 11 Therefore, because of your trampling upon the poor,
Taking a tribute of grain from him,

Hewn-stone houses you shall build,
But shall not live in them;

Pleasant vineyards you shall plant,
But shall not drink their wine.

Amos 5:12

Amos 5:12 does not appear to be integral to the poem immediately preceding it in 5:10-11. Since 5:13 is clearly prose, it does not continue the poetry of 5:12, although it may be described as a prose conclusion thereto.

With only the conjunction omitted, the poem is presented here as a unit, in normal Qinah meter and normal parallelism. The meter may be described schematically as:

couplet 1:b
couplet 1:b

Reconstructed Text: 5:12

yada^{c}*tī rabbīm piša*^{c}*ēkim*	9	⌜⌝ידעתי רבמ פשעכמ
^{c}*aṣūmīm ḥaṭṭōtēkim*	7	⌜⌝עצממ חטאתכמ
ṣōrirē ṣaddīq lōqiḥē kopr	9	צררי צדק לקחי כפר
'ibyōnīm baša^{c}*r hiṭṭū*	7	⌜⌝אבינמ בשער הטו

Translation

5:12 I know how many are your transgressions,
How great are your sins,

Afflictors of the righteous, accepters of bribes,
Who turn aside the needy at the gate.

Amos 5:16b-17

This short poem is self-contained and transparently metrical. With the exception of the deletion of *waws* at the beginning of cola and the editorial phrase *'amar yahwē* in v. 17, no emendations are required. The meter may be represented schematically as follows:

couplet	1:1
couplet	1:1
couplet	1:1

Reconstructed Text: 5:16b-17

v. 16b	*bakol raḥōbōt mispēd*	7	בכל רחבת מספד
	baḥuṣōt yō'marū hō hō	8	ב⌝⌜חצת יאמרו הה הה[19]
	qara'ū 'ikkār 'el 'ibl	7	⌝⌜קראו אכר אל אבל
	mispēd 'el yōdiᶜē nᵉhī	8	⌝⌜מספד אל ידעי נהי
v. 17	*bakol karamīm mispēd*	7	בכל כרממ מספד
	kī 'eᶜbōr baqirbeka	7	כי אעבר בקרבכ [ ][20]

Translation

v. 16b In all the squares there shall be wailing,
In the streets they shall say, "Alas, Alas."

They shall call the mourner to mourning,[21]
Wailing to those skilled in lamentation.

v. 17 In all the vineyards there shall be wailing
When I pass through your midst.

Amos 6:12

Except for the widely accepted revocalization of the consonants in the second colon of this oracle, no major emendation is called for. The meter is regular and balanced.

It may be represented schematically as follows:

couplet 1:1
couplet 1:1

Reconstructed Text: 6:12

hayiqṣūrūn salᶜ basusīm	8	הי⟨קצר⟩נ סלע ⟨ב⟩ ססמ
'im yiḥḥarēš babaqar yam	8	אמ יחרש בבקר ימ[22]
kī hapaktim larō'š mišpaṭ	8	כי הפכתמ לראש משפט
pxrī ṣadaqā lalaᶜnā	8	י⌝פרי צדקה ללענה

Translation

Does one reap rocks with horses?
Is the sea plowed with oxen?

Indeed, you have turned justice into poison,
The fruit of righteousness into wormwood.

Amos 8:7-8

The warning to Israel of its impending doom in Amos 8:7-8 is not clearly connected to the pericope in vv. 9-10 (q.v.) although it is of the same general nature. We shall treat the two poems separately, as the editor of Amos did in essence by separating the two by means of a prose introduction to verse 9.

The final three cola of 8:7-8 are repeated in the oracle found in 9:5, a happy circumstance for two reasons: the text of 8:8 is sufficiently corrupt as to need correction from a parallel, and the comparison of the two versions shows the kinds of minor changes that may be wrought upon a basic formula for the sake of adapting it to a slightly different meter or tune. Strictly speaking, a formula does not vary metrically; it always contains a precise number of syllables. In practice, however, formulae appear to be adaptable to different metrical contexts. With Lord and Parry, we may refer to formulae which are thus adapted as *similar* but not *identical* to their original or unadapted forms.[23]

The structure of 8:7-8 may be diagrammed as follows:

couplet	1:1
couplet	1:1
couplet	1:1

Reconstructed Text: 8:7-8

v. 7	*nišbaᶜ yahwē baga'ōn yaᶜqōb*	9	נשבע יהוה בגאנ יעקב
	'im 'eškaḥ laniṣḥ maᶜaśēhim	9	אמ אשכח לנצח מעשהמ
v. 8	*haᶜal zō't tirgaz 'arṣ*	7	העל זאת תרגז ארצ
	wa'abal kol yōšēb bā	7	ואבל כל ישב בה
	ᶜalatā kaya'ōr kullā	8	⌜עלתה כיאר כלה[24]
	šaqaᶜā kaya'ōr miṣraym	8	⌜שקעה כיאר מצרימ[25]

Translation

v. 7 Yahweh has sworn by the pride of Jacob,
"If I ever forget their deeds . . ."

v. 8 Shall not the land tremble because of this,
And mourn every one who lives in it?

All of it shall rise like the Nile,
It shall sink like the Nile of Egypt.

Amos 8:9-10

The uncertain connection between this oracle and that of 8:7-8 has been discussed in the introduction to the latter. The oracle contains four precisely balanced 1:1 couplets. Each couplet begins with a l.c.s. *Qal* verb in the prophetic perfect. As this is not the case in the poem in 8:7-8 the distinctiveness of the passages is reinforced.

The meter may be described as follows:

couplet	1:1	v. 9
couplet	1:1	v. 10
couplet	1:1	
couplet	1:1	

Reconstructed Text: 8:9-10

v. 9	*habē'tī šamš baṣaḥaraym*	8	⸢הבאתי שמש בצהרים
	haḥšaktī la'arṣ bayawm 'ōr	8	⸢החשכתי לארץ ביום אר
v. 10	*hapaktī ḥaggēkim la'ibl*	8	⸢הפכתי חגכמ לאבל
	wakol šīrēkim laqīnā	8	וכל שרכמ לקנה
	ha^{c}lītī ^{c}al motnaym śaq	7	⸢העלתי על ⸢מתנים[26] שק
	wa^{c}alē kol rō'š qorḥā	7	ועלי כל ראש קרחה
	śamtīha ka'ibl yaḥīd	7	⸢שמתה כאבל יחד
	wa'aḥritā kayawm mar	7	ואחרתה כיום מר

Translation

v. 9 I will make the sun go down at noon,
I will darken the earth at broad daylight.

v. 10 I will turn your feasts into mourning,
And all your songs into lamentation.

I will bring upon the loins sackcloth,
And upon every head baldness.

I will make it like the mourning for an only child,
And the end of it like a bitter day.

Amos 9:5-6

The sense of this oracle depends upon recognizing that Yahweh is the subject of the majority of the verbs. The subject is explicit only in v. 5a. Yet it is inadvisable to treat the introductory line (v. 5a) as part of the poem proper for two reasons: editorial endings and introductions to oracles employing the full name *yahwē ṣ^{e}ba'ōt 'elōhē yiśra'ēl* or approximations thereof abound in Amos,[27] and there is textual uncertainty as to the exact content of the title name since the LXX reads *yhwh 'lhy ṣb't* as compared to the MT *'dny yhwh hṣb't*. In this pericope the Vulgate and Syriac follow the MT fairly closely, while the Targum is heavily expansionistic. The LXX differs from the MT only at the points of introduction and ending which surround the poem, having in the case of the ending a much expanded divine title, *'dny yhwh ṣb't*.

The meter may be described as follows:[28]

couplet	1:1	v. 5
couplet	1:1	
couplet	1:1	v. 6
couplet	1:1	

Reconstructed Text: 9:5-6

v. 5	*hanōgē^{c} ba'arṣ watamōg*	8	הנגע בארץ ותמג
	'abalū kol yōšibē bā	8	⌜⌝אבלו כל ישבי בה[29]
	^{c}alatā kaya'ōr kullā	8	⌜⌝עלתה כיאר כלה
	šaqa^{c}ā kaya'ōr miṣraym	8	⌜⌝שקעה כיאר מצרים[30]
v. 6	*habōnē bašamaym ma^{c}lōtāw*	9	הבנה בשמים מעלתו
	'aguddatō ^{c}al 'arṣ yasadā	9	⌜⌝אגדתה על ארץ יסדה
	haqōrē' lamē yam ^{c}umud	8	הקרא למי ים ⟨עמד⟩[31]
	wayišpōkēm ^{c}al panē 'arṣ	8	וישפכם על פני ארץ

Translation

v. 5 Who touches the earth so it melts,
All who dwell in it mourn.

All of it rises like the Nile
It sinks like the Nile of Egypt.

v. 6 Who builds in the heavens his high rooms,
His vault upon the nether world he founds.

Who calls to the waters of the sea, "Stand!"
And pours them out upon the face of the earth.

Amos 9:13

In this verse is contained the last bit of poetic material in the book of Amos. It is introduced by a prose sentence, "Behold the days are coming, oracle of Yahweh . . .", upon which it is not quite dependent, but which helps define the intent of the oracle. It is followed by a prose oracle in vv. 14-15, which ends the book.

Our poem contains two couplets in precise metrical parallelism. The only emendations proposed in our reconstructed version are common, the deletion of unnecessary conjunctions and prose particles.

The meter may be outlined as follows:

couplet	1:1
couplet	1:1

Reconstructed Text: 9:13

niggaš ḥōrēš baqōṣēr	7	⌜⌝נגש חרש[32] בקצר[33]
dōrēk ^{c}anabīm bamōšēk zar^c	7	⌜⌝דרכ ענבמ במשכ זרע
hiṭṭīpū harrīm ^{c}asīs	7	⌜⌝הטפו ⌜⌝הרמ עסס
giba^{c}ōt titmōgagna	7	⌜⌝[34]גבעת תתמגגנה

Translation

The ploughman shall overtake the reaper,
The treader of grapes him who sows seed,

The mountains shall drip sweet wine,
The hills shall flow.

NOTES

The Poetry of Amos

[1]For the later (post-Biblical) poetry see now Ehlen, *The Poetic Structure of a Hodayah from Qumran*, unpublished Harvard University dissertation, 1970.

[2]I.e., all or parts of the following verses: 1:2; 1:3-2:7; 2:8 (?), 9, 11; 3:3-6, 8, 9, 11, 14; 4:4, 5; 5:3, 6, 7, 8, 10, 11, 12, 16, 17, 21-24; 6:1-7, 8, 11, 12; 7:17; 8:4-6, 7-8, 9-10; 9:1, 2-4, 5, 6, 13.

[3]Primarily 8:7-8; 9:5-6; but cf. 3:3-6, 5:16-17, and 8:9-10.

[4]See W. F. Albright, *Yahweh and the Gods of Canaan*, 1-52.

[5]See the comments on 9:5-6. The "editor" could be the prophet, his disciples, a later compiler, or in some cases even a copyist.

[6]See Cross and Freedman, *EHO*, 47-50, 56-7, 58-60, *et passim*.

[7]No exception to this is the situation of the grossly unbalanced couplet where an element or two is obviously missing due to haplography, or an element has obviously been added through dittography or deliberate harmonization. In such cases there exists a need to emend from the standpoint of *any* theory of meter, as well as the demands of the parallelism. An example is the restoration of *bilti 'im* in 3:4, which although supported textually only by the Vulgate, is clearly superior to the shorter MT *wa...'ēn*.

[8]This interpretation assumes that neither verse 7 nor verse 8 is to be understood as related to the poem in 3:3-6 in other than a general way. Verse 7 is a prose statement of an explanatory nature, and verse 8 is a separate poem of different meter and topic.

[9]To preserve the parallelism of the first lines, it is preferable to read *bilti 'im* here rather than MT *wa...'ēn*. There is limited textual support for this emendation, however. The meter of the MT version would be 7:4 without emendation, which is possible (cf. Exodus 15:10a). Our emendation is supported by the Vulgate's reading of *nisi* in the first three couplets but *absque* in the fourth.

[10]MT *mm*^{c}*ntw* renders the line unusually long (12 syllables) and should be omitted. Lions do not normally take prey in their own lairs.

[11]Omit MT *paḥ* with the LXX, copied into this position from the following couplet and out of place here. Omit the prosaic article as well.

[12]Omit *'dwny* of the MT as editorial. Such a form is highly suspect in the ancient poetry.

[13]However, the use of *dršwny wḥyw* in the MT of 5:4b is not related originally to the triplet and couplet which comprise 5:5 but rather must be understood as editorial. This parallels *lbyt yśr'l* which occurs in 5:3, 5:4, 5:6, etc.

[14]Lack of reference to Beer-sheba in this couplet is likely due more to the demands of prosody than to deliberate omission.

[15]Insert the preposition, with many commentators. It is called for by the sense of the line.

[16]Omit MT *lbyt yśr'l* as editorial. See note 13.

[17]Or "against."

[18]Read the alternate, shorter, form of *minnu*, which varied with *mimmennu/mimminnu* in the earlier period as *minnī* with *mimminnī*. Cf. II Samuel 22:9 above.

[18a]Read the fuller form of the suffix which we know varied with the shorter form, as commonly between II Samuel 22 and Psalm 18.

[19]Omit *kl* as vertical dittography. This element is typical of those added into the text in the course of transmission. Cross estimates that as much as ninety percent of the occurrences of *kol* in I and II Samuel may be secondary.

[20]Omit *'mr yhwh* as editorial. Cf. 1:5, 1:8, 1:15, etc.

[21]The meaning of these lines is generally clear. *'kr* must have a meaning other than "farmer" judging from the context. It is even possible that *'kr* should be taken as a noun parallel to *mispēd*, and that *'bl* should be vocalized as a participle, parallel to *yōdiᶜē nxhī*.

[22]On the emendation of the first line see Sperber, *Historical Grammar of Biblical Hebrew*, p. 657. In the second line, we adopt a commonly accepted redivision and revocalization of the MT. The versions support the consonantal text, with the possible exception of the Syriac, which is periphrastic. *ḥrš* could also be read in the *Piel*, with the translation, "Does one plow...?" or the like.

[23]The formula in question is that of the second colon in 8:8 which is singular and begins with *waw*: *wa'abal kol yōšēb bā*, and the second colon in 9:5, which is plural and omits the *waw*: *'abalū kol yōšibē bā*. In the former case seven syllables were required to match the accompanying line of the couplet;

in the latter, eight syllables were needed. One may thus say that a single formula is adapted in two ways, or that we have here two similar but not identical formulae. Lord and Parry would prefer the latter description.

[24]The parallel in 9:5 shows that the *waw* is to be omitted.

[25]This couplet is reconstructed with the help of the parallel in 9:5. It is likely that in both contexts the couplet was invariable. There is the flavor of repetitive parallelism in the use of *ky'r* twice, reminiscent of the earlier poetry.

[26]Omit *kol* as an addition to the text. Cf. note 19, and v. 10 above. Several times in Amos *kol* is added to the first colon of a couplet, where it does not belong, from the second colon, where it is proper.

[27]E.g. 1:8, 3:11, 4:5, 4:13, 5:3, 5:14, 5:16, 5:27, 6:8, 6:14, etc.

[28]If the original title name in 5a were spoken in poetic context, it is not impossible that it may have had a meter of its own consistent with the poem which follows since both the MT *'adōnay yahwē ṣ^{e}bā'ôt* (without the prosaic article) and the LXX *yahwē 'elōhē ṣ^{e}ba'ōt* have eight syllables. This may be no more than coincidence, however, in light of the frequent editorial use of these phrases extra-metrically elsewhere.

[29]As the versions confirm, the difference between the singular of 8:8 and the plural of 9:5 is not a problem of text but an example of deliberate alteration in the oral delivery of a formula or formulae. As argued in the discussion accompanying 8:8, it seems that this comparison of the poems reveals the kind of interchangeability or adaptability of formulae available to the prophet for his use as the metrical context requires.

[30]Note the touch of repetitive parallelism again, in the re-use of *ky'r*. Although the couplet is identical to the one in 8:8b it must be considered legitimate in both oracles and not merely a doublet copied into one of the contexts for purposes of harmonization.

[31]A word has apparently been dropped from the end of this colon by haplography. Cross suggests reading *^{c}md* or the like here, consonant with the similar image in Job 38:8-11, Jeremiah 5:22, Proverbs 8:27-29, etc. of Yahweh's setting the limits of the sea. The vocalization *^{c}imdū* is also possible.

[32]Or, with the LXX it is possible to read *ḥarīš*, "ploughing time," with no change in meter.

[33]Or read *qaṣīr*, "harvest time," with no change in meter.

[34]Omit MT *wakol-ha*...as a typical string of additions to the text, none of which is original.

CONCLUSION

A continuity is evident from Ugaritic to early Hebrew poetry. Both apparently descend from a common poetic tradition and thus share the following features: predominantly balanced couplets and triplets; thoroughly mixed meter; the free variation of couplets and triplets without discernable pattern; similar length of cola, the slightly shorter Hebrew cola being due primarily to the loss of case endings; no formal indication of strophic composition; and oral composition, with frequent use of formulae.

In Hebrew poetry the earmarks of formulaic composition are most visible in the parallel transmission of the tribal blessings in Genesis 49 and Deuteronomy 33, and the parallel texts of II Samuel 22 and Psalm 18. It may be assumed that parallel texts of other early Hebrew poems would show as much variation if they were extant. Careful textual study has uncovered a number of variant formulae even within a single text.

Meter is usually mixed in Hebrew poetry, just as in Ugaritic. Only rarely do we find sequences of several couplets which all contain the same meter. It may even have been the mark of a superior poet that he fully mixed his metrical patterns.

The basic unit of this early poetry was the couplet. The triplet was used less frequently, but appears in typical unpredictable fashion in nearly all poetry of any length. Patterns other than the couplet or triplet exist, but are much less common.

In the great majority of Ugaritic and early Hebrew couplets and triplets the cola are equal to one another in number of syllables. Differences of one syllable are infrequent, and differences of more than one syllable are rare. An exception is the meter of the purposely uneven Qinah, in which balance is found between couplets rather than within couplets. Many unbalanced couplets, moreover, are problematic in regard to either textual integrity or cesura. The normal pattern is unquestionably that of balanced cola.

Two distinct lengths of cola, clearly purposeful, may be isolated: "short" and "long," or "b" and "l." The short meter shows internal parallelism within cola, and nearly always is found in patterns of b:b::b:b or in the case of triplets, b:b::b:b::b:b. Short meter is, in effect, composed of couplets within couplets, the discernable units of composition averaging about five syllables, and never containing more than seven. Long meter shows no such complex internal parallelism. The patterns of such meter are simply l:l or l:l:l, with cola of rarely more than ten, and always more than five syllables.

Many poems contain no short meter, and only occasionally is a half-couplet (b:b) in the short meter to be found. A full b:b::b:b couplet may often have more syllables than a l:l couplet, even though the individual units of composition are shorter.

The average length of an l colon in Hebrew poetry is almost eight syllables. In Ugaritic it is a little more than nine. Early Hebrew couplets range from 4:4 to 11:11 (half of a b:b::b:b couplet to a lengthy l:l couplet). Ugaritic couplets range from 5:5 to 13:13.

Short meter occurs in very early material in Hebrew (e.g. Exodus 15) as well as in the latest material surveyed, that of Amos. Chronological patterns are not visible. In the tenth century, for example, the Lament of David contains predominantly b:b::b:b meter while II Samuel 22=Psalm 18 has none. The long meter is generally more common than the short meter in early Hebrew poems. It occurs in both early and relatively late material.

The poetry of Amos differs from the earlier poetry primarily in total length. Oracular poetry is a specific form, relatively short in duration. Most of Amos' oracles thus comprise only a few couplets. Even Balaam's first four oracles, short for the early poetry, are considerably longer. Ugaritic poems and most early Hebrew poems are much longer still, composed of lengthy strings of couplets and triplets.

Few serious metrical problems are found in relatively sound texts such as that of the Song of the Sea. Many more are present in a somewhat corrupt text such as that of the Song of

Deborah. Most are subject to resolution with the careful application of textual criticism, in Ugaritic as well as in Hebrew. Enough is now known of the history of the Hebrew text and of formulaic oral composition to confirm the necessity of reconstruction prior to any attempt at scansion.

We have studied the meter of most early Hebrew poetry, and of much Ugaritic poetry. We have presented a scansion based on the overall quantity of syllables per colon, as the most satisfactory approach to the meter of early Hebrew poems. Many problems and uncertainties remain without immediate solution. It is now likely, however, that the method of composition used by the ancient musical poet is within our grasp, and that we may with more confidence reproduce the rhythm of his songs.

APPENDIX I

TABLE OF COMPARATIVE SCANSIONS OF COUPLETS AND TRIPLETS IN EARLY HEBREW POEMS

The following table is designed to provide a rough comparison of syllabic meter with the meters of the traditional, semantic parallelism, and alternating meter schools. It is exceedingly difficult to give an accurate account of each school's treatment of a given couplet or triplet. Individual members of the various schools often differ with one another, and many members of all the schools would take exception to the emendations and stichometries adopted in the foregoing study. For example, where we have isolated b:b::b:b::b:b triplets, other scholars might render their scansion in the equivalent of l:l:l meter, producing a very different count. Most would not recognize a b:b::b:b::b:b triplet as a single unit, and might scan, for example, three 2:2 couplets. Nevertheless we have tried to set out the general correspondences between syllabic meter and the meter of the prevailing schools, avoiding any debate over stichometry, by treating each b:b half-couplet, l:l couplet, and l:l:l triplet as a unit, determining the correspondence on that basis.

Frequently it is impossible to determine how a member of a given school would scan a specific couplet or triplet. We then must give either a conjectural scansion or two equally possible scansions. We assume that members of the major schools of meter would vocalize according to the MT, but that they are adopting our emendations as they appear in the poems in Chapter III. Individual entries are presented largely in the order that the poems from which they are taken appear in the study. Exceptions are the brief poems in Genesis and Judges, whose position is adjusted here for easier reference. The couplets and triplets are arranged in ascending order of length of cola.

	Traditional	*Sem. Parallelism*	*Alternating*
3:5			
Ju. 5:25	2+2	2+2	2+2/3

	Traditional	Sem. Parallelism	Alternating
4:4			
Ex. 15:1b	2+2	2+2	2+2
:3	2+2	2+2	2+2
:9a	2+2	2+2	2+2
Ju. 5:28b	2+2	2+2	2+2
:28c	2+2	2+2	2+2
:30	2+2	2+2	2/3+2/3
Am. 3:8a	2+2	2+2	2+2
4:5			
Ex. 15:9	2+2	2+2	2+2/3
:15a	2+2	2+2	2+2/3
:15b	2+2	2+2	2+3
:15c	2+2	2+2	2+2/3
:18	2+2	2+2	2+2/3
II Sam. 1:20c	2+2	2+2	2+2/3
:20d	2+2	2+2	2+2/3
:21a	2+2	2+2	2+2/3
:21b	2+2	2+2	2+2/3
:21c	2+2	2+2	2+2/3
:21d	2+2	2+2	2+3
:22b	2+2	2+2	2+2/3
:22c	2+2	2+2	2+2/3
:26c	2+2	2+2	2+2/3
Am. 3:8b	2+2	2+2	2+2/3
4:6			
Ex. 15:17c	2+2	2+2	2+3
Ju. 5:4b	2+2	2+2	2/3+3
II Sam. 1:20a	2+2	2+2	2+3
5:4			
Ex. 15:4a	2+2	2+2	2/3+2
5:5			
Ex. 15:1a	2+2	2+2	2/3+2/3
:4b	2+2	2+2	2/3+2/3
:9b	2+2	2+2	2/3+2/3
:16a	2+2	2+2	2/3+3

	Traditional	Sem. Parallelism	Alternating
5:5 (cont.)			
Ju. 5:4c-5a	2+2	2+2	2/3+2/3
:6a	2+2	2+2	2/3+2/3
:25	2+2	2+2	2/3+2/3
15:16a	2+2	2+2	2/3+2/3
:16b	2+2/3	2+3	2/3+3
II Sam. 1:20a	2+2	2+2	3+3
:22a	2+2	2+2	2/3+2/3
:26a	2+2	2+2	2/3+2/3
5:6			
Ju. 5:5b	2+2	2+2	2/3+3
:5c	2+2	2+2	2/3+3
:30a	2+2	2+2	2/3+3
16:24	2+2	2+2	2/3+3
6:4			
Ex. 15:6a	2+2	2+2	3+2
:6b	2+2	2+2	3+2
II Sam. 1:26b	2+2	2+2	3+2
6:5			
Ex. 15:7a	2+2	2+2	3+2/3
:10b	2+2	2+2	3+3
:16b	2+2	2+2	3/4+3
:17b	2+2	2+2	3+2/3
Ju. 5:26	2+2	2+2	3+2/3
6:6			
Ex. 15:17a	2/3+2	2+2	3+3
Nu. 21:29a	3+3	3+3	3+3
23:23	3+3	3+3	3/4+3/4
Ju. 5:3a	2+2	2+2	3+3
:3b	2+2	2+2	3+3
:3c	2+2	2+2	3+3
:15b	2/3+2/3	2+2	3+3
:21	3+3	3+3	3/4+3/4
:26	2+2	2+2	3+3
14:18a	2/3+2/3	2/3+2/3	3+3

	Traditional	*Sem. Parallelism*	*Alternating*
6:6 (cont.)			
Ju. 16:23a	2+2	2+2	3+3
:23b	2+2	2+2	3+3
Gn. 49:7a	3+2/3	3+2	3+3
:10b	3+3	3+3	3+3
:13a	3+3	3+3	3+3
:14	3+3	3+3	3+3/4
:16	3+3	3+3	3+3/4
:17a	3+2	3+2	3+3/4
:26a	3+3	3+3	3/4+3/4
Dt. 33:3a	2/3+2/3	2/3+2/3	3+3
:11a	3+3	3+3	3+3
:13b	3+3	3+3	3/4+3/4
:14	3+3	3+3	3/4+4
:15	3+3	3+3	3/4+3
:17a	3+3	3+3	3/4+3/4
:17b	3+3	3+3	3+3
:17c	3+3	3+3	3+3
:22	3+3	3+2	3+3
:28a	3+3	3+3	3+3
:29a	2/3+3	2+3	3+3
II Sam. 22:24	3+2/3	3+2	3+3
:26	2/3+2/3	2/3+2/3	3+3
:27	2/3+2/3	2/3+2/3	3+3
II Sam. 1:23a	2+2	2+2	3+3
Am. 5:5b	3+3	3+3	3+3/4
:11c	3+2	3+2	4+3
6:7			
Ju. 5:23	3+3	3+3	3+3
Gn. 49:9a	3+3	3+3	3+4
II Sam. 1:23c	2+2/3	2+2	3+3
6:6:6			
Dt. 33:2a	3+2+3	3+2+2/3	3+3+3
:23	3+3+3	3+3+3	3+3+3
:26	3+3+2/3	3+3+2	3+3+3
Am. 5:5a	2+2+2	2+2+2	3+3+3

	Traditional	*Sem. Parallelism*	*Alternating*
6:6:7			
Ju. 5:6b	2/3+2/3+2/3	2+2+2	3+3+3/4
Gn. 49:27	3+3+3	3+3+3	3/4+3/4+4
7:4			
Ex. 15:10a	2/3+2	2+2	3/4+2
7:5			
Ex. 15:12	2/3+2	2+2	3/4+3
:13a	2/3+2	2+2	3/4+2/3
Am. 3:4a	3+2	3+2	4+3
:4b	3+2	3+2	4+3
:5a	3+2	3+2	4+3
7:6			
Ex. 15:7b	2/3+2	2+2	3/4+3
:13b	2/3+2	2+2	3/4+3
Ju. 5:12a	3+3	3+3	3/4+3
Am. 3:6b	3+2	3+2	4+3
7:7			
Gn. 2:23a	3+3	3/4+3	4+3/4
:23b	3+3	3+3	3/4+3/4
4:23b	3+2/3	3+2	3/4+3/4
:24	3+3	3+3	4+4
25:23a	3+3	3+3	3/4+3/4
:23b	3+4	3+4	4+4
Nu. 21:27	3+3	3+3	3/4+3/4
:28a	3+3	3+3	3/4+3/4
:28b	3+3	3+3	3/4+3/4
23:7b	3+3	3+3	4+4
:10	3+3	3+3	3/4+4
:19a	3+3	3+3	3/4+3/4
:20	3+3	3+2	3/4+3/4
Nu. 23:21b	3+3	3+3	3/4+3/4
:22	3+3	3+3	3/4+3/4
:24a	3+3	3+2	3/4+3/4
:24b	3+3	3+3	4+3/4
24:4b	3+3	3+3	4+3/4

	Traditional	Sem. Parallelism	Alternating
7:7 (cont.)			
Nu. 24:6a	3+3	2+2	3/4+3/4
:6b	3+3	2+2	3/4+3/4
:7a	3+3	3+3	4+4
:7b	3+3	3+3	4+3/4
:8a	3+3	3+3	4+4
:8b	3+3	3+2	3/4+3/4
:9b	2/3+2/3	2+2	3/4+3/4
:16b	3+3	3+3	3/4+3/4
:17a	3+3	3+3	3/4+3/4
:17b	3+3	3+3	3/4+3/4
:17c	3+2/3	3+3	3/4+3/4
:18b	3+3	3+3	3/4+3/4
Ju. 14:14	3+3	3+3	3/4+3/4
Gn. 49:5	3+3	3+3	3/4+3/4
:7b	2/3+2/3	2+2	3/4+3/4
:8a	3+3	3+3	3/4+4
:11b	3+3	3+2/3	3/4+3/4
:12	3+3	3+3	3/4+3/4
:13b	3+3	3+3	3/4+3/4
:15a	3+3	3+3	3/4+4
:15b	3+3	3+3	4+3/4
:17b	3+3	2/3+3	3/4+3/4
:19	3+3	3+3	3/4+3/4
:20	3+3/4	3+3	3/4+4
:23	2/3+3	2+2/3	3/4+3/4
:24b	3+3	3+3	3/4+4
:26b	3+3	3+3	3/4+3/4
:26c	3+3	3+3	3/4+3/4
Dt. 33:3b	3+2/3	2+2	3/4+3/4
:6	3+3	3+3	3/4+3/4
:7b	3+3	3+3	3/4+3/4
:9c	2/3+2/3	2+2	3/4+3/4
:11b	3+3	3+3	3/4+3/4
:16a	3+3	3+3	4+3/4
:16b	3+3	3+3/4	3/4+3/4
:19a	3+3	3+3/4	3/4+4

	Traditional	Sem. Parallelism	Alternating
7:7 (cont.)			
Dt. 33:19b	3+3	3+3	3/4+3/4
:20b	3+3	3+3	3/4+3/4
:21a	3+3	3+3	3/4+3/4
:27a	3+3	3+3	4+3/4
:28b	3+3	3+3	4+3/4
:29b	3+3	3+3	3/4+4
II Sam. 22:7a	3+3	3+2/3	3/4+3/4
:10	3+3	3+3	4+4
:11	3+3	3+3	3/4+3/4
:12	3+3	3+3	4+4
:13	3+3	3+3	3/4+3/4
:14	3+3	3+3	4+3/4
:16b	2/3+3	2+3	3/4+3/4
:17	3+3	3+3	3/4+4
:28	3+3	3/4+3	3/4+4
:29	3+3	3+3	3/4+3/4
:43	3+3	3+3	4+3/4
:47	3+3	3+3	3/4+3/4
:51	3+3	3+3	3/4+4
Am. 5:11b	3+2/3	3+2	3/4+3/4
:17	3+2/3	3+2/3	3/4+3/4
8:8a	3+3	3+3	4+3/4
:10b	3+3	3+3	4+3/4
:10c	3+3	3+3	4+3/4
9:13a	3+4	3+4	3/4+4
:13b	3+2/3	3+2	3/4+3/4
7:8			
Am. 5:10	3+3	3+3	4+4
:11a	3/4+3/4	4+4	4+4
:16b	3+3	3+3	3/4+4
:16c	3+3	3+3	4+4
7:9			
II Sam. 22:20	2/3+3	2+3	3/4+4/5
7:6:6			
Dt. 33:24	3+3+3	3+3+3	3/4+3+3/4

	Traditional	Sem. Parallelism	Alternating
7:7:7			
Nu. 21:29b	3+3+3	3+2+3	3/4+3+3/4
24:3-4a	3+3+3	3+3/4+3	4+4+4
:15-16a	3+3+3	3+3+3	4+4+4
:18a	3+3+3	3+3+3	3/4+3/4+3/4
Ju. 5:30c	3+3+3	3+3+3	3/4+3/4+3/4
Gn. 49:25b	3+3+3	3+3+3	4+3/4+4
Dt. 33:5	3+3+3	3+3+3	4+3/4+3/4
:21b	3+3+3	3+3+2/3	3/4+3/4+3/4
II Sam. 22:31	3+3+3	3+3+3	3/4+3/4+3/4
:48-49a	3+3+2/3	3+3+2	3/4+3/4+3/4
7:7:8			
II Sam. 22:9	3+3+3	3+3+3	3/4+3/4+4
7:8:8			
II Sam. 22:8	3+3+3	3+3+3	4+4+4
8:6			
Am. 3:3	3+2	3+2	4+3
:5b	3+2	3+2	4+3
:6a	3+2	3+2	4+3
8:8			
Ex. 15:14	3+3	3+3/4	4+4/5
:16c	3+3	3+3/4	4+4
Nu. 23:7a	3+3	3+3	4+4
:8	3+3	3+3	4+4
:9a	3+3	3+2	4+4
:10b	3+3	3/4+3	4+4
:18	3+3	3+3	4+4
:19b	3+3	3/4+3	4+4
:21a	3+3	3+3	4+4
:23b	3+3	3+3	4+4
Nu. 24:5	3+3	3+2	4+4
:9a	3+3	3+3/4	4+4
Ju. 5:4a	3+3	3+3	4+4
:17a	3/4+3/4	4+4	4+4
:17b	3/4+3	4+3	4+4

	Traditional	*Sem. Parallelism*	*Alternating*
8:8 (cont.)			
Ju. 5:24	3+3	3+3	4+4
Gn. 49:6	3+3	3+3	4+4
:9b	3+3	3+3	4+4
:11a	3+3	3+2	4+4
:21	3+3	3+3	4+4
Dt. 33:4	3+3	3/4+3	4+4
:7a	3+3	3+2/3	4+4
:8a	3+3	3+3	4+4
II Sam. 22:6	3+3	3+3	4+4
:7b	3+3	3+3	4+4
:15	3+3	3+3	4+4
:16a	3+3	3+3	4+4
:22	3+3	3+2	4+4
:23	3+3	3+3	4+4
:37	3+3	3+3	4+4
:41	3+3	3+2	3/5+4
:42	3+3	3+3	4+4
:45b-46b	3/4+3	3/4+2	4/5+4
:49b	3+3	2+3	4+4
:50	3+3	3+3	4+4
Am. 6:12a	3+3	3+3	4+4
:12b	3+3	3+3	4+4
8:8b	3+3	3+3	4+4
:9	3+3	3+3	4+4
:10a	3+3	3+3	4+4
9:5a	3+3	3+3	4+4
:5b	3+3	3+3	4+4
:6b	3/4+3	3/4+3	4+4
8:9			
Ju. 5:8	3+3	3+3	4+4
8:7:7			
Gn. 49:3	3+3+3/4	3+3+4	4+3/4+4
8:8:7			
Ju. 5:27	3+3+3	3+3+3	4+4+4
Dt. 33:12	4+4+3	4+4+3	4+4+3/4

	Traditional	Sem. Parallelism	Alternating
8:8:8			
Ju. 5:19a	3+3+3	3+3+3	4+4+4
II Sam. 22:36	3/4+2/3+2/3	3/4+2+2	4+4+4
1:19	3+3+3	3+2/3+3	4+4+4
:25	3+3+3	3+2/3+2/3	4+4+4
:27	3+3+3	3+2/3+3	4+4+4
9:7			
Ju. 14:18b	3+3	3+2/3	4+3/4
II Sam. 22:21	3+3	3+3	4/5+3/4
:39	3/4+3	3+3	4/5+4
:40	3+3	3+3	4/5+3/4
Am. 5:12a	3+3	3+2	4/5+4
:12b	4+3/4	4+3	4/5+4
9:8			
Ju. 5:8	3+3	3+3	4/5+4
9:9			
Gn. 4:23a	3/4+3/4	3/4+3/4	4/5+4/5
Ju. 5:13	3+3	3+3	4/5+4/5
:16	3/4+3	3/4+3	4/5+4/5
:20	3+3	3+2/3	4/5+4/5
:23	3+3	3+3	4/5+4/5
:26	3+3	3+3	4/5+4/5
:29	3+3	3+3	4/5+4/5
Gn. 49:4b	3+3	3+3	4/5+4/5
:8b	3+3	3+3	4/5+4/5
:10a	3+3	3+3	4/5+4/5
:24	3+3	3+2/3	4/5+4/5
:25a	3+3	3+3	4/5+4/5
Dt. 33:2b	3+3	3+3	4/5+4/5
:10a	3+3	3+2	4/5+4/5
:10b	3+3	3+3	4/5+4/5
:18	3+3	3+2	4/5+4/5
:27b	3+3	3+3	4/5+4/5
II Sam. 22:5	3+3	3+3	4/5+4/5
:19	3+3	3+3	4/5+4/5

	Traditional	*Sem. Parallelism*	*Alternating*
9:9 (cont.)			
II Sam. 22:32	3/4+3/4	3/4+3/4	4/5+4/5
:35	3+4	3+4	4/5+5
:38	3+3	3+3	4/5+4/5
:44	3+3	3+3	4/5+4/5
:44c-45a	3+3	3+3	4/5+4/5
Am. 5:7	3+3	3+3	4/5+4/5
8:7	4+3/4	4+3	4/5+4/5
9:6a	3+3	3+3	4/5+4/5
9:7:7			
Ju. 5:15	3+3+3	3+3+3	4/5+3/4+3/4
9:8:8			
Ex. 15:11	3+3+3/4	3+3+4	4/5+4/5+4/5
9:9:9			
Ex. 15:8	3/4+3+3	3/4+3+3/4	5+4/5+4/5
Ju. 5:7	3+3+3	3+3+3	4/5+4/5+4/5
:9-10	3+3+3	3+3+3	4/5+4/5+4/5
:21b-22	3+3+3	3+3+3	4/5+4/5+4/5
Am. 5:6	3+4+3	3+4+3	4/5+4/5+4/5
10:10			
Ex. 15:5	3/4+3/4	3+3	5+5
Ju. 5:2	3+3	3+3	5+5
:13	3+3	3+3	5+5
:18	4+4	4+4	5+5
:28	3+3	3/4+3	5+5
Dt. 33:29c	3/4+3/4	3+3	5+5
10:10:10			
Gn. 49:1b-2	3+4+3	3+4+3	5+5+5
11:11			
Ju. 5:14b	3/4+3/4	3+4	5+5
II Sam. 22:18	4+4	3+3	5+5

APPENDIX II

EVIDENCE OF SYLLABIC METER IN AN OLD BABYLONIAN POEM

In the recent edition of an early copy of the Old Babylonian Atrahasis Epic,[1] one may isolate a few sections of well-preserved, syllabically-written Babylonian poetry. A few features of classical Babylonian scansion have long been agreed upon: for example, that each line normally ends in a trochee. No indication has to date been forthcoming, however, that any Babylonian poetry might have been composed in a syllabic meter.

Within the Atrahasis text there are a few sections which seem, remarkably, to display the signs of syllabic meter. Even a cursory survey of the epic's best preserved sections discloses the earmarks of oral composition: formulae abound, there is almost no enjambment of lines, and the composition is markedly thematic. Thus we should not, perhaps, be surprised to find at least one or two points at which the syllable count tends to form a discernable pattern.

We must be cautious in our conclusions relative to the possible metrical composition of Akaadian poems. While the following excerpt does seem to suggest some purposeful, conscious metrical composition, most Babylonian poems, and most sections of the Atrahasis Epic do not so easily scan. Thus we offer these lines as a means of calling attention to the phenomenon of metrical balance in a Babylonian oral epic, and withhold judgment as to whether this is real or apparent. We do not know just how widespread such a phenomenon might have been, if at all.

Atrahasis Tablet I, Col. I[2]

39.	[*i-da-bu*]*-bu-ma i-ik-ka-lu ka-ar-ṣi*	They were grumbling and criticizing,
	19 (10+9)	
40.	[*ut-ta-az*]*-za-mu i-na ka-la-ak-ki*	They were complaining in the ditches.
41.	[*be-el*]*-ni gu-za-lá i-ni-im-ḫu-ur-ma*	Let us approach our lord, the overseer.

19 (9+10)

42. *[ka-ab]-tam du-ul-la-ni li-šá-si-ik el-ni* — Let him remove from us our severe corvee.

43. *ma-li-ik i-li qú-ra-dam* — The valiant counsellor of the gods

19 (7+12)

44. *[al-ka]-nim i-ni-iš-ši-a i-na šu-ub-ti-šu* — Come, let us raise from off his seat;

45. *ma-li-ik i-li qú-ra-dam* — " "

19 (7+12)

46. *[al-ka]-nim i-ni-iš-ši-a i-na šu-ub-ti-šu* — " "

47. *[i-lu] pí-a-šu i-pu-ša-am-ma* — A god opened his mouth and

19 (9+10)

48. *[iz-za-kàr] a-na i-li aḫ-ḫi-šu* — Speaks to the gods, his brothers:

(break begins)

Col. II

1. *ma-li-[ik] i-[li] qú-ra-dam* — The valiant counsellor of the gods

18 (7+11)

2. *al-[ka] ⌈i⌉-ni-iš-ši-a i-na šu-ub-ti-šu* — Come let us raise up off his seat

3. *ᵈEn-⌈líl⌉ i-li qú-ra-dam* — The valiant Enlil of the gods

18 (7+11)

4. *al-[ka] i-ni-iš-ši-a i-na šu-ub-ti-šu* — Come let us raise up off his seat.

5. *a-nu-um-ma ti-si-a tu-[qú]-um-tam* — Now then, call for war,

18 (9+9)

6. *ta-ḫa-za i-ni-ib-lu-la qá-ab-la-am* — Let us mix battle and war.

7. *i-lu iš-mu-ú zi-ki-ir-šu* — The gods heard his word;

18 (7+11)

8. *i-ša-tam ne-pí-ši-šu-nu id-du-ú-ma* — They set fire to their tools.

9. *ma-ar-ri-šu-nu-⌈ti⌉ i-ša-ta-am* — Fire to their shovels,

18 (8+10)

10. *šu-ub-ši-ik-ki-šu-nu* *ᵈBIL.GI (Gibil/Girra)* — Flame to their carrying-baskets

11. *it-ta-ak-šu* — they put.

12.	*i-ta-aḫ-zu-nim i-il-la-ku-nim*	18 (8+10)	They held them as they went off
13.	*ba-bi ša-at-ma-ni qú-ra-di* ^{d}*en-lîl*		To the gate of the valiant Enlil's dwelling.
14.	*⸢mi⸣-ši-il ma-aṣ-ṣa-ar-ti mu-šum i-ba-aš-ši*	19 (10+9)	It is night, the middle of the watch,
15.	*É* *(bitum)* *la-wi i-lu ú-ul i-de*		The house is surrounded, the god does not know it.
16.	*mi-ši-il ma-aṣ-ṣa-ar-ti mu-šum i-ba-aš-ši*	19 (10+9)	It is night, the middle of the watch,
17.	*É.KUR* *(Ekur)* *la-wi* ^{d}*En-lîl ú-ul i-de*		Ekur is surrounded, Enlil does not know it.
18.	*ú-te-eq-qí* ^{d}*KALKAL* *(kalkal)* *ú-te-[ši]*	16 (8+8)	On watch was Kalkal, disturbed.
19.	*il-pu-uṭ si-ik-ku-ra i-ḫi-iṭ*		He pushed the bolt and peered out.
20.	^{d}*KALKAL* *(kalkal)* *id-de-ki* ^{d}*[PA.LU] (nusku)*	16 (7+9)	Kalkal roused Nusku
21.	*ri-ig-ma i-še-em-mu-ú ša [*^{d}*i-gi-gi]*		They hear the clamor of the Igigi.
22.	^{d}*NUSKU id-di-ki be-[el-šu]*	16 (7+9)	Nusku roused his lord,
23.	*i-na ma-ia-li ú-še-et-[bi-šu]*		He got him out of bed.
24.	*be-lí la-wi bi-[it-ka]*	16 (6+10)	My lord, your house is surrounded,
25.	*qá-ab-lum i-ru-ṣa a-[na ba-bi-ka]*		The battle has rushed to your gate!
26.	^{d}*en-lîl la-[wi bi-it]-ka*	16 (6+10)	Enlil, your house is surrounded,
27.	*qá-ab-[lum i-ru-ṣa] a-na [ba]-bi-ka*		The battle has rushed to your gate!
28.	^{d}*en-lil [...]*[3] *u-ša-ar-di a-na šu-ub-ti-šu*[4]		He led Enlil to his own dwelling place.
29.	^{d}*en-lîl ⸢pî⸣-a-šu i-pu-ša-am-ma*	19 (9+10)	Enlil opened his mouth and
30.	*a-na SUKAL* *(sukallim)* ^{d}*NUSKU iz-za-kàr*		Says to the vizier Nusku,

31.	*^{d}NUSKU e-di-il ba-ab-ka*	Nusku, lock your gate!
	16 (6+10)	
32.	*ka-ak-ki-ka li-qí i-zi-iz ma-aḫ-ri-ia*	Take your weapons, stand in front of me!
33.	*^{d}NUSKU i-di-il ba-ab-šu*	Nusku locked his gate,
	18 (6+12)	
34.	*ka-ak-ki-šu il-qí it-ta-zi-iz ma-ḫar*(!)[5] *^{d}en-líl*	He took his weapons, he stood before (?) Enlil.
35.	*^{d}NUSKU pí-a-šu i-pu-ša-am-ma*	Nusku opened his mouth and
	19 (9+10)	
36.	*iz-za-kàr a-na qú-ra-di ^{d}en-líl*	Says to the valiant Enlil:
37.	*be-lí bi-nu bu-nu-ka*	My lord, the children are your creation!
	17 (7+10)	
38.	*ma-ru ra-ma-ni-ka mi-in-šu ta-du-ur*	Why are you afraid of your own sons?
39.	*^{d}en-líl bi-nu bu-nu-ka*	Enlil, the children are your creation!
	17 (7+10)	
40.	*ma-ru ra-ma-ni-ka mi-in-šu ta-du-ur*	Why are you afraid of your own sons?
41.	*šu-pu-ur a-nam li-še-ri-du-* [*nik-ku*]	Send, let them bring down Anu to you,
	21 (10+11)	
42.	*^{d}en-ki*[6] *li-ib-bi-ku-nim a-na m*[*a-aḫ-ri-k*]*a*	Let them lead Enki into your presence.
43.	*iš-pu-ur a-nam ú-še-ri-*[*du-ni-iš*]*-šu*	He sent. They brought down Anu to him,
	21 (10+11)	
44.	*^{d}en-ki ib-bi-ku-nim a-na ma-*[*aḫ-ri*]*-šu*	They led Enki into his presence.
45.	*wa-ši-ib a-nu šar-ri* [*ša*]*-me-e*	Anu, king of heaven is seated;
	18 (8+10)	
46.	*šar-ri ap-si-i ^{d}en-ki i-*[*im-me-re-ek*]*-*⌜*ki*⌝	The king of the Apsu, Enki, is at hand.
47.	*ra-bu-tum ^{d}a-nun-*[*na-ku wa*]*-aš-bu*	The great Anunaki are seated.
	18 (9+9)?	
48.	*^{d}en-líl it-bi-ma ša* [. . .] *-di/ki-nu* *ša puḫri x-di/ki-nu*	Enlil stood up . . . (the assembly bows?)

49.	^{d}*en-líl pí-a-šu i*[*-pu-ša-a*]*m-ma*	19 (9+10)	Enlil opened his mouth and
50.	*iz-za-kàr a-na* [*i-li ra-b*]*u -tim*		Says to the great gods,
51.	*ia-a-ši-im-ma-a* [it?]- . . .	19 (9+10)?	To me . . .
52.	⌜*ta*⌝*-ḫa-za e-ep-pu-uš ša* [*la ma-ḫa-ri*]		I will make war which cannot be opposed.
53.	*i-ni mi-na-a a-mu-ur a-na-ku*	19 (9+10)	What did I see with my own eye?
54.	*qá-ab-lum i-ru-ṣa a-na ba-bi-ia*		The battle rushed to my gate.
55.	*a-nu pí-a-šu i-pu-ša-am-ma*	19 (9+10)	Anu opened his mouth and
56.	*iz-za-kàr a-na qú-ra-di* ^{d}*en-líl*		Says to the valiant Enlil:
57.	⌜*zi*⌝*-ik-ra ša* ^{d}*i-gi-gu*	19 (6+5+8) ?	As for the report that the Igigi
58.	*il-mu-ú ba-bi-iš-ka*		Gathered around your gate,
I iii 1.	*li-ṣi-ma* [^{d}*NUSKU SUKAL* (*su-ka-al-lu?*)[7] *su-ka-al-li-šu*] ?		Let Nusku, his vizier, go out.
2.	*te-er-ta-*[*ka li-ip-šu-ur a-na i-li*][7]	19 (9+10)	Let him give your oracles to the gods,
3.	*a-na ma-*[*ri ra-ma-ni-ka li-iq-bi*]		Let him speak to your sons.

etc.[8]

NOTES

APPENDIX II

[1]CT 46, 1965; Lambert, W. G., and Millard, A. R., *Atrahasis: The Babylonian Story of the Flood*, Oxford, Clarendon Press, 1969.

[2]Our transliteration is based on Millard's copy in CT 46. The line numbers follow the plates of that edition. In some places we differ with the transliteration and translation of Lambert and Millard in their 1969 work.

[3]A word (two or more signs) is missing at the break. Millard's copy suggests that he thought he could see *il-qí*.

[4]Whatever its count syllabically, this line may not be part of the metrical pattern. It stands alone, without parallel, and may be a stage direction or the like.

[5]The text in CT 46 seems to have *ma-aḫ* ^{d}*en-líl*. The line may have been either miscopied or misdictated.

[6]The text mistakenly reads ^{d}*en-líl*. Meter is unaffected.

[7]Restored from text 12.

[8]The text becomes increasingly more difficult and fragmentary after this point. ^{d}*en-líl pí-a-šu* follows, indicating a nineteen-syllable couplet.

BIBLIOGRAPHY

Albright, W. F. "The Earliest Forms of Hebrew Verse," *JPOS* 2 (1922), 69-86.

________. "The Gezer Calendar," *BASOR* 92 (1943), 16-26.

________. "The Oracles of Balaam," *JBL* 63 (1944), 207-33.

________. "The Phoenician Inscriptions of the Tenth Century B.C. from Byblus," *JAOS* 67 (1947), 153-60.

________. "The Psalm of Habakkuk," *Studies in Old Testament Prophecy presented to T. H. Robinson*. Ed. H. H. Rowley. Edinburgh, 1950, 1-18.

________. "Dwarf Craftsmen in the Keret Epic and Elsewhere in the North-west Semitic Mythology," *IEJ* 4 (1954), 1-4.

________. "Archaic Survivals in the Text of Canticles," *Hebrew and Semitic Studies Submitted to G. R. Driver*. Ed. D. W. Thomas and W. D. McHardy. Oxford, 1963, 1-7.

________. *Yahweh and the Gods of Canaan*. Garden City: Doubleday, 1968.

Anderson, F. I. "Orthography in Repetitive Parallelism," *JBL* 89 (1970), 343-44.

Baars, W. *New Syro-Hexaplaric Texts*. Leiden, 1968.

Bellermann, J. *Versuch über die Metrik der Hebräer*. Berlin, 1813.

Bickell, G. *Metrices Biblicae regulae exemplis illustrae*. Innsbruck, 1879.

________. "Die hebräischen Metrik," *ZDMG* (1880), 557ff.

Blake, F. R. *A Resurvey of the Hebrew Tenses*. Rome, 1951.

Boling, R. "Synonymous Parallelism in the Psalms," *JSS* 5 (1960), 221-55.

Brønno, E. *Studien über hebräischen Morphologie und Vokalismus*. Leipzig, 1943.

Budde, K. "Das hebräische Klagelied," *ZAW* 2 (1882), 1-52.

________. *Der Segen Mose's*. Tübingen, 1922.

Chomsky, W. "The History of our Vowel-System in Hebrew," *JQR* N.S. 32 (1941-42), 27-49.

Clifford, R. *The Cosmic Mountain in Canaan and the Old Testament*. Cambridge: Harvard University Press, 1972.

Cobb, W. *A Criticism of Systems of Hebrew Metre*. Oxford, 1905.

Cross, F. M. *The Ancient Library of Qumran*. Garden City: Doubleday Anchor Books, 1961.

________. *Canaanite Myth and Hebrew Epic*. Cambridge: Harvard University Press, 1973.

________. "The History of the Biblical Text in the Light of Discoveries in the Judean Desert," *HTR* 57 (1964), 281-99.

________. "Leaves from an Epigraphist's Notebook," *CBQ* 36:4 (1964), 486-94.

________. "Note on the Ammonite Inscription from Tell Sīrān," *BASOR* 212 (1973), 12-15.

________. "The Oldest Manuscripts from Qumran," *JBL* 74 (1955), 147-72.

________. "Prose and Poetry in the Mythic and Epic Texts from Ugarit," *HTR* 67 (1974), 1-15.

________. "The Song of the Sea and Canaanite Myth," *Journal for Theology and the Church* 5 (1968), 1-25.

________. "Yahweh and the God of the Patriarchs," *HTR* 55 (1962), 225-59.

________ and Freedman, D. N. "The Blessing of Moses," *JBL* 67 (1948), 191-210.

________ and ________. *Studies in Ancient Yahwistic Poetry*. Missoula, Montana: Scholars Press, 1975.

________ and ________. *Early Hebrew Orthography*. New Haven: American Oriental Society, 1952.

________ and ________. "A Royal Psalm of Thanksgiving: II Samuel 22=Psalm 18," *JBL* 72 (1953), 15-34.

________ and ________. "The Song of Miriam," *JNES* 14 (1955), 237-50.

________ and ________. "Some Observations of Early Hebrew," *Biblica* 53 (1972), 413-20.

________ and Saley, R. "Phoenician Incantations on a Plaque of the Seventh Century B.C. from Arslan Tash in Upper Syria," *BASOR* 197 (1970), 42-49.

Culley, R. C. *Oral Formulaic Language in the Biblical Psalms*. Toronto: University of Toronto Press, 1967.

Culley, R. C. "Metrical Analysis of Classical Hebrew Poetry," *Essays on the Ancient Semitic World*. Ed. J. W. Wevers, D. B. Redford. Toronto: University of Toronto Press, 1970, 12-28.

Dahood, M. "A New Metrical Pattern in Biblical Poetry," *CBQ* 29 (1967), 574-79.

________. *Psalms I, II, III, The Anchor Bible*. Vols. 16, 17, 17a. Garden City: Doubleday, 1966, 68, 70.

________. *Ugaritic-Hebrew Philology*. Rome, 1965.

Driver, S. R. *Notes on the Hebrew Text and the Topography of the Books of Samuel*. Oxford, 1913.

Ehlen, A. "The Poetic Structure of a Hodayah from Qumran," Ph.D. dissertation, Harvard University, 1970.

Eissfeldt, O. "Der Gott Tabor," *Archiv für Religionswissenschaft* 31 (1934), 14-41.

Ewald, H. *Die Dichter des Alten Bundes*. Göttingen, Vol. I: 1866. Vol. II: 1867. Vol. III: 1874.

Fishbane, M. "Additional Remarks on *Rḥmyw* (Amos 1:11)," *JBL* 91 (1972), 391-93.

Freedman, D. N. "Acrostics and Metrics," *HTR* 65 (1972), 367-92.

________. "Archaic Forms in Early Hebrew Poetry," *ZAW* 72 (1960), 101-07.

________. Prolegomenon to Gray, G. B. *The Forms of Hebrew Poetry*. Reprint. New York: KTAV, 1972.

________. "The Refrain in David's Lament Over Saul and Jonathan," *Ex Orbe Religionum. Studia Geo Widengren*. Ed. J. Bergman, K. Drynjeff, H. Ringgren. (Studies in the History of Religions, Vol. 12 [1972]), 115-26.

________. "Strophe and Meter in the Song of the Sea," *A Light Unto My Path: Old Testament Studies in Honor of J. M. Myers*. Ed. H. N. Bream, R. D. Helm, C. A. Moore (1974), 163-203.

________. "The Structure of Psalm 137," *Near Eastern Studies in Honor of William Foxwell Albright*. Ed. H. Goedicke. Baltimore: Johns Hopkins Press, 1971, 187-205.

________ and Hyland, C. F. "Psalm 29: A Structural Analysis," *HTR* 66 (1973), 237-56.

Gaster, T. H. "An Ancient Eulogy on Israel: Deuteronomy 33: 3-5, 26-29," *JBL* 66 (1947), 53-62.

Gevirtz, S. *Patterns in the Early Poetry of Israel*. Chicago: University of Chicago Press, 1963.

Gevirtz, S. "A New Look at an Old Crux: Amos 5:26," *JBL* 87 (1968), 267-76.

Ginsberg, H. L. "A Ugaritic Parallel to II Samuel 1:21," *JBL* 57 (1938), 209-13.

________. *The Legend of King Keret. BASOR Supplementary Series Nos. 2-3.* New Haven, 1946.

Globe, A. "The Literary Structure and Unity of the Song of Deborah," *JBL* 93 (1974), 493-512.

Goodwin, W. and Gulick, C. *Greek Grammar.* Boston: Ginn and Co., 1958.

Gordis, R. "Critical Notes on the Blessing of Moses (Deut. 33)," *JTS* 34 (1933), 390-92.

Gordon, C. H. *Ugaritic Textbook.* 4 vols. Rome, 1965.

Gottwald, N. K. "Hebrew Prosody," *IDB*, Vol. III. New York: Abingdon Press, 1962, 829-38.

Gray, G. B. *The Book of Numbers. ICC*, Vol. IV. Oxford: 1903.

________. *The Forms of Hebrew Poetry.* Reprint. New York: KTAV, 1972.

Hanson, P. "The Song of Heshbon and David's *Nîr*," *HTR* 61 (1968), 297-320.

Harris, Z. *A Grammar of the Phoenician Language.* New Haven: 1936.

________. *The Development of the Canaanite Dialects.* New Haven, 1939.

Haupt, P. "The Poetic Form of the First Psalm," *AJSL* 19 (1903), 129-42.

________. "Moses' Song of Triumph," *AJSL* 20 (1904), 149-72.

________. *Biblische Liebeslieder.* Baltimore: Johns Hopkins Press, 1907.

________. "Critical Notes on Micah," *AJSL* 26 (1910), 201-52.

Held, M. "Philological Notes on Mari Covenant Rituals," *BASOR* 200 (1970), 32-40.

Hölscher, G. *Hesekiel.* Giessen, 1924.

________. *Das Buch Hiob.* Tübingen, 1937.

Housman, A. E. *Selected Prose.* Ed. J. Carter, Cambridge, 1962.

Hummel, H. D. "Enclitic *Mem* in Early Northwest Semitic, especially Hebrew," *JBL* 76 (1957), 85-107.

Idelsohn, A. *Jewish Music in its Historical Development*. New York: Holt, Rinehart and Winston, 1929.

Jakobson, R. *Selected Writings*, Vol. I. The Hague, 1962.

________. "Grammatical Parallelism and its Russian Facet," *Language* 42 (1966), 399-429.

Lord, A. *The Singer of Tales*. New York: Atheneum, 1968.

Lowth, R. *The Sacred Poetry of the Hebrews*. New York, 1829.

Ley, J. *Die Metrischen Formen der hebräischen Poesie*. Leipzig, 1886.

________. *Grundzüge des Rhythmus, des Vers- und Strophenbaues in der hebräischen Poesie*. Halle, 1875.

________. *Leitfaden der Metrik der hebräischen Poesie*. Halle, 1887.

Meier, E. *Die Form der hebräischen Poesie*. Tübingen, 1853.

________. *Das Hohelied*. Tübingen, 1854.

________. *Die Poetischen Bücher*. Tübingen, 1854.

Mendenhall, G. "The Census Lists of Numbers 1 and 26," *JBL* 77 (1958), 52-66.

Miller, P. D., Jr. "Two Critical Notes on Psalm 68 and Deuteronomy 33," *HTR* 57 (1964), 240-43.

Moran, W. L. "Genesis 49:10 and its use in Ezekiel 21:32," *Biblica* 39 (1958), 405-25.

________. "The Hebrew Language in its Northwest Semitic Background," *The Bible and the Ancient Near East*. Ed. G. E. Wright. Garden City: Doubleday, 1961, 54-72.

Mowinckel, S. "Zum Problem der hebräischen Metrik," *Festschrift Alfred Bertholet*. Tübingen, 1950, 379-94.

________. "Zur hebräischen Metrik II," *Studia Theologica* VII (1953), 54-85.

________. *The Psalms in Israel's Worship*. Vols. I and II. Trans. D. R. Ap-Thomas. New York: Abingdon, 1967.

Orlinsky, H. "The Textual Criticism of the Old Testament," *The Bible and the Ancient Near East*. Ed. G. E. Wright. Garden City: Doubleday, 1961, 113-32.

Orlinsky, H. "The Masoretic Text: A Critical Evaluation." Prolegomenon to C. D. Ginsburg, *Introduction to the Massoretico-Critical Edition of the Hebrew Bible*. Reprint, New York: KTAV, 1966.

Parry, M. *L'Epithète traditionelle dans Homère*. Paris, 1928.

________. "Studies in the Epic Technique of Oral Verse-Mak-Making." I: *Harvard Studies in Comparative Literature* 41: 73-147 (1930); II: *Harvard Studies in Comparative Literature* 42: 1-50 (1932).

________ and Lord, A. *Serbocroatian Heroic Songs*. Cambridge: Harvard University Press, 1954.

Pope, M. H. "Ugaritic Enclitic *-m*," *JCS* 5 (1961), 123-28.

Pythian-Adams, J. W. "On the Date of the 'Blessing of Moses'," *JPOS* 3 (1923), 158-66.

Revell, E. J. "Studies in the Palestinian Vocalization of Hebrew," *Essays on the Ancient Semitic World*. Ed. J. W. Wevers, D. B. Redford. Toronto: University of Toronto Press, 1970, 51-100.

________. "The Placing of the Accent Signs in Biblical Texts with Palestinian Pointing," *Studies on the Ancient Palestinian World*. Ed. J. W. Wevers, D. B. Redford. Toronto: University of Toronto Press, 1971, 34-45.

Robertson, D. *Linguistic Evidence in Dating Early Hebrew Poetry*. Missoula, Montana: Scholars Press, 1972.

Robinson, T. H. *The Poetry of the Old Testament*. London, 1948.

________. "Basic Principles of Hebrew Poetic Form," *Festschrift Alfred Bertholet*. Tübingen, 1950, 438-50.

________. "Hebrew Poetic Form," *Supplements to Vetus Testamentum* I (1953), 128-49.

Saalschütz, J. *Von der Form der hebräischen Poesie*. Königsberg, 1825.

________. *Form und Geist der biblisch-hebräischen Poesie*. Königsberg, 1852.

Sarna, N. "Some Instances of the Enclitic *-m* in Job," *JJS* 6 (1955), 108-10.

Segert, S. "Vorarbeiten zur hebräischen Metrik," *ArOr* 21 (1953), 481-510.

________. "Zur Habakkuk-Rolle aus dem Funde vom Toten-Meer, IV: (F. 'Metrisches')," *ArOr* 23 (1955), 178-83.

________. "Problems of Hebrew Prosody," *Supplements to Vetus Testamentum* VII (1960), 283-91.

Sievers, E. *Metrische Studien*, Vol. I: *Studien zur hebräischen Metrik*. Leipzig, 1901; Vol. II: *Die hebräischen Genesis*. Leipzig, 1904.

Speiser, E. "The Pronunciation of Hebrew According to the Transliterations in the Hexapla, Chapters I-II," *JQR* 16 (1925-6), 343-82; "Chapter II continued," *JQR* 23 (1932-33), 233-65; "Chapter III," *JQR* 24 (1933-34), 9-46.

________. *Genesis*. *The Anchor Bible*, Vol. I. Garden City: Doubleday, 1964.

Sperber, A. "Hebrew Based upon Greek and Latin Transliterations," *HUCA* 12-13 (1937-38), 103-274.

________. "Hebrew Based upon Biblical Passages in Transmission," *HUCA* 14 (1939), 153-249.

________. *Grammar of Masoretic Hebrew*. Copenhagen, 1959.

________. *A Historical Grammar of Biblical Hebrew*. Leiden, 1966.

Strugnell, J. Review of Goshen-Gottstein, M. H., *Text and Language*, *JBL* 80 (1961), 199-200.

________. "Notes on the Text and Transmission of the Apocryphal Psalms 151, 154, 155," *HTR* 59 (1966), 257-81.

________. "Notes on IQS 1, 17-18; 8, 3-4 and IQM 17, 8-9," *CBQ* 29 (1967), 580-82.

________. Review of Di Lella, *The Hebrew Text of Sirach*, *CBQ* 30 (1968), 88-91.

Watson, D. W. *Text-Restoration Methods in Contemporary U.S.A. Biblical Scholarship*. Naples, 1969.

Wellhausen, J. *Der Text der Bücher Samuelis*. Göttingen, 1871.

Werner, E. "Masoretic Accents," *IDB*, Vol. III, 295-99.

Whitaker, R. "A Formulaic Analysis of Ugaritic Poetry," Ph.D. dissertation, Harvard University, 1970.

Wright, G. E. (ed.). *The Bible and the Ancient Near East: Essays in Honor of William Foxwell Albright*. Garden City: Doubleday, 1961.